Good Ted, Bad Ted

The Two Faces of Edward M. Kennedy

Lester David

A BIRCH LANE PRESS BOOK
Published by Carol Publishing Group

FOR IRENE
whose tireless help, shrewd guidance
and collaboration on many parts of this book
were invaluable

AND FOR
Sarah and Michael Rosen
and Alexander and Jessica Lewin

A Birch Lane Press Book
Published by Carol Publishing Group
Birch Lane Press is a registered trademark of Carol Communications, Inc.
Editorial Offices: 600 Madison Avenue, New York, N.Y. 10022
Sales & Distribution Offices: 120 Enterprise Avenue, Secaucus, N.J. 07094
In Canada: Canadian Manda Group, P.O. Box 920 Station U, Toronto,
    Ontario M8Z 5P9
Queries regarding rights and permissions should be addressed to
Carol Publishing Group, 600 Madison Avenue, New York, N.Y. 10022

Carol Publishing Group books are available at special discounts for bulk purchases,
for sales promotions, fund-raising, or educational purposes. Special editions can be created to
specifications. For details contact: Special Sales Department, Carol Publishing Group, 120
Enterprise Avenue, Secaucus, N.J. 07094

Manufactured in the United States of America
10 9 8 7 6 5 4 3 2 1

Library of Congress Cataloging-in-Publication Data

David, Lester.
    Good Ted, bad Ted : the two faces of Edward M. Kennedy / by Lester
David.
        p.   ;   cm.
    "A Birch Lane Press book."
    ISBN 1-55972-167-7
    1. Kennedy, Edward Moore, 1932–   2. Legislators—United
States—Biography.   3. United States. Congress. Senate—Biography.
I. Title.
E840.8.K35D29   1993
328.73'092—dc20
    [B]   92-39544
                                                            CIP

Contents

Author's Note

As a journalist and biographer, I have covered the Kennedys for nearly thirty years. During that time, I have talked with many members of the "clan," a term I know they dislike, but which has been—and will be—ineradicably attached to the most celebrated political family of the century.

Dr. David Burner, professor of history at the State University of New York at Stony Brook, and Dr. Thomas R. West, associate professor of history at the Catholic University of America, have been kind enough to say that I "probably have more information at [my] command about the Kennedys than anyone else." Over the decades, I have interviewed Edward M. Kennedy many times in Washington and Cape Cod, have had innumerable private conversations with Joan Kennedy, and count myself a friend of Rose Kennedy.

I have also had conversations with Eunice Shriver; Kathleen Kennedy; Joseph Gargan, Ted's cousin, and his wife Betty; Edwin Schlossberg, Caroline's husband; and hundreds of people who have known the family since John F. Kennedy's first run for Congress, including David F. Powers; Kenneth P. O'Donnell; Kirk LeMoyne

Billings; Pierre Salinger; Frank Mankiewicz; John Seigenthaler; Luella Hennessey Donovan; Candace McMurrey, Joan's sister; Doris Reggie, Ted's mother-in-law; and a large number of Kennedy historians and biographers. I am especially grateful to Dr. Thomas C. Reeves of the University of Wisconsin, Dr. Garry Wills of Northwestern University, and Professor Herbert Parmet of Queensborough Community College. Their contributions, and those of the many scores of other scholars interviewed, appear in the notes. Many of the sources to whom I spoke over the years I covered the Kennedys have been reinterviewed for this book.

I am deeply indebted to my many journalistic colleagues who gave so freely of their valuable time to answer my endless questions. I must make special mention of Ken Chandler and Richard Kaplan, to whom I owe much gratitude for their unstinting help.

Thanks also to the archivists at the John F. Kennedy Library in Columbia Point, south of Boston, for making available their vast store of research materials. References to the numerous magazines and newspapers consulted appear in the notes. Finally, and hardly least, I am grateful to my editor, Hillel Black, for his encouragement, guidance, and suggestions while this book was gestating.

To Begin

To understand Ted Kennedy, I found it essential in some chapters to explore the crucible in which his character was forged. No man or woman develops a personality, ideology, and a behavior pattern in a vacuum. As Oscar Hammerstein II wrote: "You've got to be taught." I believe, after studying the youngest Kennedy all these years, that he is a victim of the family mystique, a reluctant torch-bearer who, by tragic accident, became the patriarch, a role for which he was unsuited.

Until its sudden end, the Kennedy administration, which Jacqueline Kennedy herself had named Camelot, caught the romantic imagination of the country. It was a rare and wonderful time of magic, when youthful verve, excitement, and glamour replaced the stodginess of the Eisenhower years.

Scores of books and hundreds of magazine articles were published about the family. Millions of women copied Jackie's coiffure and pillbox hat. Jack Kennedy's witty press conferences drew huge radio audiences.

Few cared that this Camelot was as much a fantasy as its predecessor. The nation—indeed, the entire world—dazzled by its new King Arthur, willed it to be real. It was virtually impossible to escape its magic spell. Few cared or even knew that the king wore a hollow crown and that his court was deeply flawed. His charm made all forgivable. The youth of America adored him, and as many commentators said, he made everyone old feel young again.

No matter that his efforts to overthrow Fidel Castro through the invasion at the Bay of Pigs turned into a monumental fiasco. No matter that, as many historians claim, he brought the world to the brink of nuclear catastrophe during the Cuban missile crisis of 1962. Yet JFK was not criticized, but acclaimed as a bold leader. If he initiated a war in Vietnam, few showed concern.

Some of Kennedy's accomplishments were meaningful. He established the Peace Corps, promoted space exploration, and brought the Soviet Union to the conference table to sign a nuclear test-ban treaty. He initiated civil rights legislation that would ban discrimination in public places and in programs that were federally assisted and would permit lawsuits to be brought in federal courts against persons and places which refused to serve people because of their race. It was the most far-reaching measure ever proposed to Congress in U.S. history.

But Kennedy's faults outweighed his achievements by a considerable margin. His personal conduct was perhaps the most scandalous of any president in history. Few outside a small Washington circle knew or talked about the Central Intelligence Agency plot to assassinate Fidel Castro, using Mafia chieftains who were promised $150,000 for the "hit." No hard evidence has ever implicated Jack and Bobby in the assassination attempt.

The clandestine operation to hire Mafia killers was revealed to a stunned nation in 1975 by a bipartisan Senate committee headed by Senator Frank Church. Barry Goldwater declared that the CIA could never have plotted against the life of any foreign leader without presidential approval. In 1992 Chuck Giancana, Sam's younger brother, quoted the Chicago mob boss as saying he was given the "contract" by the CIA.

But the Kennedys brought glamour to America. Jackie put her imprint on the White House: sophistication, grace, wit, vitality, and style. She coaxed René Verdon, a famous French chef, to head the kitchen and prepare the cuisine: consommé, madrilène iranien, lobster en Bellevue, stuffed bar polignac, supreme of capon Demidoff, vol-au-vent Maryland, and the rarest of wines.

Jackie refurbished the White House so that it glittered. Nobel Prize winners, internationally famed poets, artists, playwrights, and musicians were invited to the Executive Mansion to participate in a cultural renaissance.

In counterpoint to the glamour of the White House was the madness at Hickory Hill. The nation watched with fascination as Bobby, Ethel, and their children and guests cavorted at the estate. "The house and grounds were anarchic," said one close friend. "Orderliness was unheard of. Children and animals were everywhere, inside and outside. You'd see the kids charging around the lawn, riding horses, splashing in the pool, and blowing up balloons, which they would burst behind you." A jukebox played at full volume at the pool. No guest was safe from practical jokes: even a member of European royalty was sprayed in the face with shaving cream by Ethel. The theatrical producer Leland Hayward quipped that Hickory Hill would make the damnedest musical comedy the Broadway stage had ever seen.

After Jack Kennedy's brutal murder in Dallas, the Camelot legend was solidified. Since that tragic November day in 1963, America's worship of the Kennedy family has intensified. Almost everything they do, bad or good, is news. In a study published in 1973, psychohistorian Nancy Gager Clinch called America's worship of the Kennedy family a national neurosis.

And the legend endures, despite searching examination by such serious scholars as Dr. Thomas C. Reeves of the University of Wisconsin, Dr. Garry Wills of Northwestern University, Herbert S. Parmet of Queensborough Community College, and investigating journalists Peter Collier and David Horowitz, and Joan and Clay Blair, Jr. These, and others, document that the reality of John F. Kennedy's life was unlike the popular perception, and that the legacy he left was part myth, part illusion, and part cultist hero worship.

Liberals studying Kennedy's record have learned to their dismay that while his rhetoric was glorious, his actions were less so. Dr. David Burner, a historian at the State University of New York at Stony Brook, calls him "ambivalently liberal." On civil rights, JFK moved so slowly that he became "the reluctant emancipator." In October 1960, during the election campaign, JFK promised to end segregation in public housing by "one stroke of a pen," but once elected, he delayed for two years before signing an executive order. Meanwhile, proponents of the order sent thousands of pens and gallons of ink to him at the White House. Angrily, Kennedy sent the gifts to Harris Wofford, his special assistant for civil rights, who had suggested the pledge. Wofford kept them stacked in his office until JFK finally signed the order.

Despite the outrages in Birmingham, Selma, and the University of Mississippi, Kennedy enacted little civil-rights legislation. An ugly crowd estimated at between one and three thousand had savagely beaten the Freedom Riders in Birmingham on May 6, 1961, when they traveled through the South to integrate public facilities. In Selma, six hundred blacks marching in a voter registration drive were tear-gassed by mounted state troopers and in September 1961, violence erupted on the campus of "Ole Miss," when James Howard Meredith, twenty-nine, became the first black to enroll. When the rioting finally ended, 2 people were dead, 166 U.S. marshals and 40 soldiers and guardsman had been injured, 200 rioters were in jail, and burned and wrecked vehicles littered the campus.

The Rev. Martin Luther King, Jr., bitterly condemned the administration for its legislative inaction. Meredith was scornful. "Jack Kennedy," he said, "was a typical rich Irishman who did whatever he did from political necessity."

Bobby and Ted, as an integral part of the legend, were unable to stand apart from it. It is doubtful that either of them knew it was flawed or that their older brother had handed them a dimly lit torch.

Bobby, as conservative in his views as his father, moved sharply to the left. The liberalism with which Bobby has become identified came only in the last seven years of his life, when his eyes were opened to the poverty of those who had been bypassed by social and economic progress.

Bobby had been an open supporter of Joseph R. McCarthy, had served for a time as assistant counsel and staff director of the senator's Red-hunting Senate Permanent Investigating Subcommittee, and soon had become "passionately devoted" to the crusade, according to *New York Times* columnist Arthur Krock. Jack tried to dissuade his brother from accepting the position, but Bobby, knowing that his father wanted him to take the job, refused to budge.

"Oh, hell," Jack had said, "you can't fight the old man."

Bobby wept when Joe McCarthy died in 1957, went to his funeral in Appleton, Wisconsin, and never disavowed him, though he deplored his tactics. Even Bobby's closest friends have never been able to resolve the paradox.

Ted persisted in the liberal ideology year after year. He changed only when other paths had to be taken to achieve the same goals. "Edward is the most philosophically complete of the three," commented Drs. Burner and West.

Ted has worked harder in the Senate than either of his brothers; he is a better speaker, and he has become far more skillful in the legislative process that turns ideas into laws.

Edward Kennedy has become a good—some say great—United States senator. His legislative accomplishments are an important part of this book.

At the same time, in his personal life, Teddy has acted as a man without morality. *New York Times* columnist Anna Quindlen said: "The trouble with Teddy is that he's like the little girl with the curl in the middle of her forehead. When he's good, he's better than anyone else, but when he's bad—oh, boy!"

This book chronicles—and explains—those two facets of one of the most unusual political leaders of our time.

One

The Anointed

What the hell is that guy jabbering about?" Ted Kennedy wondered as he listened to the announcer's frenetic shouting, mingled with snatches of prayer, on his car radio. He was returning to his San Francisco hotel, weary after a long day of overseeing the northern California operations in his brother Bobby's campaign for the Democratic presidential nomination.

It was a few minutes after midnight on June 5, 1968, the end of a day when everything had gone wrong. Voting machines in many areas of the city and suburbs had broken down, and Ted had had to send squads of poll watchers to make sure the problems were straightened out so that Bobby would not be cheated of precious ballots. Earlier, some of the end-of-campaign rallies had been so rough that Ted had been threatened with physical violence. At one particularly disorderly meeting, David Burke, his administrative assistant, became worried that Ted would be injured by the crowds that pulled and tugged at him in a municipal auditorium.

Many in the throng were protesting the arrest of Huey P. Newton, the cofounder of the Black Panther party, on charges of slaying a policeman in Oakland, California.

"People kept yelling and screaming, and I frankly felt very uncomfortable for Edward Kennedy," Burke said. "I told him, 'Hey, let's get out of here, fast.'"

Burke, the son of a policeman, had grown up with a sense of alertness to possible danger. He knew Ted was vulnerable and often kidded him about it. "Look, whenever you and I go out in public, I'm going to draw a large arrow on a placard and write on it in big letters: 'It's him, not me.'"

Late that might, Ted had spoken to a much friendlier crowd at Masonic Hall, then left for his suite at the Fairmont Hotel, atop Nob Hill. In the car he drew a deep breath. It was now clear that Bobby had won the most important primary election since he entered the presidential nomination race March 14, after agonizing for months over the wisdom of his move.

Late in 1967 Bobby had seemed incapable of deciding whether to seek the presidency, despite urging by close advisers. Lyndon Johnson had been damaged seriously by the backlash over his conduct of the Vietnam War. Senator Eugene McCarthy of Minnesota, an unlikely contender and upstart, had made the national discontent only too plain with his stunning performance in the New Hampshire primary, where he won 42.2 percent of the Democratic vote to Johnson's 49.4 percent. On March 31, nineteen days later, Johnson announced that he would not seek reelection.

In the car behind Ted and Dave Burke, John Seigenthaler, Bobby's administrative assistant, listened to the same incoherent babbling. "This must be some kind of sick joke," he thought, but after thirty seconds he finally made out what the man was saying. Bobby Kennedy had been shot. Seigenthaler, listening hard while maneuvering through heavy traffic, almost wrecked the car. Finally he pulled up in front of the Fairmont. He told his wife Dolores and their thirteen-year-old son David to go up to their suite, then bolted into an elevator.

"When I got to Teddy's suite on the fourth floor, he was standing in front of the television screen, his coat in his hand, his tie loosened, staring at the scene in the Embassy Ballroom at the Hotel Ambassador in Los Angeles," Seigenthaler recalled. Steven Smith, the slender, preppy-faced husband of Ted's sister Jean, had taken the microphone at the podium. Although inwardly agitated, the politically shrewd Smith kept his voice level as he asked the crowd, which had just heard Bobby's victory address, to leave quietly.

Many did, wondering what was happening; others milled around the foot-high platform, moaning and crying as word filtered out that something terrible had occurred.

Behind the platform, in a narrow serving kitchen and pantry, Bobby Kennedy was lying on the concrete floor, a quizzical look on his face, arms outstretched, eyes staring, blood oozing from the right side of his head. He had left the stage from the rear, taking a shortcut through the pantry to the Colonial Room, where newspeople were impatiently waiting for him to appear at a press conference. He had only gone a few feet when Sirhan Bishara Sirhan, a swarthy twenty-four-year-old Jordanian immigrant, fired eight shots from a .22 caliber Iver-Johnson revolver from a distance of only four feet.

Three bullets had struck Bobby; one in his right armpit, another in his neck, and the third tearing through the right mastoid bone behind the ear, scattering bone fragments throughout the lower part of his brain.

At the Fairmont, Ted snapped out of his near-hypnotic state. He told Burke: "We've got to get down there. Get us a plane." He called Los Angeles, where he reached Pierre Salinger, Bobby's press aide, at the Ambassador while Burke rushed to the desk of the assistant manager.

Salinger told Ted: "He was alive when the ambulance took him away. Nobody knows yet how bad the wounds are." Downstairs, Burke and the assistant manager had no luck with private airlines and charter companies. Finally Burke reached Hamilton Air Force Base in Marin, twenty miles to the north. The operations officer said they would provide a military jet fighter.

Burke raced back to the rooms to tell Ted. By this time, Seigenthaler had arrived. Kennedy, Burke, Seigenthaler, and Kennedy cousin Robert Fitzgerald drove to the field in a California Highway Patrol car, escorted by four motorcycles. Aboard the plane, they learned that Bobby had been taken first to Central Receiving Hospital on Valencia Street for emergency treatment, then to the Hospital of the Good Samaritan on West Sixth Street.

"There was a lot of silent praying going on," Seigenthaler said. "Ted, sitting in front of me, turned to ask me to make sure Bobby's children would be notified and that someone would be with each of them when they learned. He didn't want them to be all alone when they heard the news."

At the Los Angeles Airport, a helicopter waited, its blades whirring. In minutes it had set down on Good Samaritan's parking lot. Ted was taken to the fifth floor, where he embraced a tearful Ethel, Bobby's wife, and with Steve and Jean Smith and other close friends, remained throughout that long night while surgeons worked to repair Bobby's bullet-lacerated brain.

At 6:20 A.M., Bobby was brought to the intensive care unit on the fifth floor. Ted and Ethel sat by his bedside, hoping and praying. But there was no hope. Dr. Henry Cuneo, a prominent Los Angeles neurosurgeon who had headed the surgical team, had said that it was only a matter of time before Bobby died.

One of his top aides said afterward that he saw Ted Kennedy standing alone in the bathroom of the hospital room where Bobby lay, his head swathed in bandages. Through the half-open door, the aide could see Ted leaning over the washbasin, his hands clutching the sides, his head bowed.

The aide recalled: "I never expect, for the rest of my life, to see more agony on anyone's face. There are no English words to describe it. That is a vision that comes to me when I think how he has lived his life since."

On June 5, Ted selected Bobby's coffin himself. It was African mahogany, over which a maroon pall would be draped. He remained with it all during the flight aboard the Boeing 707 that President Johnson had sent to carry the body back to New York.

On the trip to New York, NBC newsman Sandor Vanocur quietly entered the narrow front compartment next to the cockpit where the coffin had been secured. He found Ted asleep, his right hand on the pall and tightly gripping a wreath of flowers. Earlier, after the coffin had been lifted onto the hydraulically operated loading platform in Los Angeles, the wreath had slipped off. Ted, watching, left the plane, picked up the flowers from the tarmac, and replaced them before the takeoff.

Jackie Kennedy had been awakened in New York at 4:30 A.M. and flown to Los Angeles to be at the bedside. On her arrival she learned Bobby had died and that his body would be returned to New York. When the big blue-and-white Boeing 707 came into view, Jackie turned white and began to tremble.

It looked to her exactly like Air Force One, which had carried the body of President Kennedy from Love Field, Texas, to Andrews Air Force Base in 1963.

She shrank back, wondering whether this was the same aircraft in which she had flown next to her husband's coffin in the cramped tail compartment five years before, still in her blood-splattered pink suit. Seated there, she had sobbed uncontrollably for the first time (that November day, turning her anguished face to Kenneth O'Donnell, one of JFK's closest aides, asking, "Kenny, Kenny, what do we do now?"

Tough, sardonic Kenny had replied, "I don't give a goddamn."

"I couldn't go on that plane again," she whispered to a crewman.

He assured her, "It's not the same one, Mrs. Kennedy. You see, there are six planes assigned to the Chief Executive, all looking the same. Only one is Air Force One. That was Number 26000. This is 86972, Air Force Two."

Reassured, Jackie boarded and at 1:38 P.M. on June 6, the 707 roared down the runway.

On June 7 in St. Patrick's Cathedral in New York, a six-man honor guard kept a twenty-four-hour vigil around the flag-draped coffin. They included former U.S. Secretary of Defense Robert McNamara, President of the United Auto Workers Walter Reuther, poet Robert Lowell, former Supreme Court Justice and Ambassador to the United Nations Arthur Goldberg, Kennedy speechwriter and biographer Ted Sorensen, actor Sidney Poitier, and novelists Budd Schulberg and William Styron. The others took their stations in half-hour relays, but Ted remained all during the night. He sat, head bowed; he paced up and down the aisle; he knelt in prayer. When dawn broke, he was still there. Only when morning came did he go to Ethel's home for a few hours' sleep.

At the funeral service in St. Patrick's on June 8, Ted stunned the 2,300 invited guests by rising to deliver the eulogy. Dave Burke had been appalled when, the day before, Kennedy decided to do it. Burke didn't think that any human being could go through what Ted Kennedy had and then stand up in that cathedral and speak over the body of his brother. He told Ted bluntly, "I think it's a terrible decision, and I want no part in the planning."

But Ted wouldn't be deterred from paying homage to his brother. With the help of Adam Walinsky, one of Bobby's speechwriters, and Milton Gwirtzman, an aide, he spent most of the day preparing the eulogy. A few minutes after 10:00 A.M., he rose from the front pew, where he was sitting with Ethel, his mother, and other family members, and stood before the lectern.

The eulogy he spoke that morning over the coffin of his brother was one of Edward Kennedy's finest public addresses. Part must be repeated here because of the inner strength it took to make it at all, because of the compassion for humanity it contained, and—perhaps most important—because it marked a watershed in his life.

A few minutes after he began, his voice broke. Dave Burke shut his eyes.

Ted paused, gained a measure of control, and went on. He recalled the role of the Kennedy dead in years past: his oldest brother Joe, his sister Kathleen, his Brother Jack. and now Bobby. In a tremulous voice, he talked of Bobby.

"He gave us strength in time of trouble, wisdom in time of uncertainty, and sharing in time of happiness. He will always be by our side."

Most of the eulogy was devoted to a reading of Bobby's own speeches expressing his ideals of helping the helpless and being the voice of the voiceless. A hushed cathedral heard Ted quote from a speech made by Bobby two years before:

> "There is discrimination in this world, and slavery and slaughter and starvation. Governments repress their people. Millions are trapped in poverty, while the nation grows rich and wealth is lavished on armaments everywhere.... "Each time a man stands for an ideal, or acts to improve the lot of others, or strikes out against injustice, he sends forth a tiny ripple of hope. And crossing each other from a million different centers of energy and daring, those ripples build a current that can sweep down the mightiest walls of oppression and resistance...."

As he neared the close, Ted Kennedy was clearly at the point of tears; he paused, tightened his lips, then continued, concluding with the quotation from George Bernard Shaw with which Bobby ended his speeches on his presidential campaign:

> "Those of us who loved him and who take him to his rest today pray that what he was to us, and what he wished for others, will someday come to pass for all the world. As he said many times, in

many parts of this nation, to those he touched and who sought to touch him:

"'Some men see things as they are and say, why. I dream of things that never were and say, why not.'"

Then the huge bronze doors of the Gothic cathedral swung open and, as Handel's Hallelujah Chorus swelled from the great organ, the coffin of Robert Kennedy was borne by his friends and placed in a hearse. Tens of thousands of people lined Fifth Avenue, most of them weeping, as the cortège moved downtown to Pennsylvania Station to board a train that would bear the body to Washington. Robert Kennedy would be buried in Arlington National Cemetery alongside his brother.

On the twenty-one-car funeral train, Ted Kennedy walked through the cars to greet the two thousand invited mourners personally. Later, in the darkness, he watched the coffin being lowered into a grave fifty feet down the slope from where John F. Kennedy lay.

The next day, Ted Kennedy left for his summer home on Squaw Island near the compound at the end of Scudder Avenue in Hyannis Port. With him were his wife Joan and his daughter Kara, then seven, and sons Teddy, Jr., six, and Patrick, fifteen months. Ted had lapsed into a grief so profound he was barely aware of their presence. He would enter and leave the eleven-room shingled house overlooking Nantucket Sound without saying a word, ignoring the calls of his children, who were bewildered by the change in the man who had always had time for roughhouse play and storytelling. Joan, too, was helpless. "Bobby's death hit him so hard I couldn't talk to him." She would speak to him but he wouldn't answer.

He was unable to share his mourning with anyone. All he wanted was total seclusion, to sit alone on the terrace gazing for hours at the sound, reflexively having his meals there, not knowing what he was eating.

Like Bobby, Ted had a strain of Celtic melancholy, but while Bobby's was always close to the surface, Ted's pensiveness was buried so deep within his psyche neither he nor anyone else in the family had suspected it was there. Bobby had a morbid preoccupation all his life with death and dying. "I don't know that it makes any difference what I do," Bobby said a year after Jack's death. "Maybe we're all doomed anyway."

Ted, who loved life and living, never was heard to express hopelessness; for him the glass was always at least half-full.

When Jack was killed, Bobby's spirit was dimmed to the point where his boyhood friend David Hackett called him "a lifeless man going through the motions of living. It was as though someone had turned off his switch," Hackett said. Upon Bobby's death, Ted was affected the same way. The once-vibrant, enthusiastic young senator's life force was extinguished.

After Jack's death, Bobby would dash out of his home in the middle of the night and drive deep into Virginia, not knowing or caring where he was going, returning at down, red-eyed and white-faced, dressing to go to work at his job as attorney general. In his cavernous office, he would sit at his desk, staring out the window.

After Bobby's murder, Ted sought consolation from the sea aboard the *Mira*, a rented yawl, sailing alone westward on Nantucket Sound, past Wood's Hole and up into Buzzard's Bay. Or would cruise north along the coast, as far as Maine, for days at a time, watching the changeless sea. Toward nightfall he would head for a marina where he would tie up and try to sleep. At night, he would drink, seeking solace in liquor but finding none; he would pick up women but find no comfort in his brief companionship with them.

Richard Drayne, his handsome, bespectacled press secretary, usually cheerfully efficient, visited Ted at marinas and was uncharacteristically subdued when he returned to Washington. "I have never seen any human being so devastated," he said. "I thought to myself: 'How can that man ever be the same again?'"

Now and then, Ted called his office, but Drayne and other aides clearly saw that he was barely interested in what was happening. Late in July, Ted had to return to Washington to sign some important papers, but after sitting in his car outside the old Senate Office Building, he drove back to the Cape. "I just couldn't go in and face them all," he said.

Sometimes he would take young John F. Kennedy, Jr., then eight, and his own children on a long sail, but they probably didn't like it much because of his prolonged silences. Rita Dallas, his father's nurse, surmised that Ted's world, once shared with his father and brothers, no longer existed for him. "He was left in a lonely universe of fatherless children, grieving widows, and aging parents," she said.

Once Dallas saw him on the porch of Joe's house on the Kennedy compound, watching Bobby's children at play. "From the pain in his eyes, I could tell he knew there was no way to replace their losses. He tried valiantly, but it was too much."

At one point, after almost ten days of lonely sailing, he returned home and went to the compound to visit his parents. Old Joe, who had suffered a debilitating stroke in 1961 and could neither speak nor walk, was startled when Ted, his hair down to his shoulders and with a two-week beard on his face, entered his father's bedroom.

His eyes wide with surprise, Joe pointed a finger at his son, his hair and beard, his torn old sweater. Rose told Ted to shave at once, or she would get a razor and do it herself. That wouldn't be necessary, Ted said, and ducked into a bathroom. He emerged clean-shaven. "We all had a good laugh afterward," Ted recalled, "and seeing my father laugh like that at last, my mother said, 'I wish we could do that every day.'"

The murder of Robert was an emotional blow that hit Edward Moore Kennedy harder than did any other family tragedy. It changed not only the person but the course of his life.

Ted had joyously played the game of politics, earning high praise from President Kennedy, who called him "the best politician in the family." Ted was the reincarnation of John J. "Honey Fitz" Fitzgerald, Rose Kennedy's father, the magnetic former Boston mayor, who, JFK once said, could charm the birds from the trees and the votes from anyone who ever heard him speak.

Ted would go anywhere and do anything to help his brothers win elections. As Rocky Mountain and Western States Coordinator for Jack's presidential race, he once mounted a bronco with a reputation for meanness and on another occasion made an 180-foot ski jump, neither of which he'd ever done before. He sang Irish songs, danced Irish jigs; his boundless exuberance was so infectious that many times farmers yelled from the crowd: "Hey, Ted, why ain't you the one who's running?"

John Kennedy, reading about these dangerous exploits, telephoned his impulsive brother. Ted recalled the conversation: "He said he had just spoken with the state Democratic chairman in Wyoming who told him I was coming there. They were arranging to have a sharpshooter shoot a cigarette out of my mouth at twenty yards. Jack said casually that he didn't think I had to go through with that if I didn't want to, but...,"

After ten weeks of solitary bereavement, Ted Kennedy, speaking in public for the first time since the funeral of Bobby Kennedy, made a solemn pledge. He committed himself to carrying on Bobby's un-finished work, to helping the poor, and hungry, the disfranchised, the oppressed, in all areas of American life.

In Worcester, Massachusetts, Ted talked about the war in Vietnam, where America was still staying the course, on the protests sweeping the nation and about himself.

"Today," he said, "I assume my public responsibilities, like my brothers before me. I pick up a fallen standard. Sustained by the memory of our priceless years together, I shall try to carry forward that special commitment—to justice, excellence and to courage—that distinguished their lives.

Having moved up, death by death, in the family hierarchy, Edward Moore Kennedy accepted the burden of restoring Camelot to its former grandeur.

Badly wounded emotionally, was he entering a world he never really wanted and should have shunned? Did he have the inner strength to pursue, as passionately as Bobby, the causes to which his brother had devoted the last years of his life? Did he have the will to achieve the family's goal, drilled daily into his sons by the patriarch, that Kennedys must win, at whatever cost, everything from sailing races and football games to the highest office in the land?

It cannot be doubted he meant what he said that day in Worcester. Several times in the years that followed, he spoke to me about the injustices in the country and the world. Using Bobby's words, he said he wanted to be the spokesman for the "voiceless and powerless, the helpless and hopeless. I'd like to be their senator. There is so much suffering around us, so much that is wrong. When my brother Bobby held a poor, sick Indian child in his arms, he cried. I cry, too, at the sick who cannot be helped. I want to help."

But could he? He was the youngest brother, adrift, in choppy seas, with no pilot to guide him and no safe haven where he could dock. Joe Kennedy had brought up his sons to be connected emotionally. "John, campaigning, had Robert to work for him," said Garry Wills, professor of history at Northwestern University. "Robert had Edward to advise [him] and be his surrogate. Edward has no one but ghosts at his side."

Ted had relied on his brothers to help him deal with important problems; they were the older, wiser figures in whom he had confidence. But they were now only memories and constant reminders of his own vulnerability.

Many times he was heard to say that he would be the next target. "It's me now," he would say. And "It's me for the bullet, it's me for the brass ring." And "I know I'm going to have my ass shot off someday."

Ted would shudder at any noise that sounded like a gunshot. A cannon signaling the start of a political parade in Haverhill, Massachusetts, caused him to double up as though in pain and to fall down, white-faced and trembling.

Six years before, when he was only thirty years old, Ted had also lost the guidance of his father, who had suffered a stroke. Indeed, Ted became father to Old Joe, helping to care for him and easing his stresses. Rose, although wonderful in her role as campaigner, was never counselor to the boys; Ted's wife Joan, unable to compete with the other Kennedy women, needed reassurance herself.

Jack and Joe, Jr.,* his oldest brother, had been Ted's heroes and protectors, and while he mourned their loss deeply, the death of Bobby hit him hardest because he was closer to him and had looked upon him all his life as a "second father." As a small boy, when he was scared, Ted had run to Bobby, six years older, who would put his arm around him and provide the comfort he could not get from his father, who was away from home much of the time, or from his mother, who watched what he ate, how he conformed to his faith, his health and schoolwork; she saw herself primarily as a teacher and disciplinarian.

A comment Ted made at the age of six is revealing. At the Sloane Street School for Boys, which he and Bobby attended while Joe, Sr., was ambassador to Great Britain, he told a classmate who wanted to be his "best friend" that he already had one, his brother Bobby, but the boy could be his "second-best friend."

In March 1938, Joe had taken Rose and five of his children to London, installing them in the thirty-six-room official residence at Princes Gate, a quiet little street opposite Kensington Gardens. Luella Hennessy, a diminutive but tough registered nurse, hired by the Kennedys two years before, had come to supervise the children. Luella, who remained with the Kennedy family for the next half-century, was present at the birth of twenty-eight of the twenty-nine grandchildren of Joe and Rose. Luella, now living in a retirement home near Boston, recalled:

"The boys had always been close, but in London they were together most of their free time. I could see that they truly *liked*

---

*Joe, Jr., was killed during World War II when his explosive-packed PBY4 exploded in the air over the English Channel while he was flying a top-secret mission to knock out German rocket-launching sites in Pas de Calais, France.

each other, which is rare between brothers. So many other siblings bicker and shut one another out from their games. Bobby always included Ted when some of his schoolmates came to play, even though they were twice his age."

At the back of the ambassador's residence, a large formal garden had been transformed into a playing field for racing, tumbling, baseball, and, of course, the much-publicized football games. A marble terrace several hundred feet long stretched across the other houses on the street. It was an ideal bicycle path. Ted, Bobby, and Luella would ride up and down the terrace, racing each other, the boys shrieking with glee when they would beat Luella, which was almost all the time.

"Always," Luella said, "there seemed to be something very special between the two boys. They were so different, Bobby the intense one and Ted so easy-going, and yet they understood each other so well."

As the result of his brothers' assassinations, Ted had become father to sixteen children. He had three of his own, and now was surrogate father to two of his brother John's and eleven of Bobby's, including one as yet unborn. He took this role seriously. When Ethel gave birth to her last child, Rory, by cesarean section, Ted was in the operating room in a surgical gown and mask.

With the family support system gone, could Ted Kennedy, by himself, carry the standard thrust into his hands?

Two Teddys

Ted Kennedy is the Dr. Jekyll and Mr. Hyde of American politics, a complex amalgam of good and bad, one side of his personality seeming to have no command of, or relationship with, the other. He is a good, some say superb, senator; but in the quarter-century after the murder of Bobby he has also exhibited a dark side. Judging by his public behavior, which he has made little effort to conceal, he has been an uninhibited pleasure-seeker, driving too fast, drinking too much, and wenching whenever the mood struck, which was often.

As he passed his sixtieth birthday on February 22, 1992, friends, enemies, and impartial observers agreed that the youngest Kennedy's personal life had become a mess.

Looking at him up close in mid-1991, I was shocked. When I interviewed Kennedy in the 1970s and observed him throughout that decade and the early 1980s, his face was a healthy pink, his blue eyes clear, his walk a confident stride; he was moving into his mature years, still handsome as a movie star.

Now, as 1990 opened, his face had turned puffy, blotched with shades of pink and crimson. His jowls hung loose, his nose was red and misshapen, his eyes were narrowed and bloodshot, and he was grossly overweight. ·

His life is a modern-day Rashomon tale: Different observers, all qualified to render judgment, see him in ways that differ astonishingly.

James Wooten, the newspaper and television journalist, wrote: "Edward Moore Kennedy is simultaneously becoming not only America's favorite son, but its favorite son-of-a-bitch as well."

Bad Ted has also elicited these comments:

Dr. Thomas C. Reeves, professor of history at the University of Wisconsin and author of a best selling book, *A Question of Character: The Life of John F. Kennedy*, said, "Ted Kennedy is a drunk, he is a womanizer, he is a tragedy as a husband. In fact, his whole life is a tragedy."

"He is the nation's oldest juvenile delinquent."—Howie Carr, columnist for the *Boston Herald*.

"He is a dried-out and hollowed-out husk…an aging Irish boyo clutching a bottle and diddling a blonde."—Michael Kelly in *GQ* magazine.

"He has been utterly shameless, brazen and indifferent to what should be his internal conscience"—Howard Phillips, chairman of the Conservative Caucus.

The *New York Times* called him a "hard-drinking roué." *Newsweek* said he is "the disreputable Kennedy," adding: "Once the carrier of the family flame, he has become the living symbol of its flaws."

Dr. Garry Wills of Northwestern University, who has studied and written extensively about the Kennedys for years, said, "He is neither immoral, amoral, or immature. He knows exactly what he is doing, but does it anyway. He has become an object of pity for those who watch him up close. He is a weak man with neither the drive nor tremendous ambition of his brothers."

Bad Ted is the butt of countless jokes. For example:

"How many Ted Kennedys does it take to change a light bulb?" "Three. One to hold the bulb and two to drink until the room starts spinning."

Political satarist Mark Russell convulsed audiences when he said, "Ted Kennedy has said he's going to clean up his act. Since he's approaching his sixtieth birthday, the decision to slow down may not be his. Mother Nature is taking care of that."

During the Palm Beach rape scandal, this one went the rounds:

Willie Smith meets a girl in a bar and invites her to the family mansion where the attack was alleged to have taken place.

"How will I get back?" the girl asks.

"Don't worry," Willie says. "My uncle will drive you home."*

But there is an entirely different Ted Kennedy: a legislator who commands and retains the respect and admiration of political colleagues on both sides of the aisle.

Senator Orrin Hatch of Utah, the ranking Republican on the Labor and Human Resources Committee, which Kennedy chairs, said in 1990, "He's becoming the statesman that we all hoped he would be. Whether you agree with him or not, he's becoming one of our all-time great senators."

Conservative Republican senator John Warner of Virginia said, "He works twelve to fourteen hours a day. In the deepness of his heart he believes in what he is doing, which you cannot say for everybody around here."

"He is a man driven in all his pursuits, nothing if not a political phoenix," said the *Boston Globe*. "Scrappy, inquisitive, tireless, and single-minded, he has been successful in an institution his two bothers never took seriously."

Thomas P. O'Neill, former speaker of the House, who has spent a lifetime in politics, believes that Ted is one of a few leaders in America who will go down in history as a legislator of true distinction. O'Neill rates Teddy an "excellent" senator. "He excels as a liberal in government and has a considerable knowledge of government and how it works. Most importantly, he has the ability to get things done."

But Tip O'Neill is a Democrat and a Kennedy friend, and thus his assessment can be viewed as biased. Consider, then, the opinion of Senator Alan K. Simpson of Wyoming, a Republican who is often at odds with Kennedy on public issues. As a fellow member of the Senate Judiciary Committee, Simpson has had close contact with Ted over the years. In his judgment, "Ted is a very steady and able legislator, performing a heavy task extremely well. He is extraordinarily well versed in parliamentary procedure and understands the pitfalls of the legislative process."

Once Simpson tried to get Senate approval for a measure but without success. He told Ted of his problem. "Ted read the bill carefully,"

---

*William Kennedy Smith, Ted's nephew, was acquitted in December 1991, on charges of sexual battery (the legal definition of rape in Florida) against a young woman he picked up in an exclusive Palm Beach bar after Uncle Ted had taken him and Ted's son Patrick for a postmidnight bout of drinking. The scandal is discussed in chapter 20.

Simpson related, "and told me that if I changed just four words, it would go through. I did, and it was passed."

Kennedy is a hero to liberals and those who work for progressive causes. Declared Judith Lichtman, president of the Women's Legal Defense Fund, "He's the best legislator I know. He's up early, works all day, and calls in the middle of the night to make sure he's got it right." Lichtman speaks from a background of a quarter-century's work with Kennedy on health and child care, sex discrimination, and civil rights.

Good Ted worked long hours behind the scenes late in 1991 to forge the compromise that finally won President Bush's approval of a civil-rights bill, then refused to take the credit for his accomplishment; he gave the lion's share to Senator John Danforth, a Missouri Republican. Bad Ted affronts public decorum often and brazenly and doesn't seem to give a damn.

Good Ted is a devoted surrogate father. All through their youth, he visited Ethel's home at Hickory Hill to play with Bobby's children, help them with schoolwork, and listen to their problems. Sometimes he would arrive in a semi-inebriated state, but they neither noticed nor cared.

Bad Ted arose at a dinner party on Cape Cod and shocked the guests with a lewd toast.

Good Ted works harder than most other senators. "Lots of times—too many times," says a staff aide ruefully, yet with strong admiration for his boss, "there are all-nighters in his home. We work in that beautiful family room he has, with the purple and blue couch and a tall stone fireplace, thrashing out strategies and prepping the boss for hearings the next day. He's fresh and bright in the morning. The rest of us drag our asses back to the office."

Bad Ted humiliated his wife Joan on many occasions at parties, ignoring her while he danced and flirted with pretty young women. Good Ted has for years been the Senate's only champion of women's rights, prompting Ann Lewis, a Democratic activist, to say, "His advocacy is so valuable that it more than makes up for any concern about his private life."

Watch Good Ted on the floor of the Senate.

On January 21, 1992, the Senate convenes at 11:30 A.M. for the second half of the 102nd Congress. Senator Joseph I. Lieberman, Connecticut, is presiding and bangs the gavel; Chaplain Richard C. Halverson calls upon God to guide their deliberations, and the debate begins.

Ted Kennedy is at his desk in the back row. As fifth in seniority, having served in the Senate for thirty years, he is entitled to a choice desk as far front as he wishes, but he prefers the rear. Explains Melody Miller, his deputy press secretary, "He wants to sit there because it's easier for him to get in and out when urgent business comes up elsewhere, and also, from that vantage point, he can address the whole Senate without turning around. It's also easier on his back."*

About 1:00 P.M., Ted rises to introduce his newest bill, S.2137, the "Emergency Anti-Recession Act of 1992," providing $40 billion for job retraining, construction projects, and assistance to jobless workers. He looks tall and commanding as he faces the members. He has dropped about thirty pounds, his face has lost its pudginess, and his voice, which sounds like a high-decibel klaxon, is strong and vigorous.

Kennedy speaks for twelve minutes, underscoring his abiding concern with people and their human needs. His plan to end the recession calls for a substantial short-term stimulus "and a commitment to make long-term investments to create jobs and meet the nation's fundamental needs in education, job training, research and development, health care, and other top priorities..."

Increased federal, state, and local spending, he said, may be the only way to guarantee a start to recovery. Under his proposal, the $40 billion in new funds should start flowing as soon as possible and should go to existing programs, divided equally between infrastructure repair and human needs. While President Bill Clinton did not mention Kennedy, these ideas were part of the economic program he proposed to Congress in mid-February 1993.

Ted remained in the chamber about twenty minutes after he had finished speaking. Then, glancing at several three-by-five-inch cards stapled together, he slipped out and hurried to the Dirksen Building at First and C streets. The Labor and Human Resources Committee, which he chairs, was holding hearings on proposed legislation to provide affordable health care for all Americans and to reduce health-care costs.

These index cards dictate Kennedy's day. On them his staff types where he must be, minute by minute, hour by hour. He carries the

---

*Kennedy has worn a back brace ever since he was severely injured in a near-fatal air crash in 1965. See chapter 9.

cards in an inside jacket pocket and has said he couldn't function without them. One day, some years ago, my name had appeared on the cards with the notation that I would tag along wherever he went. By 6:30 P.M., I was exhausted, but Kennedy's day, which had begun at 8:30 A.M., had not ended.

Nor was it finished on that January in 1992 when he returned to his office at Number 315 in the Russell Building at First and C streets. He conferred with aides, made a dozen phone calls, picked up his briefcase, and drove home to McLean, Virginia.

The "bag," as everyone in his office calls it, is an important part of Ted Kennedy's working life. It is so worn that one can barely see the gold-stamped EMK on the front, and so jammed that most times it cannot be closed. Into the bag go the memos he must read and comment upon, letters of varying degrees of urgency that must have replies, transcripts of debates and hearings—anything and everything that calls for his attention.

He opens the briefcase on the drive home, works on its contents, often until 1:00 or 2:00 A.M., and again on his way to work. Usually, everything inside is completed by the following morning.

Three

The Baleful Influence

T ed's great-grandfather, the first Kennedy on America's shores, was a brawny lad named Patrick Kennedy, who stepped off a packet boat in Boston in 1849 with a rope-tied suitcase and about a hundred dollars in his pocket. He had endured a six-week, storm-tossed journey in steerage, cramped into a tiny cell-like room with seven other men, breathing foul air and close to starvation from rigidly rationing the food he had brought along.

Patrick, who was twenty-five, had come from Dunganstown near New Ross, a port city in southeastern Ireland where his family owned a once-prosperous farm. Some 750 other passengers landed with him at Noddles Island in Boston Harbor. About 80 others had died en route of dysentery, typhus, and cholera aboard the aptly named "coffin ship."

Patrick, and thousands like him, were fleeing the devastating typhus epidemic and potato famine that would claim a million Irish lives before they had run their course. A few months later, he married Bridget Murphy, a pretty colleen who had "caught the boat" with him at New Ross.

The immigrants who were scorned in Boston as "famine Irish" and "the scum of creation," could find employment only as laborers, dockhands, coal heavers, ditchdiggers, and other low-paid construction workers. The women, termed "biddies" and "kitchen canaries," were hired as domestic servants.

Struggling to survive, Patrick became a barrel maker. Bridget bore him four children; three girls and a son, Patrick Joseph, who was only six when his father died of cholera at the age of thirty-three.

A muscular man like his father, Patrick Joseph left school early and went to work on the Boston docks, saving every dollar until he had enough to set up a small liquor business. He made more money and bought a saloon, then another. His liquor company and saloons were successful; so was the new career to which Patrick turned: politics. A genial and friendly man, he ran for and was easily elected to the Massachusetts State Legislature when he was only twenty-eight. He eventually served five terms.

Patrick married Mary Augusta Hickey in 1887 and the following year threw a huge party in one of his saloons to celebrate the birth of his first child, a red-haired son he named Joseph Patrick. Joseph squalled a lot in infancy, probably from colic, and had stomach problems all his life. His digestive system may have been delicate, but his will was strong and his manner imperious.

Now a wealthy man, Patrick gave his children—two daughters, Loretta and Margaret, were born later—a fine home in East Boston. He sent Joe to the prestigious Boston Latin School, the oldest public school in America, established in 1635, and later to Harvard.

Patrick's slender reddish-haired son never took to politics; he preferred money. A friend since boyhood days recalled that Joe's favorite—and frequently asked question, was "How can we make some money?" He learned how early. At fifteen, he was the founder of a baseball team in East Boston, scrounging contributions to buy uniforms, then renting a small ballpark and charging admission. He made a profit on each game. He sold candy and ice cream to hungry and thirsty passengers on excursion boats, charging double what he paid. Joe vowed he would be a millionaire before he was thirty-five. He reached his goal before he turned thirty.

Ted's great-grandfather on his mother Rose's side, Thomas Fitzgerald, arrived three years after Patrick Kennedy. Their paths never crossed—not in Ireland, nor in Boston. In 1857, Tom, who had opened a grocery and liquor store, married twenty-two-year-old Rosanna Cox and produced a family of eleven children, one of whom was the redoubtable

John Francis "Honey Fitz" Fitzgerald three-times a congressman and twice mayor of Boston.

In 1889 Honey Fitz fell in love with a slender, petite girl named Mary Josephine Hannon, whose brown hair framed beautifully chiseled features. He beat out a phalanx of competitors for her hand. On July 12, 1890, an unbearably hot summer night, a dark-haired daughter was born in the kitchen of their home in Garden Court in Boston's North End. They named her Rose Elizabeth. She would become the matriarch of the Kennedy clan.

The paths of the Kennedys and the Fitzgeralds crossed for the first time at Old Orchard Beach, Maine, when Rose was seven and Joe was nine. Afterward, Joe met Rose at social events and the two began seeing each other. Honey Fitz, then the mayor, didn't like the idea of his daughter going to cotillions with the son of a saloonkeeper, even though Joe's father was also a member of the state legislature. Joe simply wasn't good enough for Rose.

For seven years Honey Fitz tried to keep Joe and Rose apart, even sending Rose and her younger sister on a European trip and then enrolling them in a convent school in Germany. Rose, however, slipped a photograph of Joe into her suitcase and kept it on her nightstand the whole time she was away. Back home, Joe and Rose were equally ingenious at keeping their rendezvous secret. Joe would fill up her dance card with phony initials and then claim her for those numbers. They would meet casually at the home of friends or at the library. Even the family chauffeur conspired to help them. He would take Rose for a drive, and suddenly Joe would appear. They would leave to have tea, visit friends, skate in winter, or go for walk. Later the chauffeur would meet them and drive Rose home.

When Joe, at twenty-five, became the youngest bank president in the United States, Honey Fitz finally relented, and his daughter's engagement was announced. Joe and Rose were married on October 7, 1914, in the private chapel of William Cardinal O'Connell. The marriage united two prominent Boston political families and began the dynasty that would become the most celebrated in U.S. political history.

After the wedding, the young couple moved into a small house at 83 Beals Street in Brookline, and the children began arriving, on average of one every eighteen months between 1915 and 1932.

Joe's wealth grew rapidly through shrewd investments in the stock market and real estate, through cheap movies produced on the lowest of budgets during a five-year venture into the motion-picture business, and through the liquor business. By 1926, at the age of thirty-eight, he was a multimillionaire. Seven years later, convinced that Prohibition would be repealed, he made a deal in England with Haig and Haig, Ltd., John Denver and Son, Ltd., and Gordon's Dry Gin Co. for exclusive rights to handle their liquor in the United States. Through his friendship with Franklin D. Roosevelt, Jr., Joe obtained medicinal licenses to import alcoholic beverages, bringing in vast quantities of liquor which he stockpiled in warehouses. When Utah became the thirty-sixth state to ratify the Twenty-first Amendment, repealing Prohibition, Joe was the first businessman in the country ready to distribute liquor legally around the country.

Countless stories have surfaced that, during Prohibition, Joe Kennedy was a bootlegger who imported liquor illicitly, but no conclusive evidence has ever been produced. Doris Kearns Goodwin, author of *The Fitzgeralds and the Kennedys*, speculates that while Kennedy may have been one of many small liquor importers at the start of the 1920s, "it is harder to imagine Kennedy still involved during the middle or late twenties after the criminal gangs had taken over and fundamentally changed the nature of the illicit trade." Joe was much too busy in motion pictures; moreover, there was little reason for him to be involved in liquor when he was reaping such huge profits from his speculations in Wall Street.

But Joe's wealth did not impress the Boston Brahmins. The Kennedys were not their kind of people; they were not accepted in the best circles. As ambitious socially as financially, Joe smoldered. Finally, when the Cohasset Country Club, the city's most prestigious, rejected him, he exploded.

"Boston is no place to bring up Irish children," he told Rose. In 1922, Joe packed his family and their belongings into a private railroad car and moved to Riverdale, an exclusive section of the Bronx, north of Manhattan, which he felt would be more hospitable to Irish Catholics.

Four years later, the Kennedys moved again, this time into a mansion in the elegant Westchester suburb of Bronxville, a solidly Republican enclave, derided by outsiders as "a hotbed of social rest" and hailed in verse:

Here's to Westchester County
Society's uppermost shelf.
Where Scarsdale speaks only to Bronxville,
And Bronxville just talks to itself.

By 1950, Joe Kennedy had amassed a fortune estimated at $400 million.*

"There are few people in this world who have bigger incomes than I've got," he once said. But the acquisition of wealth was only part of his master plan. Power for his sons was the other half. So while Rose fed them on sturdy New England fare—clam chowder, fish, chicken, roast beef, lobster, gallons of milk, and chocolate cake—Joe fed them on ambition and competitive drive.

Lose a sailing race, and a boy would be exiled to the kitchen that evening to have his dinner alone. Work at his job to near-exhaustion, or a son would receive a verbal lashing. Once Bobby, who had worked for three months nonstop as investigator for the Senate Rackets Committee, came to the Cape for a weekend of rest and, still bone-weary, decided to stay another day. Joe saw him lounging in the living room. His face turned beet red as he thundered at his son: "Get up off your ass and get back to your job in Washington, where you should be!" Bobby packed and left.

Joe Kennedy's mania for winning no matter what the cost is familiar to everyone who has followed the family saga. But there was a master plan in his demands for competitiveness that he voiced aloud, probably for the first and only time, on a humid afternoon in early August of 1960.

He was sitting on the wide, shaded porch of the big three-gabled house in Hyannis Port, sipping iced tea as he talked to author and journalist Joe McCarthy, a close family friend. (With the full cooperation of the family, McCarthy would later write the bestseller *Johnny, We Hardly Knew Ye*, about the late president.) McCarthy had come to Hyannis Port that day at Joe's invitation to gather material for another book, *The Remarkable Kennedys*, published in 1962; it was one of the first family-authorized biographies.

---

*See chapter 22 for a discussion of the Kennedy wealth, past and present.

In 1978 I visited Joe McCarthy, whom I had known since World War II days, at his home in Blue Point, Long Island. We were reminiscing about the early Kennedy years, and Joe told the story of that day at Hyannis Port.

"The old man let down his guard that afternoon," McCarthy said. "Jack had just been there, visiting his grandmother Josie, who was ninety-five and in poor health. Joe was saying how sick Jack had been as a kid and how he was now heading for the country's number-one job. He went on to Bobby and Teddy, and how brilliant they all were, how capable and talented and all that, and what he had in mind for them.

"I was taking notes, but then I stopped because it was getting clear to me that Joe wasn't even aware of what he was saying and certainly never intended me to put his remarks in a book. I never wrote what he said because I didn't think it was fair to take advantage of the old man that way. He was a tough SOB, that's for sure, and I knew he broke people in business and never missed a second's sleep. But still, I had this journalistic integrity hangup. Besides, I knew that if I wrote it, the old man would deny he ever said it.

"I don't recall his exact words, but they went like this: 'Each of those three kids is going to be president of the United States. There would have been four if Joe had lived. Hell, Joe, that's three presidents named Kennedy going down in the history books, one after the other.'

"He gave a little laugh when he said that three Kennedys beat two Adamses."

As the years went on, Joe's master plan became increasingly clear to historians and political commentators, but never once did he put it explicitly as he did that day at Hyannis Port. McCarthy asked me not to publish the incident, "at least, not while I'm alive. The Kennedys wouldn't like it at all, and I'm still writing about them." He died in 1980.

It wasn't the only time Joe Kennedy blurted out his feelings without recognizing their news value.

The most famous of these blunders occurred during World War II, and it ended his diplomatic career.

The ambassador to the Court of St. James had returned to the United States in the fall of 1940 to deliver a personal report to President Roosevelt on the fast-moving events in Europe.

In a New York hotel in November of 1940, Joe Kennedy couldn't keep his mouth shut. While Britain endured nightly bombing attacks, he was being interviewed by a *Boston Globe* reporter. While the reporter, Louis M. Lyons, scribbled notes, Kennedy flailed away at the British.

"Democracy is dead in England," he said. "It isn't that she's fighting for democracy. That's the bunk. She's fighting for self-preservation, just as we will if it comes to us."

Pacing the floor and devouring cheese-topped apple pie, Joe praised Col. Charles A. Lindbergh, who had made no secret of his isolationist views, and expressed low regard for the intelligence of the British cabinet.

At the end, he wasn't aware of what he had said. "Well, I'm afraid you didn't get much of a story," he told Lyons.

It was indeed a story. Published all over the world, the Lyons interview made big headlines. The British were infuriated by the remark that democracy was dead in their country.

Joe Kennedy's ambassadorship and his relationship with President Roosevelt had ended. FDR summoned Joe to his estate at Hyde Park, New York, talked to him for about ten minutes, then told his wife Eleanor, "I never want to see that son-of-a-bitch again as long as I live." Joe resigned, and FDR accepted his resignation at once.

Edward Moore Kennedy was born February 22, 1932, but not in Bronxville. Rose insisted on having her ninth baby at St. Margaret's Hospital in Dorchester, south of Boston. He was delivered by Dr. Frederick L. Good, the city's most prestigious obstetrician.

Rose remained in the hospital almost two weeks. While there she received a short, unsigned note on stationery from the Choate Preparatory School in Wallingford, Connecticut, where Jack was enrolled.

> Dear Mother,
> It is the night before exams, so I
> will write you Wednesday. Lots of love,
> P.S. Can I be Godfather to the baby?

A month later, John Kennedy, fifteen years old and painfully thin, neat and solemn in a dark blue suit, made the Profession of Faith at the baptism of his baby brother. The boy was christened Edward Moore Kennedy, for the plump and faithful Eddie Moore, whom Joe had met in the early 1920s and who remained his lifelong friend, troubleshooter, and confidential secretary.

Rose took Teddy back to Bronxville. Because of his father's peripatetic lifestyle, Teddy attended nine separate schools before he entered Harvard, where Joe had decided he must go. He began in the kindergarten at Lawrence Park Country Day School in Bronxville, attended two schools in London during his father's ambassadorship, and one each year after that until he completed his secondary education at Milton Academy.

In 1940, after Joe's resignation, the family moved into the sprawling Hyannis Port house, where Teddy joined the boot-camp regimen Joe ordered for his children when they were on vacation. Joe had a schedule posted on the outside wall near the entrance, each child was instructed to read it in the evening and memorize where he or she must be the next day, and when.

A typical one read:

7:00 A.M. wake up time
7:20 to 8:00 setting up exercises on the lawn.
8:00 breakfast
9:00 to 10:00 tennis
10:00 to 11:00 basketball
11:00 to 12:00 touch football
12:00 to 1:00 lunch
1:00 to 2:30 rest
2:30 to 6:00 water sports
7:30 dinner
9:00 bedtime for the younger children
10:00 bedtime for the older ones

Joe appointed Eunice, his second-oldest daughter, to supervise the program; afterward, he hired an athletic instructor to take charge.

Joe Kennedy's belief in the virtue of winning took root in Jack and Bobby. Early in 1960, John Kennedy's hopes for getting the Democratic presidential nomination seemed dim to Associated Press correspondent Jack Bell, who suggested several times that Kennedy aim no higher than vice-president. Kennedy was enraged. He dashed off a note to Bell: "I wish you'd get those words out of your typewriter because I'm never going to take second place."

Bobby was even more tenacious in his pursuit of excellence. "He was a feisty guy, tough on himself. Tougher then hell," said Dr. John Knowles, a classmate at Milton Academy, who later became director of Massachusetts General Hospital. Weighing only 150 pounds, Bobby was never a good football player, but he struggled to improve with an energy and determination that amazed his friends and coaches. At Milton, players who outweighed him by fifty pounds or more would smash into him continually at practice sessions, but he would always get up to take more punishment. Freshman coach Harry Lamar said, "You'd have to kill him to make him quit."

Bobby's competitiveness sometimes went to hilarious extremes. Once, during a softball game at Hickory Hill, his daughter Kerry, then six, came to bat. It was the last of the ninth, the score tied, two out and two on base. Bobby wanted to win the game, and he did. Instead of tossing an easy one to Kerry, he threw her a hard, fast pitch. Kerry never saw the ball go past. When Rose heard the story that evening, she was aghast. "Bobby," she said, "you didn't!"

Bobby shrugged. "Can I help it if Kerry is a sucker for an inside fastball?"

Ted, however, had a problem with his father's insistence on winning. As a child, he was good-natured and easygoing, with a choirboy smile, trotting around after his three brothers like an adoring puppy. Recalled Luella, the family nurse, "Teddy always had the happiest disposition. I never saw him moody. He was always gentle, always agreeable." He never complained, not even when Joe, Jr., in a fit of anger, tossed him overboard from a sailboat—at the age of six!—when he failed to obey an order to pull in the jib.

Teddy grew up loving sports but was perfectly content to play for the fun of it and if he lost—well, so what? Luella said, "Bobby always groused and worried whenever he lost a game but Teddy never cared."

Actually, none of the Kennedy boys quite understood why they had to win. Said Dr. James MacGregor Burns, professor of government at Williams College, "How to win, the price to be paid for winning, the rules and practices to be followed, were never quite clear [to them]. Nor was the ultimate aim of competition clear—was it for some higher purpose, like money? Or was it worthy and rewarding in itself?" A search through their statements over the decades reveals nothing on record from any of the four brothers that they knew Joe's insistence on the highest degree of competitiveness was to fulfill his dream of four Kennedy presidents.

"Like the others, especially the boys, Teddy was expected to live up to parental expectations of constant achievement and victory," said psychohistorian Nancy Gager Clinch. "At first, the focus was centered on the older brothers," Ms. Clinch asserted, "and the demands on Teddy were less immediate."

Nor was the discipline as strict. Rose had grown tired by the time Teddy came along. Having borne nine children in seventeen years, she was easier on Ted than she had been on the others.

But Joe didn't let up. When Fessenden, one of the boarding schools Ted attended, sent home a notice to all parents asking permission to give students a paddling for infractions, Joe was the first one to send it back, approved. Once, when Ted and a friend went on an overnight sailing trip, they were caught in a storm and spent the night on board, buffeted by wind and soaked by rain. Too exhausted to sail back, they rowed to shore the next morning in a small boat, found a telephone, and called home. One of the Kennedy employees drove down and took them back.

Joe spotted Ted straggling upstairs, asked why, and sent him out again. "When you start something," he told Ted, "finish it. You don't ever quit on the job." Ted, then eleven years old, returned to the boat and sailed it home.

Ted did not resent the order because he was growing up with the conviction that his father was right in the demands he was making on his children. He had unbounded admiration for his father who, he said, was "eminently successful, extraordinarily knowledgeable, and thoroughly enjoyable." He admired, too, his "strong and firm handshake," his "broad smile, warmth, and generosity."

He admitted that his father was a "hard taskmaster," quick to scold them for mistakes which he would tolerate once, but never a second time. "We were ashamed to do less than our best," Ted asserted, "because of our respect and feelings for him."

Father and youngest son doted on each other. Joe told everyone Teddy was his "sunshine." When Joe was in a dark mood, especially after his stroke, Teddy would burst into his father's room and at the sight of him, Mr. Kennedy's face would light up, "'Hi, Dad,' he'd say, 'havin' any fun?' Joe would wink and beam at him," said Rita Dallas, Joe's nurse.

When Joe suffered his stroke, he was rushed to St. Mary's Hospital in Palm Beach. He had fallen into a deep coma and was given the last rites of the Catholic Church. Ted flew down from Boston and remained at his father's bedside throughout the day and night, sleeping and eating there, holding Joe's hand, caressing his brow, staring intently at him for signs of awakening.

The next afternoon, Joe's eyelids flickered. Teddy leaned toward him; Joe's eyes opened and saw his son. Teddy's face broke into a wide grin. For a long moment, he held his father's hand, then called his brother Jack, who was staying nearby. The president rushed to St. Mary's. Thereafter, Ted came to see his father as often as he could, conferring constantly with doctors on rehabilitation procedures. He was impatient when physical therapists would be even a couple of minutes late and would bark at them to be on time.

Once, at Hyannis Port, Joe was being given an electrocardiogram as part of a physical examination. The technician applied the electrodes and turned on the machine, but it wouldn't work. Teddy waited less than a minute.

"Quit fooling with that damned thing and buy a new one!" he yelled. The solution was simple: the technician had neglected to plug the instrument into an electric socket.

In 1965, after the plane crash in which he broke his back, punctured a lung, and cracked several ribs, Teddy spent almost six months immobilized in a metal frame, unable to move anything but his head, hands, and feet. During that time, he produced a book, *The Fruitful Bough*, consisting of reminiscences by the Kennedy family and also his father's friends.* Ted got the idea for the tribute from *As We Remember Joe*, the volume of recollections that Jack had put together in 1945 in memory of their oldest brother. Joe Kennedy could never read that book. "I cry nearly every time I open it," he said. But he could—and did—read the volume of reminiscences Ted had collected. He cried again, this time from happiness.

---

*Ted took the title from Genesis XLIX:22,24: "Joseph is a fruitful bough, even a fruitful bough by a well; whose branches run over a wall;... But his bow abode in strength, and the arms of his hands were made strong by the hands of the mighty God of Jacob...."

As Joe lay dying in the fall of 1969, Ted slept on the floor of the bedroom in a sleeping bag. He was at his father's bedside, his head bowed, weeping, when Rose kneeled at the bed and gently placed a rosary in his hand.

When a news magazine published an obituary containing sharply critical comments, Ted lashed out in cold fury. He wrote a blistering letter in longhand to the editor. Said an aide, "I never saw the boss so pissed."

Joe's efforts to mold Teddy into a hard-charting, go-go Kennedy ultimately proved disastrous to the boy. Ted sought his father's approval all his life, but he was too amiable, too friendly, too innately *nice* to become what his father said he must.

Bobby would bellow about a disputed call in tennis but, said Meyer Feldman, a former JFK aide: "Teddy bends over backward to be fair, is scrupulous about the calls, always giving the advantage to his opponent—and I haven't seen that in any other Kennedy." Teddy would never dream of striking out a six-year-old to win a ball game!

"The seeds of Ted Kennedy's problems in later life, and they were monumental, were planted in him by his father who, quite literally, charted the lives and careers of his sons," said Dr. Thomas C. Reeves of the University of Wisconsin.

"Trying to adapt himself to Joe's standards, Teddy was thrust into a world he never wanted and couldn't handle. Raised by a father who drove him to compete and succeed, whatever the cost, Teddy was left in a moral vacuum."

The tug-of-war within Teddy was responsible for this first serious misstep, which would haunt him for the rest of this life.

Four

First Fumble

A happy, friendly little boy, Ted Kennedy grew up into a husky, happy, still friendly, young man, who loved sports, chased—and caught—young women anytime he wanted one, but found little time for academic studies.

At Milton Academy, south of Boston, where he enrolled in 1946, Ted was popular with the students because of his sunny nature but won no plaudits from his teachers, even though they recognized his efforts. "I was never a quick study," Ted said later. He tried to make up by plugging away at the books, but while he managed Bs in European and American history, his average hovered closer to a C in most other subjects.

To earn even those, Ted had to spend a couple of hours most evenings with Kernel Holloway, a special teacher whose job at the academy was to help floundering students. Said Arthur Hall, dean of students during Ted's Milton years, "He was Kernel's favorite customer."

Ted could never master foreign languages. Since Milton required three years of a second language for graduation, Teddy elected what he thought—and his friends advised him—was the simplest: Spanish. He had trouble with the subject each of the three years he took it, but not nearly as much as he would have only a short time later.

Teddy graduated in June 1950 with a C average and the tag "Smilin' Ed" beneath his picture in *The Orange and Blue*, Milton's yearbook. Few classmates foresaw much of a political future for him; he received only four votes as "class politician."

Brother Jack, on the other hand, was voted "most likely to succeed" by his senior class at Choate, a fact which mother Rose noted proudly in her autobiography *Times to Remember* in 1974. Unknown to Rose, however, and probably most everyone else, Jack rigged the election. He conspired with his friend Ralph (Rip) Horton to lobby for him.

Rip did a magnificent job. He spoke to every senior, pleading Jack's cause. Most went along, because while Kennedy had demonstrated virtually no qualities that would lead anyone to believe he would succeed in later life, his popular approval rating was high. When the results were announced, the Kennedys were delighted, but the Choate faculty was stunned. Said Seymour St. John, who succeeded his father, George St. John, as headmaster in 1947; "If you'd have asked the teachers where Kennedy would stand, I'd expect they would have put him well below the middle."

Of the four sons, Joe, Jr. was the only brilliant student. Declared Dr. Seymour St. John, "He was the golden boy. He did everything right. He was extraordinarily popular, an excellent student and a terrific athlete. The young man was amazing."

Jack, who followed Joe to Choate, also graduated with a C average, his years there marred by a seemingly endless succession of illnesses. He suffered feverish colds, conjunctivitis, mumps, boils, fallen arches, painful knees, and bouts of extreme weakness, the first signs of what eventually turned out to be Addison's disease.* While Jack was an omnivorous reader, he neglected his studies. Hugh L. Packard, his French teacher, said, "He was frequently unprepared and his homework was sloppy and badly done." Owen Morris, his Latin instructor, declared, "His work was passing but poor." The final assessment by the faculty was that his low marks were far below his intelligence and potential.

---

*Addison's disease destroys the cortex of the adrenal glands, which become unable to produce sufficient hormones, resulting in weight loss, poor appetite, extreme weakness, and low blood pressure. Kennedy was close to death in London in August of 1945, and again in Vietnam while on a global journey with Bobby. Later that year, the diagnosis was made. Lifelong treatment with cortisone, a synthetic hormone discovered about that time, kept him in a state of fairly good health. See chapter 11.

Nor was Bobby an academic achiever. At Portsmouth Priory, a Catholic boarding school in Rhode Island, where he spent two-and-one-half years, his grades were only fair—averaging 75 for the 1941–42 school year, his last at the Priory. He did worse when he transferred to Milton, where he scored a D in English, an E-minus in French, and failed Latin in his final year. Albert Norris, his housemaster, suggested tutoring in his senior year, and Rose agreed.

All four boys went to Harvard. Joe decreed Cambridge, and there they enrolled. Despite poor grades, both Bobby and Teddy were academic "legacies" by virtue of being preceded at Harvard by a father and two brothers. Their Milton diplomas and the influence of Joe Kennedy, who called the right people, were also compelling reasons.

In his freshman year, Ted earned a C in general education, a B-minus in social sciences, B-minus in one naval-science course, and a C in another. He drew an "unsatisfactory" in a foreign-language course; the reason will be discussed shortly.

His grades as a senior were better, though not remarkable. He received four Bs, one B-plus, one A-minus, an A, and a C, for a B average. He did well enough in two government courses to win approval from the distinguished professor Arthur N. Holcombe, Eaton Professor of the Science of Government.

Dr. Holcombe was the only Harvard professor who, in his long tenure at the university, taught all of the five Kennedy men who attended there, Joe, Joe Jr., Jack, Bobby, and Teddy. I talked at length with Dr. Holcombe in Germantown, Pennsylvania, where he lived following his retirement form the university. Dr. Holcombe's comments about the Kennedys—and especially about Teddy—are illuminating:

"Edward was in great demand socially by ambitious mothers in Boston society to attend all of the important functions, and that, of course, made great demands on his time. During the football season, he had even less time to devote to study. He did just what was necessary to remain in good academic standing.

"He never had time for the kind of work Jack did, for example. Jack got very much interested in the research work done in the course (American National Government, ed).* During Christmas vacation,

---

*Dr. Holcombe supervised John Kennedy's honors thesis, which he later expanded into the book *Why England Slept*. With considerable assistance from his father, who enlisted the help of the distinguished *New York Times* columnist Arthur Krock, the book became a bestseller.

Jack went to Washington to make contacts down there and pursue further research. Ted didn't ever have time for that sort of thing."

Professor Holcombe said that, academically, Ted "didn't think he was in the same class as his older brothers." Still, he added, "I have no doubt that Edward could have graduated with high distinction if he had wanted to."

At Harvard, Teddy lived at Winthrop House, known around the campus as the "jock house" where the athletes roomed. A brawny 200-pounder who stood 6'2", he was at home with the others, many of whom outweighed him and were one to three inches taller.

He found football and girls a good deal more interesting than studies. Once, after an argument about a touch-football game, Teddy told one of his roommates, Edward (Ted) Carey he'd prefer to have Carey go away—far, far away—as far away as Africa. Ted said he'd like to send him there if Carey would go, which he doubted very much.

Carey, who had never been much farther away than his hometown of Westfield, Massachusetts, accepted the dare. "You put me on a plane, and I'll go anywhere you say."

Done. Ted agreed to supply an airplane ticket to Cairo, provided that Carey got back to Cambridge by himself. Later, Ted Carey admitted he had little money but figured he would get a job on a freighter to pay for his passage home.

The following day, Kennedy handed him a one-way ticket to Cairo, purchased on his credit card, and three days after the whole silly thing had been hatched, he and a few friends drove Carey to the airport, where he boarded a plane for New York where he would take a connecting flight to Cairo.

Kennedy watched him fly off with growing trepidation. Recalled George Anderson, another roommate, "He began worrying about what his father would say, and what the newspapers would print about a senator's brother pulling such a stunt." He called the airport in New York and told Carey to come on back, that he'd taken the dare and won. But Carey refused to return.

Kennedy paled and went back to Winthrop House. Meanwhile, Carey, who wasn't about to go off to Cairo anyway, returned to Westfield, where he remained overnight. He showed up at Winthrop on Saturday, relieving an anxious Ted Kennedy.

"He was always making these wacky bets," Carey said. "He was willing to bet on anything, like who could hit a golf ball across the

Charles River. He usually bet a couple of dollars or, if you lost, you had to pick up his laundry for a week."

Once Carey found himself in trouble with the law, thanks to a bet with Teddy. John Arnold, a classmate, recalled: "We were all sitting in the room one January night, and Kennedy said, 'Gee, it's cold outside,' Carey said it wasn't cold, and that was all Kennedy needed to hear.

"'Okay,' said Kennedy, 'I'll bet you won't run nude over the footbridge in front of the business school and back.' Carey said, 'The hell I won't,'" and dashed outside.

"As soon as he was gone, Teddy called the campus police and told then that some guy was running around in front without any clothes on. The cops arrived in a couple of minutes, searched the area for half an hour, and left. Spotting them, Carey had hidden in the bushes until they left. Shivering with cold, he returned to the house. He never found out that it was Ted who called the police."

As for girls, Ted never went out with one girl more than a few times; he would go off with his pals to Scollay Square, a disreputable area in Boston known as "the combat zone" because of its taverns where frequent battles would erupt. When he met a young woman he fancied, he would make his intentions clear almost from the start. If the girl indicated that she did not intend to sleep with him—at least not that night—he would leave her abruptly and seek someone else.

His sex life at Harvard was as active as Jack's had been. In his sophomore year (1938), Jack wrote to Lemoyne K. Billings, his room-mate at Choate who remained a lifelong family friend, that he could "get tail as often and as free as I want." Jack never again had to pay for sex after their first sex experience in a Harlem brothel while they were students at Choate.

Billings, who attended Princeton, had invited Jack for a weekend which would, of course, be spent in the company of women. Jack asked Billings to make sure his room was as far removed as possible from Lem's. "I don't want you coming in for a chat in the middle of the night," he wrote, "and discussing how sore my cock is." Another time he gave Lem a further report: "JJ has never been in better shape or doing better service" he wrote. "JJ" was Jack's pet name for his penis.

Bobby was entirely different. A moralist all his life, he had little patience with classmates who went to parties to drink and "just waste time doing nothing worthwhile." Said Nicholas Rodis, a Harvard friend who later became athletic director at Brandeis University, "Bobby wasn't a party boy." And Samuel Adams, who had gone to Milton with Bobby and entered Harvard the same year, said that Bobby would never accompany the other boys on their periodic visits to Boston's houses of prostitution and neither did he.

It was in football, however, the family fixation, that Teddy performed better than his brothers.

Joe, Jr., made the varsity but never was awarded the Harvard letter which, by tradition, was given to squad members who played, however briefly, in the end-of-season Yale game.

Jack made the junior varsity but dropped out because he had suffered a spinal injury during his sophomore year.

Bobby was on the sixth and seventh squads most of his years but, because of his ferocity and scrappiness, finally made the varsity in his senior year. He played in the opening game of the season against Western Maryland, catching the first and only touchdown pass of his collegiate career.

A week after the game, he was scrimmaging side by side with Kenny O'Donnell, the team captain. After a half hour, he collapsed on the field. "He had been playing with a broken leg all that time," Kenny said. It healed in time for him to be sent into the Yale game at the season's end, so he earned his letter.

Brawny Ted easily made the freshman or "yardling" team, playing left end in nearly every game. He lacked speed, the Harvard *Crimson* wrote, but his blocking and tackling were highly praised.

He observed training rules rigidly, eating only the foods the coach instructed the team to have and made sure he got plenty of sleep. His goal was to make the varsity and win his letter.

He was also aware that his father prized gridiron success above all other athletic accomplishments. A measure of what football meant to Joe Kennedy could be adduced from the memorable scene he made during the Yale game when, in his senior year, his son Joe was warming the bench. Joe became increasingly agitated as the game neared the end and coach Dick Harlow gave no indication of sending young Joe onto the field. With the game over, Joe wouldn't receive his letter and Joe, Sr., white with rage, ran into the locker room. Before the entire team and with young Joe red from embarrassment, Joe scathingly castigated the astounded coach for not putting his son into the game.

Joe Kennedy never realized that the family obsession with football, and the value he placed on athletic success, was mainly responsible for

Ted's much-publicized 1950 attempt to cheat on a Spanish test at the end of his freshman year.

University rules dictated that freshmen unable to demonstrate proficiency in a foreign language would be barred from playing on any athletic team in their sophomore year. Fearful of flunking the Spanish final, eager to continue playing football and of winning his father's approval, Ted became increasingly apprehensive as the exams neared.

At Winthrop one of the students suggested that he hire somebody better versed in Spanish to take the test for him. After all, it was argued, faculty members are never present at the exams, which are proctored by graduate students or teaching fellows. Moreover, finals are given in the larger classroom and lecture halls, with students taking different tests in the same rooms. The chances of being detected were almost nonexistent, they told Ted.

The jocks at Winthrop who were in on the "deed," as one called it, told me that Ted's need to continue to play football was the prime motive. Later, I asked Ted Kennedy, "Were they right? Was that why you did it?"

He replied, "That's the story. They told it to you straight. That was the only reason."

He paused a moment, then added, "It seemed so important them."

One of the jocks brought up the name of Billy Frate, a husky, affable guard who roomed at Dunster Hall. "He's a Spanish whiz." Billy was approached and agreed to take the test for Ted.

Billy Frate went to the assigned room, picked up an examination booklet, wrote Edward Kennedy's name, the date, and his class on the cover, and sped through the test. Ironically, it was a particularly easy one which Ted probably could have passed himself. When Billy turned in his booklet, the proctor looked up and recognized him. His eyes caught Ted's name on the cover.

Hauled before Dean Delmar Leighton that same day, both boys were summarily expelled from school. Dean Leighton told them they could reapply for admission the following year provided they could demonstrate a record of constructive and responsible citizenship.

Ted returned to his room and, for several hours, sat alone in total confusion. He had been dismissed from Harvard—the only brother so disgraced. What would he tell his father? What would his mother say? How could he explain the shame to his family? Finally he telephoned his father at Hyannis Port and blurted out the story.

He was amazed at Joe's calm reaction. Speaking as though his son had just told him about getting a ticket for a parking violation, Joe wanted to know the complete story. Ted explained as best he could.

But it was the calm before the eruption of a furious storm. When Ted came home the day after his expulsion, the full impact of the episode had struck Joe. "He went absolutely wild and went up through the roof for about five hours," Ted said. From then on, he was calm. It was just 'How can we help you?' and he never brought up the subject again."

The disgrace hit Ted Kennedy hard. He lost his bounce and buoyancy; his smile was gone. He worried about his family, himself and, by no means least, about Billy Frate, who had been pulled into the conspiracy and punished, too. The Cape was beautiful in that summer of 1951, but Ted sat staring at the sparkling sea, not caring to sail or to swim or to do anything at all but brood.

Finally, after a month, he decided to enlist in the army. He brought his papers home and showed them to his father, who read them and exploded in rage. "Don't you ever look at what you're signing!" he bellowed. Teddy hadn't looked. He had intended to enlist for a two-year hitch, but had signed for four. With truce talks in the Korean War about to start and the outcome still uncertain, he would have been sent overseas if the shooting was renewed. Joe couldn't stand the thought of yet another son going into combat. He made a few calls to the right places and had Ted's enlistment period altered to two years.

Ted's military service in France and Germany proved uneventful, except for some more feats of derring-do on his furloughs. He climbed the Matterhorn, the 14,692-foot mountain peak in the Pennine Alps on the Swiss-Italian border, and won a one-man bobsled race for novices in Switzerland; he had never before scaled a mountain or ridden a bobsled. He corresponded regularly with his family, asking many questions about the progress of Jack's 1952 campaign for the Senate. Learning that there were eight Massachusetts residents in his outfit, he campaigned for Jack and got each man to obtain and send in absentee ballots for him.

Ted was discharged in 1952 as a private first class, having turned down a bid to go to officer candidate school. He applied for readmission to Harvard and, having demonstrated the required responsible and constructive citizenship, was accepted. So, too, was Billy Frate. They graduated together.

Back at Harvard, Ted made the football varsity and, with Number 88 on the back of his jersey, had three good seasons playing right end. In his senior year, he gladdened Joe's heart—and his own—by catching a pass on Yale's seven-yard line in the final classic and scoring the Crimson's only touchdown. Joe, shivering in the stands, rose and yelled himself hoarse with the other Harvard fans. He embraced Ted after the game, pride shining in his eyes. Never mind that Yale won 21 to 7: Ted had scored Harvard's only touchdown.

After graduation, Ted applied to Harvard Law School but was rejected because his grades weren't high enough. He talked to his father, who thought it inadvisable to use his influence on Ted's behalf at this point in his career. Ted then said he wanted to go to law school at Stanford University in Palo Alto, California.

It was am important moment in his life, the start of an attempt to break away from the family's influence. There were several more to come, as we will see, but, like this one, they were aborted by his father. When Ted told Joe of his decision, his father stared at him for a full minute, then turned away with a curt "You stay in the East."

So Teddy obediently enrolled in 1956 at the University of Virginia Law School in Charlottesville, where Bobby had earned a law degree in 1951. Like Bobby, Teddy was only an average student. But Ted distinguished himself in the same two ways; bad and good.

Curiously nicknamed "Cadillac Eddie," although he drove an Oldsmobile, Ted drove recklessly, and often very foolishly, around the historic town in the foothills of the Blue Ridge Mountains. Once he passed a red light, was spotted by a patrol car and a movie-type chase ensued. Teddy sped down the street, rounded corners with tires squealing, and lost his pursuer. It made a great story back at school.

Several evenings later, Ted drove down the same street and sped past the same red light. This time, the same patrol car, driven by a lieutenant of the Charlottesville police force, was able to follow Teddy to his residence, a three-bedroom, red brick house on Barracks Road which he shared with his closest friend, Varick John Tunney, son of Gene Tunney, the heavyweight boxing champion.

Ted went down the long driveway, parked in the rear of the house and, knowing he was followed, crouched beneath the dashboard, hoping he wouldn't be seen in the dark. But he was spotted, ordered to come out, and did, "meek as a cat," the lieutenant said later. Ticketed for reckless driving, he paid a $35 fine, the first of at least two other convictions for the same offense at law school.

Teddy began drinking heavily at law school for no special reason other than to have fun. He accepted every invitation to a party, where he told jokes, did imitations of political figures and generally had a good time. But he also studied hard.

Knowing his limitations as a student—"I've got to go at a thing four times as hard and four times as long as some other fellow," he said—he woke early and studied until the law library closed. Said librarian Frances Farmer, "He and Tunney would come in at eight o'clock in the morning, study until it was time for class, then return and sit just outside my office until it was time to close the doors."

Ted's hard work got him through law school, again with a C average. His extracurricular achievements however, were notable. He teamed with Varick Tunney (who later dropped the uncommon first name at Teddy's suggestion because "John" sounded more electable) to win the prestigious moot-court tournament. They triumphed over fifty other teams and, in the finals, were judged by a panel of distinguished jurists. As at most law schools, a moot-court victory is equal in honor to editing the *Law Review*.

Ted also became president of the Student Legal Forum, an organization Bobby had rescued from near-oblivion in his student days. The forum invited noted speakers to discuss current national and international problems. Bobby had corralled Supreme Court Justice William O. Douglas, and his brother John, who was then a congressman. When Teddy took over, he invited Walter P. Reuther, president of the United Automobile Workers, Senator Hubert Humphrey, and his brother Bobby, the chief counsel to the Senate Rackets Committee.

Bobby couldn't resist a dig at his younger brother for the frequency with which he had been cited for traffic violations: "My mother wants to know on what side of the court my brother is going to appear when he gets out of law school, attorney or defendant."

In the fall of 1957, at the start of his second year, Edward Kennedy met the quintessential American beauty, blond, blue-eyed, tall, and slender. Twenty-one-year-old Virginia Joan Bennett lived with her parents and sister only a mile from the former Kennedy home in Bronxville. Joan would soon marry Ted Kennedy and begin a glamorous life which placed her near the pinnacle of power and then, all too quickly, encountered problems that almost destroyed her.

Five

Joan

Virginia Joan Bennett's family arrived in America two centuries before the Kennedys and only about twenty-five years after the *Mayflower* brought the Pilgrims to New England. Like most pioneers in the New World, the Bennetts became farmers in the Massachusetts Bay Colony and later journeyed to New Hampshire, working the land and engaging in commerce.

Throughout his long life, Joan's grandfather, Harry Bennett, Sr., sought risk and adventure. He built a railroad in Cuba, where he started a sugar-exporting business, which soon failed, bought a copper mine in New Hampshire and a gold mine in Alaska, ran a silk mill, invented a new kind of dog biscuit, and became an investment broker in New York City. Harry, Sr., made and lost several fortunes; unhappily, he was on the losing side when he died in 1952 at the age of eighty-six, leaving his second wife, Andasia, with little but fond memories.

Seventeen years earlier, on June 8, 1935, Harry Wiggin Bennett, his son and Joan's father, married Virginia Joan Stead, a slender girl, five feet four inches tall, with delicate features set in a round, beautiful face. Joan was born fifteen months later, on September 5, and was named for her mother. A second daughter, Candace, was born two years later.

Harry was an advertising man most of his life, important enough to be listed in *Who's Who in America*. Before retiring, he had been an executive with the Bryan Houston Agency, where he handled major accounts such as Colgate-Palmolive-Peet, placing some $30 million in ads annually. That was and still is serious money. Houston remembered Harry as a shrewd, extraordinarily able man who managed his staff of two dozen people easily. "He was not the stereotype of the adman you see in the movies and on TV," Bryan Houston said. "He wasn't the blustering type, but a low-key, quiet, and decent man who never made an enemy in his life."

So decent and so well liked that when a major company decided to drop the agency, the CEO waited until Harry, who was the account executive, was out of town before announcing the cancellation. "We didn't want to hurt his feelings," he told Harry's boss.

Like the Kennedys, the Bennetts lived for a while in Riverdale, then moved to Bronxville, where Harry bought a pink-and-gray home with four bedrooms, a high-ceilinged living room with a stone fireplace, a dining room, kitchen, and pantry. It was only a mile and a half from the mansion on Pondfield Road where Joe Kennedy had installed his rambunctious family a few years earlier. They had never met because Joe moved back to Massachusetts before the Bennetts came to Bronxville.

Life was pleasant for the Bennett girls. Harry and Ginny (the girls did not call their parents "mother" and "father") took them to New York City for the theater and concerts. The family belonged to the Siwanoy Country Club and had a summer home in Alsted, New Hampshire. Ginny, an accomplished pianist, began teaching Joan before she was four, and music became Joan's lifelong passion.

Joan received excellent grades in school and, in one case that remains on record, provided the sole sensible answer to a question posed by a reporter for the *Bronxville Mirror*: "If you had an extra hour in your day, anywhere in the day, to use as you like, what would you do?"

One respondent was flippant: "Swim to Bermuda." Another would play bridge; a third, do her Christmas shopping. Joan announced that she "would take a nap."

By the time she was twelve, Joan had grown to her full height of five feet seven inches. Spindle-thin, she wore braces on her teeth. At school, she was mousy-quiet, shy, and bookish. "I wasn't outgoing," she said. "I didn't like athletics. I enjoyed just coming home from school, doing my homework, reading a great deal, playing the piano, and being very much by myself."

Her younger sister, Candy, a stunning brunette, was as vivacious as Joan appeared to be unassuming. A high-school cheerleader, she was surrounded by boys, but was also liked by the girls.

Once, in the midst of her marriage, Joan blurted out to Kennedy family nurse, Luella Hennessey, "Ted should have married Candy. She was always the girl athlete who plays tennis so well and rides beautifully, while me—I'm allergic to horses!"

Joan recalled that she "didn't have boyfriends" in her early teens. "I had a few girlfriends who were quiet like me." However, as she approached her seventeenth birthday, her braces came off, she "filled out," and the boys began to take notice of the other beautiful Bennett girl.

That year Harry Bennett decided to take Joan with him on a business trip to Florida.

"I was working like crazy," he said. "Ten, twelve, fourteen hours a day. I knew that I didn't give my family enough time and attention, but I was so busy earning a living. I missed having time with my family, and I thought it might be fun to take my little girl away with me and have her all to myself, just for a week.

"I decided from the moment we left the front door of our house she would no longer be my daughter, but my date. And I wooed her all that week, and took her out, not as my daughter, but as my sweetheart, if you want to call it that.

"Joan stayed up all night with me at nightclubs for the first time in her life, and we drank champagne together for the first time. We saw everything there was to be seen in St. Petersburg, Tampa, and Gainesville. We went fishing, we went swimming, we did everything.

"She had the time of her life. And when we were on the plane coming home, she looked at me and said. 'I never knew adults could be so much fun.'"

Joan's closeness with her father continued even after her blond beauty began to be noticed and she became a sought-after date for fraternity weekends, especially at Yale.

She would send her father a card from a restaurant or nightclub. "Dear Harry," she would write. "Having such a nice time. Miss you. Joan."

In June 1954 Joan graduated from Bronxville High and entered

Manhattanville College of the Sacred Heart at Purchase, New York, where Rose Kennedy and her daughters, Eunice and Jean, were educated. Joan was an English and music major and took courses in history, science, mathematics, and religion. She had been accepted at two other women's colleges, Mount Holyoke and Smith, but chose Manhattanville because, she said, she hadn't had much training in her faith.

Joan was happy at Manhattanville, which was a short distance from her home. She made friends easily with the other students, who were bright, affluent Catholic girls like herself.

During spring break, Joan and several classmates went to Bermuda, where her fresh blond beauty and stunning figure easily won her the College Queen crown. The following year, the Bermuda Chamber of Commerce selected her from among several other college queens to preside over the island's annual floral pageant, and she rode through the streets of Hamilton in a lily-bedecked coach.

Proud of the local girl, the *Mount Vernon Daily Argus*, ran a story on March 2, 1956, with the headline BRONXVILLE GIRL TO BE QUEEN OF BERMUDA'S FLORAL PAGEANT:

> It's a Westchester Queen for the annual 1956 Bermuda Floral Pageant to be held in Hamilton on April 5. She is Joan Bennett of Bronxville, a sophomore at Manhattanville College of the Sacred Heart in Purchase.
>
> The pretty nineteen-year-old is the daughter of Mr. and Mrs. Harry Wiggin Bennett, Jr., of 14 Eastway. Joan will be accompanied by her parents and her sister Candace, seventeen, as guests of the Bermuda Chamber of Commerce....
>
> Selection of Queen Joan came about when the Chamber of Commerce decided to choose the 1956 ruler from among the college girls who visited the island last year during the Spring vacation. She had been designated Miss College Week.

That summer, Harry Bennett, who had been dealing with beautiful models for many years on his ad campaigns, suddenly realized that his own daughter was lovelier than most of them. He talked to Joan about a part-time modeling career. She agreed, not because she was intrigued by the glamour of being a model, but to earn money for a trip to Europe.

Bennett had known Candy Jones, then one of the country's best-known models and magazine cover girls, for several years. Candy, the wife of Harry Conover, director of one of the two leading model agencies in the country, was in charge of the agency's training school for young girls.

One day Candy went to Harry's office for a consultation on an upcoming ad campaign for a beauty product. After an hour and a half, Harry leaned back in his chair and said, "Candy, have I got a girl for you!"

"Sure, sure," Candy thought. "Another proud father thinking his daughter was prettier than Vivian Leigh and sexier than Raquel Welch. Sure. I acted pleased, though; I didn't want to offend Harry. I said, 'Fine, Harry, send her over. I'd love to talk to her.' All the usual things I say when an important person has a girl for me.

"But then one day this gorgeous girl walks in, an astonishing girl with a deep tan and glorious eyelashes, sort of wheat color and long. She was one of those rare beauties we get infrequently. I said to myself, 'This can't be for real.' Her hair, I could tell at one look, was real blond, not out of a bottle. She radiated beauty and glowed with good health. Oh, I said to myself, there has to be *something* wrong, like she'd probably be a lisper, or have a sibilant 's,' but she spoke in perfect cultured tones."

Candy said Joan loped like a cowgirl and was a bit too hippy for a model, but they were both faults that could be corrected. Joan easily learned the model's sinuous glide and on Candy's advice pared her hips, an old-fashioned way: lubricating her skin and running a rolling pin up along her hips and backside.

Joan was selected for some choice commercial assignments. She did photographic modeling for beauty products, food, and shampoos, as well as television commercials for Maxwell House, Revlon, and Coca-Cola. She made thousands of dollars in her eighteen-month modeling career.

Joan was in her senior year at Manhattanville when she met Ted on October 7, 1957. It was a special day on campus. The new Kennedy Physical Education Building, for which Joe had contributed a handsome sum, was to be dedicated, and Francis Cardinal Spellman would be the guest of honor at a tea and reception. Many Kennedys were there, and all seniors were required to attend.

Joan, who had an English paper due, decided to skip the ceremonies and was working busily when her roommate, Margot Murray, rushed in. She told Joan she had been missed and was about to receive demerits.

Margot said, "Maybe if you come down real fast, the student government girl who gives out the demerits will see you and assume you've been there through the whole ceremony."

Joan recalled, "So, I got out of my old bathrobe, jumped into something appropriate, and ran over. The next thing I knew I was standing with Margot, and Jean Smith, Ted's sister, came up to me and said, 'Aren't you Joan Bennett? Remember we met last August?'

"Well, when she spotted me at this reception and came over to talk to me, I didn't know Jean Smith was one of the Kennedys. *I had never even heard of the Kennedys!* I just took no interest in current events; my lowest grade in college was in current events. Jean said she'd like me to meet her little brother or her younger brother, and I'd almost expected to meet someone knee-high."

Little brother turned out to be Ted, then twenty-five, who had asked his sister to introduce him to the pretty blond. Ted had to leave to catch a flight back to Charlottesville that night. Joan and Margot drove him to LaGuardia Airport.

In the next few weeks Ted called Joan many times. During the Thanksgiving holiday, they met for lunch in New York City and Ted drove her back to Bronxville. One day he called for her at the offices of the modeling agency, where Candy Jones saw him. His football days were over, and so was the rigorous training-table dieting. Ted had put on weight. Candy asked her secretary, "Who's that fat kid with Joan? She could do better than that."

More dates followed, but Ted did not have Joan all to himself. Two other young men were strong competition, which did not please the young Kennedy, who was unused to occasional turndowns when he asked for dates during his year-long courtship. Unsure of how he stood, he finally asked the Rev. John Cavanaugh, the president of Notre Dame University, who was a close friend of both, to plead his cause.

Father Cavanaugh did, successfully. Later Joan confessed Ted had been "my first and only love" and she would have accepted with no need for an intermediary. Ted proposed as they walked along the beach at Hyannis Port.

Ted endeared himself to Harry Bennett by calling for an appointment, arriving promptly at the house and, after a few hesitant moments of small talk, asked for the hand of his daughter in marriage.

"It was kind of old-fashioned," Harry recalled, "but I was touched and impressed. He was so sincere, so obviously in love. I broke the tension by asking if he could support my daughter in the style to which she had been accustomed. He laughed, we shook hands, and the engagement was on."

On September 21, 1958, eleven and one-half months after they met and three months after Joan graduated from college, their engagement was announced. Two months later, on November 29, a blisteringly cold day, they were married at St. Joseph's Roman Catholic Church in Bronxville. Joan and Ted wanted Father Cavanaugh to perform the ceremony because, she said later, "he was the best priest-friend Ted and I ever had."

But Joe said that only a prince of the Church should officiate. Ted balked. Joe insisted. As usual, Ted lost. Joe telephoned Francis Cardinal Spellman, the spiritual leader of the New York archdiocese, who agreed to marry the couple.

Joan was stunning in a long-sleeved ivory satin wedding gown, in whose folds was hidden a small microphone. Ted, too, wore a microphone, and floodlights lit the altar. Harry Bennett had made arrangements to have the whole ceremony filmed professionally.

John Kennedy was the best man, Bobby an usher. The guests included Ted's Harvard football teammates. A reception followed at the Siwanoy Country Club. After a three-day honeymoon on Lord Beaverbrook's estate in Nassau, the newlyweds returned to Charlottesville for Ted's last year at law school. They lived in a rented three-bedroom apartment, where Joan taught herself to keep house and, with the aid of several cookbooks, to prepare edible meals. Ted even came home regularly for lunch.

Mrs. E. Gerald Tremblay, wife of a Charlottesville attorney who had been a law-school classmate of Bobby's, visited often. "Joan wanted to show she had learned to keep house, and she wanted to do it all by herself," she recalled. "Once there was a dinner party at their house, and they invited almost fifty people. Joan prepared all the food. It was a buffet, delicious and beautifully organized. She glowed with pride when we all told her how well it went."

After Ted's graduation in June 1956, he and Joan went on a long-delayed honeymoon to South America, and in late summer moved in with Rose and Joe in the Compound while they looked for a permanent home. There, in the Big House, Joan got her first real look at Kennedy-style politicking.

Their bags were still unpacked when Joe called a conclave. Besides the three brothers, the gathering included Steve Smith, Ted Sorensen, Lawrence O'Brien, one of the state's best political organizers, Pierre Salinger, who would become John Kennedy's press secretary, and Jack Baily, a power in Connecticut politics. They met in the large living room with Currier & Ives prints on the walls overlooking comfortable early American furniture. Joe set the timetable:

Jack would announce his candidacy for the Democratic presidential nomination early in 1960, and at once a campaign, fueled by Joe's fortune, would be launched for the nomination at the convention in August. Bobby would manage his campaign. Teddy would be assigned a major role.

In fact, the campaign had been going on for almost two years. Joe had told Jack to barnstorm around the country, making speeches anywhere he was invited or could arrange an invitation. Jack obeyed. He spent more time traveling around the country than in the Senate, hitting the major voting areas and gathering enthusiastic support wherever he went.

On Joe's orders, Steve Smith had already opened a campaign office in Washington and was busily making contacts in every state. Always Jack Kennedy was introduced as "the next president of the United States." Polls showed him leading all other candidates by a wide margin. By 1958 the campaign office looked like a "five-ring circus," Dr. James MacGregor Burns wrote, with people constantly bustling in and out, secretaries feverishly trying to catch up with the mountain of paper work, while answering jangling phones.

When the Kennedys closed the Big House in the fall, Joan returned to Bronxville to await the birth of her first child. Kara Ann arrived on February 27.

In January, following his father's schedule, Jack announced his candidacy. In the spring, he won nine primaries; West Virginia, Ohio, Wisconsin, Nebraska, Oregon, Indiana, Maryland, Illinois, and Pennsylvania. None of his opponents could match his wit, charm, good looks, and, certainly not least, his war record. He had won the Navy and Marine Corps Medal for rescuing crew members of his PT-109 after it had been sliced in two by a Japanese destroyer in the Solomon Islands. His five-hour swim to a tiny island, pulling a crewman with a lifebelt strap between his teeth, also aggravated a back injury which would cause him intense pain all his life and which nearly proved fatal when, in October 1954, he underwent spinal-fusion surgery.

While he recovered, Jack published his Pulitzer Prize–winning *Profiles in Courage*, a book for which he won high praise. Actually, he did not write the book: it was mainly the work of Ted Sorensen and a corps of assistants. Kennedy himself did little more than oversee the project.

However, Kennedy's behavior during the Senate's hearings on the censure of Joseph R. McCarthy, the junior senator from Wisconsin who had made reckless charges of communists and subversives in government in the early 1950s, was less than courageous. By a 67-22 vote, McCarthy charged with 46 counts of wrongdoing, became the fourth United States senator to be censured by the Upper House.

John Kennedy was the only Democrat who did not vote for censure. Roy Cohn, the lawyer closest to McCarthy, had served as counsel to his investigating subcommittee. In 1967 Cohn explained to me why Jack Kennedy was forced to act as he did:

"McCarthy was a pal of Joe Kennedy's. He had been up to the Cape any number of times, liked Kennedy, and Kennedy liked him. He had even been on several dates with Jack's sister Patricia. Joe Kennedy asked his son not to vote for censure, and Jack obeyed his father. Simple as that."

Later, Kennedy explained that he did not vote because he was ill, and senators must be present in the chamber for their votes.

After Jack won the nomination in Los Angeles, Ted became "coordinator of the eleven Rocky Mountain states." He charged around his territory, including Alaska, and then flew to Hawaii. Joan moved to San Francisco, his base of operations, where she hoped to be near him, but he was home only thirteen days in three-and-one-half months. He would have breakfast in one city, lunch in another, and dinner in a third. He made up to twenty speeches a day.

Joe called all the shots. He planted a spy in Jack's Boston office to report to him personally and confidentially on all visitors who came to see his son. He wanted to make certain that Jack wasn't seeing the wrong people who could affect his policies. Joe even had a mole in Jack's Georgetown house, a maid who regularly sent him reports.

Late one day, Joe stormed into Jack's Boston headquarters and wanted to know why he didn't see many "Vote for Kennedy" bumper stickers. Ted, who had just returned from a tour of the city which he had begun at 5:30 A.M., put a bunch of them into his car and drove to the Sumner Tunnel, where he stood at the entrance. "I'm Ted Kennedy," he said to each homebound commuter. "Do you mind if I put a bumper sticker on your car for Senator Kennedy?" Few did.

David F. Powers, Kennedy's devoted friend, companion and political adviser, who went "every foot of the campaign" with him, was effusive about Ted's courage and loyalty to his brother. "He was handsome, red-cheeked, adored Jack, and would do anything for him. In Parkersburg, West Virginia, on May 1, a Sunday, Jack lost his voice completely. When I walked into his room that day to get him up for mass, he wrote two words on a yellow pad: 'Get Ted.' The primary was on May 10, and that afternoon there was to be a big outdoor rally.

"All the Kennedys had a schedule of where they would be, and when. I looked it up, found Ted was in Charleston, West Virginia, and called him. He dropped everything, got into a car and whipped north to Parkersburg. He got there in time for the rally, and he was just great. Jack looked on and beamed at him. Ted was so enthusiastic and got so many laughs and cheers that Jack wrote a note and handed it to him: 'Don't forget who the candidate is!' Next day, at Weirton, West Virginia, Ted again substituted for Jack at a rally in a high school. On the way to the next stop, Kennedy wrote me a note: 'Teddy was great.'"

The day before the voting, Ted raced to Massachusetts to campaign in the tiny community of Mashpee, west of Hyannis Port on Cape Cod, and Washington, southeast of Pittsfield in the western part of the state. Though small, they were considered election bellweathers; their polls closed early and Massachusetts voters who read the results in the afternoon newspapers could be influenced by them.

But they were strongly Republican, and Ted wanted those first tallies to be for Kennedy. Reportedly, he went to every home in each of the towns and every store, hospital, and business. Both communities reversed their traditional party allegiances and voted for JFK.

In 1946 the Kennedys had discovered the importance of women on the stump. When Jack ran for Congress and later the Senate, Ethel, Eunice, Patricia, and Jean had dashed around the district and state, ringing doorbells, passing out handbills, and acting as hostesses at coffee and tea parties. Rose especially won hearts and votes by telling tales at rallies of her children's early years, her joys and sorrows as a mother, and her own Boston childhood.

It was inevitable that Joan would be recruited, too. She found to her surprise that she attracted larger and larger crowds, which delighted the strategists, who then gave her more and more assignments. Joan went to

West Virginia, Arizona, New Mexico, Wyoming, Washington, and California. Her shyness, thick butter-colored hair, and startling beauty won approval from men and women alike.

With the family's help and with massive infusions of Joe's money, Jack Kennedy was elected president in November, defeating Richard M. Nixon. His vote totaled only 118,550 than Nixon's, but in the Electoral College his count was 302 votes to Nixon's 219.

At the Inauguration on January 20, 1961, in snow-blanketed Washington, Ted and Joan were seated only a few rows behind the new president as he told Americans that "the torch has been passed to a new generation of Americans, born in this century, tempered by war, disciplined by a hard and bitter peace, proud of our ancient heritage, and unwilling to witness or permit the slow undoing of those human rights to which this nation has always been committed."

Ted, his ebullient spirits raised several notches by a few drinks, danced an Irish jig at one of the five Inaugural balls and sang several old Irish ballads, while Joan beamed.

Wisely, Old Joe faded into the background. He had masterminded Jack's entire campaign, engineering the largest public-relations buildup of a candidate in the history of American politics. "He fed information and granted interviews to sympathetic journalists," Dr. Thomas Reeves said. "He wooed publishers...he confided to a friend, 'We're going to sell Jack like soap flakes.'" He enlisted the support of political leaders in every state and even obtained the backing of Franklin D. Roosevelt, Jr., who campaigned in areas where FDR was still looked upon with reverence.

At the Los Angeles convention, Joe had rented a mansion once belonging to the Hollywood star Marion Davies and remained out of sight, at the same time operating a battery of phones installed near the swimming pool to keep in constant touch with Jack's headquarters. After his son won the nomination, he left town quietly. Not once during the entire campaign did he appear in public with the candidate. Joe knew his son was wildly popular, but he himself was not. He had heard—and winced at—the Republican jibe: "Jack and Bob will run the show, while Ted's in charge of hiding Joe."

Joe had little to do with helping his son select his cabinet—except for one portfolio; attorney general. Bobby had left his job as chief counsel to the Senate Select Committee on Improper Action in the Labor and Management Field—the investigation of labor racketeering—chaired by Senator John L. McClellan of Arkansas, to head up Jack's presidential campaign. The election won, Bobby was at sea. Maybe, he said, he would travel, or read, or do something: "I just didn't know."

But Joe Kennedy had a very clear idea where Bobby would go: into Jack's cabinet.

About November 15, former Senator George Smathers of Florida, who had served with Jack, gone girl chasing with him in earlier years, and remained a close friend and confidant, was lounging at poolside at the Palm Beach mansion with the newly elected president. Jack confessed that his father had been pressing him to name Bobby attorney general. The president-elect was aware that if he did choose Bobby, he would unleash a torrent of charges of nepotism. Moreover, Bobby had never practiced law; he had only served on Senate investigating committees.

Smathers came up with an idea: name Bobby assistant secretary of defense. The job, he pointed out, carried minor responsibilities, and, within a year or two, he could be promoted to secretary of defense. Bobby would not be in the cabinet—at first—thus muting the critics, but would nonetheless be close to his brother, as an adviser.

Jack pondered the suggestion for several minutes, then said, "That's a fine idea." Jack had told Smathers that his father would soon come down to join them at the pool. "Would you broach the idea to him?" he asked. Smathers agreed.

A half hour later, Joe Kennedy arrived, and Smathers offered his suggestion. Joe listened but did not reply. Instead, he turned to Jack. Shaking his finger under the nose of the next president of the United States, the patriarch barked: "I want Bobby to be attorney general. He is your blood brother. Nobody has sacrificed more of his time and energy in your behalf than your brother Bobby. And I don't want to hear any further thing about it."

Joe closed his eyes and turned his face to the sun. Jack Kennedy named Bobby attorney general.

Ted returned to Boston with Joan. They moved into their first real home, a duplex apartment in a town house in Louisburg Square, the most exclusive street in Beacon Hill. Ted went to Europe on a six-week fact-finding tour with the Senate Foreign Relations Committee. Upon his return he became an assistant district attorney in Suffolk County (Boston). His salary was one dollar a year.

They settled in as young marrieds. Ted walked to the office each morning while Joan took care of the house and baby, with two maids.

Joan was the happy little homemaker. She and Ted lived simply and entertained quietly. Ted often had speaking engagements, although he was usually back home for dinner at 7:30 P.M. Joan spent long hours in her kitchen preparing gourmet dishes until she discovered that "Ted couldn't tell the difference between frozen peas and fresh ones or between my gravies and the ones that came in cans."

In the spring of 1961, they bought their Squaw Island home on the Cape, a four-bedroom, gray-shingled house, a mile from the Kennedy compound, but linked by a special telephone line. Family members phoned and visited each other often. When Joan and Ted decided to have dinner alone one Sunday, the Kennedy sisters teased her for days about being a "recluse."

Joan was pregnant again that spring and summer. She went into labor when Ted was in Boston. She was driven to St. Elizabeth's Hospital in Boston, where Ted was told to wait at home because the birth was hours away. A heavy sleeper, when the baby was born, Ted could not be roused by the ringing of the telephone. He did not know of the coming of Edward, Jr., until his son was three hours old.

In 1961, soon after JFK took office, the Kennedy political machine was busily gearing up again: Teddy was slated to try for the Senate seat his brother John had vacated.

And Joan, handing around glasses of champagne at parties, would giggle and say that the bubbles tickled her nose.

Six

Sexual Legacy

If Joe Kennedy drew the blueprint for his sons' political careers, he was also the role model for their blatant womanizing.

For Joe Kennedy, the conquest of women was ranked just below the making of money, but higher than winning athletic contests. It was a family trait that became, as Garry Wills noted, "a very important part of the Kennedy mystique." Ted, arguably the sexiest-looking of the three brothers, devoted as much time to keeping the mystique alive at Harvard as he did to football. His conquests were undiminished at law school and later in Washington.

Nor did his marriage slow him down.

In October 1961, three years after he married Joan, Ethel and Bobby Kennedy gave a lavish party at Hickory Hill, their six-and-one-half acre estate in McLean, for friends who had helped Jack win the presidency. Among the guests was Shelley Winters, the blond actress who Columbia Pictures hoped would dethrone Marilyn Monroe as America's sex queen.

Dozens of celebrities milled around the swimming pool. Champagne and wine flowed freely, and everyone was having a Kennedy-style grand time, which included a conga line on a plank bridging the pool. A couple of hours after midnight, Shelley, gorgeous in a strapless green chiffon dress, broke the heel on her sandal and limped up the lawn to a bench near the house.

Ted Kennedy saw her leave, followed, helped remove the shoe, and then put his arms around her and kissed her—"passionately," Shelley said. Startled, she broke free and drew away, frightened.

"For God's sake!" Ted exclaimed. "I was only trying to kiss you. What did you think I was going to do?"

"Only God knows," Shelley said as she rose and hobbled back to the party. Ted, too, returned to the festivities, where he joined Joan.

"He was philandering from the moment he was married," said Richard Tuck, Bobby's astute traveling aide and a family friend.

Joe's sons knew of their father's lusty lifestyle, which he did not conceal from them. They were proud of his conquests and sought to imitate them in their own lives. However, while they had strong sex drives, it was not nature but nurture that was to blame for their behavior. "A father's sexual ethics can exert a powerful influence on his sons' attitudes toward women," declared Dr. John E. Schowalter, Albert Solnit Professor of Child Psychiatry at the Yale Child Study Center in New Haven. "Watching their fathers, seeing what they do, sets the stage for their own actions."

"If there is a piece of cake on your plate, take it," Joe Kennedy taught his sons.

They did. "The Kennedys, father and sons, had their wives and their girlfriends," said John H. Davis, Jackie's cousin. "That was the way they lived." According to novelist James Carroll, writing in the *New Republic*, "The sexual habits of the Kennedys, have revealed an emptiness at the core of their story. Those habits betray a permanent disregard for the nameless and faceless persons whose function is to submit. Females exist to submit to males."

Joe emphasized many values in raising his children, but sexual morality was not one of them.

When he was away from home, which was a good deal of the time, he would call and write scores of lengthy letters insisting on study, performance, allowing no barrier, no matter how insurmountable, to deter them from a goal. But "not once in more than two hundred letters did he put forward any ultimate moral principles for his children to contemplate," declared Doris Kearns Goodwin.

What led Joe into this moral vacuum? Ethnic studies have shown fairly conclusively that Irish Catholics, rather than espousing sexual freedom, for the most part adhere rigidly to marital vows. Professor Garry Wills, in *The Kennedy Imprisonment*, theorizes that Joe, rebelling against his Irish origins, also wanted to break the chains of sexual prudishness. "Kennedy wanted people to know that... he was a man of the world, making his own rules, getting what he wanted, ready to indulge the one sensual pleasure that interested him." It was also the only one that remained for him; because of chronically bad digestion, Joe could not indulge in the pleasures of food and drink, or even tobacco.

Joe hopped from bed to bed with amazing frequency wherever he traveled and did not hesitate to bring his women to his homes in Hyannis Port and Palm Beach. In the 1950s, he was never without a lovely young woman on his arm when he frequented nightclubs in New York, Chicago, Los Angeles, and San Francisco.

His sons followed his lead. Joe, Jr., had girls by the score in his brief life. Jack had so many women that his father once remarked wistfully, "I wish I could have his leavings."

Even shy, moralistic Bobby was tempted once, in a brief affair with Marilyn Monroe toward the end of his life, the full facts of which are still clouded in mystery.

One evening at the Big House, Joe Kennedy opened the door of a guest room and stepped inside. A young girl, who had been invited for the weekend by one of his daughters, had just gone to bed. Startled, she sat up. Joe untied his robe and let it slide to the floor. Stepping toward the bed, he said, "This is going to be something you'll always remember."

Thereafter, a grinning Jack Kennedy, who was watching through the keyhole of an adjoining room, would warn female guests when they arrived to lock their doors. "The ambassador," he said, "has a tendency to prowl at night."

Pretty girls brought home by the sons were also cautioned to look out for the old man. In 1941, after Jack was commissioned as an ensign in the U.S. Naval Reserve, he fell deeply in love with a blue-eyed honey blond from Denmark named Inga Arvad and considered marrying her. Joe was furious. "Damn it, Jack!" he howled when his son broached the notion, "She's already married." And she was—to Paul Fejos, a Hungarian film director. Jack replied that the marriage was breaking up and she would soon be free, but Joe wouldn't listen.

However, Joe wasn't adverse to an amorous fling with Inga himself.

Her son Ronald revealed that Joe "tried to hop in the sack with her" at the Big House. Inga refused. "She thought it was a totally amoral situation, that there was something incestuous about the whole family," her son said.

Jack and Ted reportedly provided their father with female companionship when he visited Washington during JFK's administration, and later throughout the 1970s. In part, they were being gracious hosts to an out-of-towner. They were also acting in self-defense. Aware of their father's strong appetite for women, they knew he wouldn't hesitate to move in on their own lady friends.

During his term in the Senate, Jack maintained a small apartment on Bowdoin Street in Boston. Joe came visiting one day. As he alighted from his car, he asked the driver, "Can't you get a stewardess to cook dinner for us up here?" The driver could: a stewardess showed up in less than an hour.

Again in Boston Joe recognized a young man walking with a pretty girl as JFK's former chauffeur. Introducing them, the young man said, "Mr. Kennedy, I'd like you to meet Iris." Joe spoke to the young man but kept his eyes fixed on Iris. "Why don't you come down to the Cape?" Joe said. "Oh, and bring Iris." When they showed up at the Compound, Joe took Iris by the arm, and eventually to his bedroom.

Joe didn't slow down until he suffered his stroke in 1961 at the age of seventy-three. Shortly before, he had invited a group of celebrities to the Cape for a big party, among them Frank Sinatra, Judy Garland and, of course, a number of attractive women. To Frank Saunders, then Kennedy chauffeur, the women "looked like whores." Saunders, expecting interesting events to unfold, kept his eyes open. He wasn't disappointed. In a hallway at the rear of the house, he spotted Joe with a giggling young girl, his body pressing hers against a wall. "Then he stood away from her, his arms extended, hands against her breasts, fingers tickling. Her silhouette showed big tits," Saunders said.

Rose's side of the family also contributed to the womanizing tradition. Her father, Honey Fitz, was a brazen flirt and philanderer. His relationship with one Elizabeth (Toodles) Ryan was revealed publicly, and he was forced to give up his campaign for a third term as mayor of Boston.

Toodles was a large-bosomed waitress, cashier, and cigarette girl at Ferncroft Inn, a popular dining and illegal gambling place frequented by local pols. When they danced, Honey Fitz would press his body against her lewdly and kiss her countless times.

James M. Curley, Fitz's archrival for the Democratic nomination (which, in Boston, was equal to the election) had counted on Fitz's promise to leave office and was infuriated when he decided to run again. Looking into every scrap of scandal they could dredge up, Curley and his staff found a gold mine in Toodles.

Curley had thousands of posters printed up announcing that he planned to deliver a series of three lectures, the first of which would be called "Graft in Ancient Times Versus Graft in Modern Times." That one didn't bother Fitz. His next lecture, Curley said, would cover "Libertines from Henry VIII to the Present Day."

And the third would deal with "Great Lovers from Cleopatra to Toodles Ryan."

That did it! In December 1914, Honey Fitz announced that he would not seek another term.

Jack lost his innocence about his father when he was only eleven. Joe had invited Gloria Swanson, the sex goddess of the 1920s and 1930s, to Cape Cod. With a house full of children, Joe could not be alone with Gloria, so he invited her for a sail on the *Rose Elizabeth*, which he had bought the year before.

They sailed out into Nantucket Sound, but with a passenger: young Jack, who had slipped onto the craft and was even then below decks. Jack never explained why he was there, but a short time later, he wished he was not.

Joe dropped anchor in the sound, and he and Gloria, their sweaters off, stretched out on the sun-drenched deck. Jack crept up the steps, took a long look at his father and the film actress and, in a panic, leaped overboard and began swimming to shore. "What he saw when he peeked up was too unexpected, too startling, too awful for anyone to live with," said Alex Madsen in *Gloria and Joe*, an account of the affair.

Startled by the splashing, Joe yelled and leaped overboard, overtook the boy, and swam back to the sailboat with him. Madsen speculates that Jack had wanted to kill himself, "rather than have to live down the shame of what he had seen."

Joe bundled the shivering boy in blankets and instructed him in what to tell the family on their return. Jack agreed. The following day, Gloria left the house.

Joe never bothered to hide from Rose the fact that his sexual appetite was being satisfied outside the marriage bed. It is difficult to imagine a more brazen act by a husband than Joe's invitation to Gloria to join him and Rose on a voyage to England. The trip followed many appearances in public with Gloria, and the year before visits to Bronxville and Hyannis Port, where she was a houseguest.

On the trip to England, they dined at the same table. Virtually ignoring Rose and Virginia Bowker, a friend whom Gloria had brought along, Joe behaved toward the star in a courtly and possessive manner. Acting very much the jealous lover, he became infuriated when a man at an adjoining table turned to look at Swanson. Joe jumped up and loudly berated the passenger, ordering him to stop staring.

Gloria was embarrassed, but Rose, to Gloria's amazement, defended Joe, saying that he had been perfectly correct in defending Gloria's right to privacy.

Swason was astonished. "Was she a fool? I asked myself as I listened with disbelief, or a saint? Or just a better actress than I was?"

Rose Kennedy understood her husband completely. She was no fool, nor was she blind. Following the birth of Ted, she told her husband there would be "no more sex" between them. She didn't want any more babies and certainly would not approve of contraception in any form. Thereafter, she told Joe, they would sleep in separate bedrooms.

Joe was then only forty-six. It is highly likely that Rose gave her husband the unspoken freedom to engage in as many extramarital relations as he wished.

Rose maintained the pretense of Joe's fidelity as long as she could. When I talked to her in 1979 about the swirl of gossip about the Kennedy men, she spoke about Joe's reputed affairs for the first time, calling them "nothing but the usual gossip."

She told me, "Yes, I know there are a great many rumors about my sons but, you know, they talked about Mr. Kennedy and me in the early years of our marriage. Oh, they talked a very great deal. But I paid no attention to it. We were always in love, long before we were married and forever after."

The following year, Swanson's book was published. Rose was silent. She was like the other Kennedy women who, although publicly humiliated by a straying husband, chose to outwardly ignore what was happening.

Although she herself slept alone, Rose knew more about the Kennedy men's private lives than any of them realized or wanted her to know. She was aware of Ted's roving eye for pretty girls during the years of his marriage to Joan. Each time the senator was linked to another woman, Rose found out and made a mental note of the latest one's name.

One day in 1980, after Joan had left their home in McLean, Virginia, to live alone in Boston, I talked to Rose about the couple. Asked if she could confirm the rumors that the marriage was breaking up, she replied frankly, "I really don't know."

"Then why has Joan gone to live up in Boston while Ted remains in Virginia?" I persisted.

A hilarious misunderstanding followed. Rose, then nearing ninety, had some impairment of hearing and did not catch my words correctly.

"Virginia?" she demanded. "Who's Virginia? I never heard of *that* one!"

John Kennedy's legendary sexual exploits need no extensive documentation here. When Jackie was out of town, he hosted nude swimming parties in the White House pool, invited girls to the upstairs living quarters, and conducted a well-publicized affair with Marilyn Monroe. At White House receptions, he would occasionally invite a pretty girl to the Oval Office to discuss "some business," consummate the business on a couch, and return to the party. "I'm not finished with a woman until I've had her three ways," he once said.

His skirt chasing was so well known that jokes went the rounds of Washington parties. Sample: One day, while visiting a midwestern city to deliver a speech, he invited a girl to his suite. She was escorted into the elevator by a Secret Service agent who, on the way up, began caressing her breasts. When the young woman indignantly asked what he thought he was doing, the agent replied, "Sorry, ma'am, but the president is on a tight schedule. He hasn't got time for foreplay."

"He had a real bad case of satyriasis," Truman Capote said. At a dinner party one evening, Capote related, a guest was regaling the men, who had retired for cigars and brandy, with stories of Las Vegas call girls. "He had their telephone numbers with what they did—how well they sucked cock, how much, and how long, how big a one they would take... how big their tits were. Everyone was very interested in tits." Kennedy, not yet president, was busily scribbling notes on a napkin. Kennedy, Capote said, had more—"*much*, much, much more"—high-priced call girls than anyone imagined.

Jack and Ted never respected each other's claims on women. They poached on each other's territory gleefully and remorselessly. They considered sleeping with one another's women a victory as commendable as scoring a goal in touch football.

Consider, for example, the affair that Jack Kennedy had with Judith Campbell Exner, then twenty-six, a dark-haired beauty to whom he was introduced by Peter Lawford, on February 7, 1960, in Las Vegas, six weeks after he announced his candidacy for president.

The following month, Exner, recently divorced from William Campbell, began a two-year relationship with Kennedy. (She later married David Exner, a golf pro.) She was also the mistress of Salvatore (Sam) Giancana, the man who had succeeded Al Capone as Chicago's crime boss, though she later denied that she was sleeping with both men at the same time. The president broke off with Exner in March 1962, after Bobby convinced him that an affair with a woman who was also close to a Mafia don was charged with potential trouble.

After they were introduced, Jack and Judith Campbell had dinner with Ted and two others, watched the show in the Copa Room, and adjourned to the lounge. Teddy, who was sitting next to Judith, leaned over and suggested they see the town. She agreed, and the two went casino hopping.

Much later, he escorted her to her room and, when the door was opened, started to follow her inside. Judith told him to "be a good boy and say goodnight." Teddy said he'd just read a magazine while she went to sleep. It didn't work. Ted started to leave, sighing, "You can't blame a guy for trying."

But he wasn't about to stop trying. At the door, he turned, told her he was off to Denver that night, and asked her to come along. Another turndown. Teddy still wouldn't give up. He told Judith he would call from the airport. And he did. He asked her to join him. She hung up, but he called back in an hour, saying he had cancelled his flight and was still waiting at the airport for her. She never showed. She was the one who got away.

Afterward, Jack exulted in his victory. "I got her, Teddy didn't," he told friends. "Teddy must be eating his heart out."

Judith Exner is no historian or social psychologist: but, unlike them, she was *there* and her views may be worth some attention. She has thought a great deal about her early dealings with the Kennedys and, at age fifty-eight, assessed them: "The father really set the pace for the boys. I used to say that the Kennedy men were morally bankrupt. And I still feel that way."

If Jack's girls were fair game for Ted, so were the wives and lovers of friends and family members, present and former. Once he made a crude overture to Patricia Seaton (later Lawford), then twenty-one, who was living with Peter Lawford after his divorce from Ted's sister Pat.

Comedian Richard Pryor had been severely burned while freebasing cocaine and was recovering in a hospital. Peter Lawford, a friend of Pryor, called Pryor's wife and asked what, if anything they could do. Mrs. Pryor explained that Richard was not permitted to have flowers or the usual assortment of gifts, but there was something: as a longtime admirer of Ted Kennedy, she said, he would be cheered by a signed picture of the senator. Pat Seaton said she thought the autograph could be obtained quite easily and called Ted's office in Washington.

Ted was as forthright as he had been with the girls he met in bars at Harvard. "Hi, kid," he said. "How are you? I hear you're the young one. You have big tits."

Ted asked her when she was coming to Boston. "The more he talked," Pat Seaton said, "the more I realized he wanted to have sex with me. I was expected to go to Boston and service the [new] patriarch." She told Ted she was living with his former brother-in-law, but Ted was unimpressed.

He repeated his suggestion that she come to Boston. "I was the new Kennedy woman," Pat Seaton said. "I was the young one with the big tits. I was the woman he was going to have because he hadn't had me yet." Ted asked her age. "Apparently he liked them young," Pat asserted.

That evening, when Peter returned from a recording session, she told him about the incident. Peter displayed no anger, no jealousy, no resentment or shock. "Maybe, he said at last, "it would be a good idea for you to go see Teddy." Apparently, to maintain good relations with the Kennedys, Peter was willing to have his lover (whom he later married) travel to Boston and have sex with his former brother-in-law. Anything, Pat Seaton concluded, to appease Ted Kennedy.

If Jack, as Capote suggested, had a serious case of satyriasis, Teddy's woman problem was probably worse. Worse still, he was even less circumspect than his brother, who at least took some minimum precautions to hide his indiscretions. On campaign trips, Jack would sneak down the back stairs of hotels to enter a woman's room. Ted was open about his flirtations, went to nightclubs where everyone— including photographers—could see him and became the most scandal-prone Kennedy of them all.

Ted's far-ranging escapades have infuriated women writers and educators. Magazine journalist Susannah Lessard was probably the first to discuss Ted Kennedy's womanizing in print. Her article, written originally for *The New Republic* in 1979, called his behavior abnormal, characteristic of a "severe case of arrested development." *The New Republic* rejected it. The piece was also turned down by a number of other magazines but finally published by the *Washington Monthly* in December 1979. Lessard's blistering analysis described Ted's incessant skirt chasing as "pathological behavior," suggesting a "mind of narcissistic intemperance, a huge babyish ego that must be constantly fed." Her conclusion was that Ted was emotionally sick.

Mary Daly, who teaches feminist ethics at Boston College, sees the Kennedy womanizing tradition "as further degeneration of brain rot. Fucking around, the use of women—it's all interrelated with sleazy politics. The Kennedys' behavior exemplifies the prevailing rapist mentality in the culture."

Other women, however, draw a distinction between Ted Kennedy's sexual ethics and his political policies: Good Ted, Bad Ted. One of the country's most prominent philanthropists put it this way:

"If they could only cut out that part of him and leave the politician, wouldn't it be wonderful?"

Seven

"Now It's Ted's Turn"

Ted's second—and more significant—rebellion against his father occurred in 1961, after Jack's election. (The first, easily quashed by Joe, was his attempt to go to law school in California.) This one came out of a gut feeling that he must remove himself from the influence of his family. The alternative was marching to the beat of the Kennedy drums for the rest of his life.

After the inauguration, on January 20, 1961, Joe told Ted to go into the Senate to fill the seat Jack had vacated. Ted politely refused. Ted, who would be twenty-nine the following month, didn't want to be a senator. He didn't feel qualified to fill such a high government post. Most important of all, Joan told me, Ted wanted to strike out for himself, move away from the family, and become his own man.

Ted informed his father that he planned to leave his job as assistant district attorney and take Joan and his daughter out west to start a new life. Joan said, "His main reason was that in a new state, among new people, he would have to succeed or fail on his own." He took Joan on a tour of a number of western states, talked glowingly about the mountains and valleys, and excitedly about the possibilities abounding there.

But Joe stifled Ted's revolt. He gave his grown son the same icy stare which had made his young children behave. He made it clear to Ted that he would stay in Massachusetts and run for the Senate the following year.

Ted obeyed. He never again attempted to free himself from his father's influence.

Although he capitulated outwardly, and indeed waged an energetic campaign once he became reconciled to the idea, he still felt the need to disengage himself from the family.

When Ted and Joan wanted a summer home, he chose one in Hyannis Port, but not inside the Compound, where Jack, Bobby, and Eunice and Sargent Striver had houses only a few yards from Joe and Rose. Ted bought his cottage a mile away on Squaw Inland for quiet and privacy. Joan was teased about it, especially by Ethel, the most Kennedy-like of all the wives, but she smiled and said nothing.

One day when the president was weekending at Hyannis Port, Joe told Jack that he wanted Teddy to take Jack's seat as senator from Massachusetts. Jack sat quietly as his father uttered those now-famous lines: "You boys have what you want now and everyone else helped you work to get it. Now it's Ted's turn." Joe had always believed the family has a proprietary claim to the seat. "Look, he said reportedly, "I paid for it. It belongs in the family."

The president tried to dissuade his father, but got nowhere. On his return to Washington, he told Kenny O'Donnell and Lawrence O'Brien. They were appalled. Both said that Ted's candidacy would do the president considerable damage. And if Ted lost, the consequences would be even worse; his defeat would be widely interpreted as a rejection of Jack himself.

Charles (Chuck) Spalding, who had known Jack and Joe, Jr., since 1940, said, "I thought it was a big mistake, that it laid the Kennedy family open to all the dynasty charges of too many Kennedys.

Charles Bartlett, then a columnist for the *Chattanooga Times*, who had "fixed up" Jack and Jackie at a dinner in his Georgetown home, agreed with the president when he said, "I don't see why the House isn't good enough for Teddy. Hell, it was good enough for me."

Steward Alsop, the distinguished political commentator, wondered in print before Election Day: "Why did Teddy do it? More important, why did the President let him run? The President started at a much lower rung on the political ladder. So why did he allow young Teddy to aim so high so soon?"

Alsop was unaware that Jack had no choice.

However, JFK was not a puppet for his father when it came to running the country. Joe's suggestions flooded the White House almost daily, arriving by letter, messenger, telegram and telephone. Jack was able to deflect the vast majority of them. Often he would say, "Sure, Dad, fine idea. I'll try," and then didn't try.

Kenny O'Donnell told me: "The old man and the president never saw eye to eye on a thing."

Jack himself once said, "My father is to the right of Herbert Hoover."

During his Senate years, Jack once bluntly told his father, who was pressing for a bill then being debated, "Look, Dad, you have your political views and I have mine. I'm going to vote exactly the way I feel I must vote. I've got great respect for you, but when it comes to voting, I'm voting my way."

Jack yielded to his father on Ted's Senate candidacy because it involved family loyalty, the sole area where he was vulnerable. He tried a last, desperate tactic: "We ought to have one playboy in the family," he told Joe. "Don't force Teddy into politics. Let him be the playboy. Let him enjoy life."

When Ted heard about Jack's argument, he didn't think it was such a bad idea. He told friends it would be pleasant to sail down to the Caribbean, wander wherever he and Joan wanted, discover new islands, then go anywhere else their fancy dictated and "just plain live."

Joe brushed aside Jack's playboy argument. He had his agenda and stood by it. However, it was now February 9, 1961, and Ted could not be appointed to Jack's vacant seat because he would not have reached the age of thirty, as specified in the Constitution, until February 22 the following year. Someone—unambitious politically—had to fill the chair until a new election was held in 1962 to complete the final two years of Jack's unexpired term.

In Boston, Governor Foster Furcolo prepared to name himself when he received a phone call from the White House. Would he tap a man named Benjamin A. Smith? Ben Smith had been a housemate of Jack's at Harvard, owned a box-making factory, and once served as a councilman and mayor of Gloucester. He had no intention of resuming a political career and would happily rise from the Senate seat to make way for a permanent replacement.

Furcolo was upset, but he could not antagonize the Kennedys. He named Smith and kept quiet.

Nobody knew for certain what the close-knit Kennedys were planning. Would Teddy seek his brother's former seat in Congress, the governorship of Massachusetts, the state attorney generalship or, just possibly, the Senate? The talk in political circles was heavily larded with dismay.

Ted's legislative experience was nonexistent. His understanding of foreign affairs consisted of what he could absorb in three whirlwind tours, which his advisers said would give him the "world vision" essential for a senator. He visited Europe, Latin America, and Africa as a tourist who wants to cover as many countries as possible in a limited time. In Europe, he whizzed through eleven countries in three-and-one-half weeks. He completed a "fact-finding" tour of Africa in two weeks and covered nine Latin and South American countries in nine weeks.

Nor was he received cordially on any of his tours. The Africans and the Irish, quickly recognizing that his visit was purely political, were resentful. Dublin newspapers were so sharply critical that Ted threw them across his hotel room in disgust. The Israeli press barely mentioned him. The heaviest coverage he received there was when he got lost after making a wrong turn in an undeveloped area.

In Italy, his advisers hired a professional television crew to film his tour, which they called "Ted Kennedy in Italy"; it was subsequently screened throughout Massachusetts. In Latin America, he wrote postcards to each delegate who had cast a ballot for a Senate nominee in the last three Democratic conventions.

A U.S. Embassy official, in charge of shepherding Ted around one country, remembered little about the "fact finding" but was enthusiastic about the "fun" aspects of the tour. Theo Lippmann, Jr., one of Ted's early biographers, quoted the official as saying, "Kennedy was a great man for nightlife."

Doubts lingered in Ted's mind all during 1961. He had talked several times with Jack, telling him that his main interest was in arms control, not in legislation. When Ted came to Washington from time to time with an idea, his big brother didn't help his self-esteem much by grabbing his head and checking behind his ears. "Hmmm," he said. "Still wet, I see."

Ted could only say, "Aw, Jack."

Bobby, too, wasn't very helpful, telling him—and everyone else in Washington—that if he doesn't have the "stuff" he wouldn't make it to the Senate.

On December 19 that year, Ted cancelled all appearances to be with Joe after his stroke. If Ted had harbored any uncertainties, they vanished. "The Senate race became a crusade for Ted," a friend said. He was going to win this one for his father.

While Ben Smith was sitting quietly in Jack's former Senate seat, Joe called Steve Smith in New York to run Teddy's still-unannounced campaign. Smith set up a headquarters at the Sheraton-Kimball Hotel and arranged for a staff of experienced professionals, most of whom had worked for Jack in previous races, to merchandise Teddy. In a few weeks, he had put together a huge staff of 240 workers, paid and unpaid.

But in Washington, the president was having serious misgivings. Edward L. McCormack, the favorite nephew of Speaker John McCormack, had also set his sights on the seat. Jack knew that without the Speaker's help, much of his legislative program would be lost in the Senate. The last thing he wanted was to antagonize the Speaker.

Moreover, Ed McCormack had an excellent résumé: editor-in-chief of *Law Review* at Boston University School of Law, where he graduated first in his class; three terms in the Boston City Council, the last as president; and Massachusetts attorney general since 1956, where his record was outstanding.

The president tried to make a deal with Ed McCormack. Jack called Thomas P. (Tip) O'Neill, then a congressman from the Eleventh District, which Jack had represented in the House, and asked him to call Kenny O'Donnell. Kenny told Tip the polls showed McCormack would be soundly beaten, an embarrassment which would roil the Speaker. The solution, Kenny explained, was to offer Ed McCormack the ambassadorship to any country of his choice if he quit the race.

That wasn't all, Kenny said. "We also understood that he's in debt for $100,000. If he gets out now, old Joe will make sure his debt would be taken care of." Then Kenny added this clincher: "Eddie will be retained as a lawyer for some of the Kennedy ventures."

But after several days, Ed McCormack said no. He would fight Ted for the seat. The battle was on.

Smith's staff arranged speaking engagements for Ted at masonic halls, fraternal and veterans' groups, at church socials, and every ethnic and religious organization they could find. They set up radio, television and newspaper interviews. They organized rallies.

Nobody outside the tight Kennedy circle knew for certain why Teddy had suddenly taken to barnstorming around the state for most of 1961, making what he said were "nonpolitical" speeches. The comment drew guffaws from politicians who were sure that Ted was aiming for some elective office or other.

Ted was told to custom-tailor his talks to ethnic groups. Reporters assigned to cover him heard Ted tell Irish groups of the great advances he had personally observed in Ireland after the "troubles," and predicted greater advances to come. He told Jews of the great advances he had personally found in Israel and of greater advances to come. He told Italians of the great advances he had witnessed at firsthand in Italy and of greater advances to come.

By the time the year ended, the secret was out.

On March 14, 1962, newspeople jammed into the small, informal flower-filled room of his house at 3 Charles River Square, where they had moved in 1961, to hear Ted, with Joan at his side, make the formal announcement of his candidacy for the Senate. Two-year-old Kara, startled at the intrusion, began wailing in her nursery off the main hallway; her nurse shut the door quickly to muffle her cries.

Ted acknowledged that he expected a barrage of nepotism charges, but added, "I am convinced, however, the people will choose the candidate they consider the most effective." Neither Jack nor Bobby would campaign for him, he said, but the rest of the family will surely come for "a visit" and "we won't keep them in a closet all the time."

He was right about the criticisms, which came in torrents.

James Reston wrote in the *New York Times* that Ted's candidacy is "an affront and a presumption. One Kennedy is a triumph, two Kennedys at the same time are a miracle, but three could easily be regarded by many voters as an invasion."

The *Chicago Tribune*, in an editorial, foresaw the future lineup of presidents as John F. Kennedy, followed by Robert and Edward. "Before you know it," the editorial said, "we are in 1964 with Caroline coming up fast and John F., Jr. just behind her."

In a 900-word letter he sent to 4,000 Massachusetts educators, Mark De Wolfe Howe, Harvard professor of constitutional law, stated: "His candidacy is both preposterous and insulting."

The National Committee for an Effective Congress criticized: "Teddy's candidacy is an affront to Congress."

Cartoonists Herb Block, Bill Mauldin, and Jules Feiffer savaged him.

The *Wall Street Journal* wrote caustically that "if a third Kennedy acquires high national office the rest of us might as well deed the country to the Kennedys." If he lost, the *Journal* warned, "he might find that at the next family dinner he would have to eat in the kitchen."

Paraphrasing a remark by Winston Churchill, the *Washington Post* editorialized that Teddy was a modest man "with much to be modest about."

Columnist Steward Alsop reported that Ted's family was surprised at the vicious attacks. He quoted one of Ted's sisters, mercifully not identifying her, as saying innocently, "After all, Teddy had to do *something.*

In March 1962, the worst possible time for Ted, the Spanish-test-cheating episode exploded into the headlines. Robert L. Healy, political editor of the *Boston Globe*, had uncovered the story after weeks of digging. "I had it," Healy said, "but there was a stumbling block. Harvard had a firm policy of not revealing any of its records. In today's world of journalistic leaks, the story would have been printed immediately, but back then we required documentation before publishing.

"I had to get the okay or forget about it. I asked the White House to open up the Harvard record and was summoned down to the Oval Office.

"I had three meetings there with the president, Ted Sorensen, McGeorge Bundy, Kenny O'Donnell and Arthur Schlesinger, Jr. Jack was pretty shrewd. He would have liked the story included in some kind of profile of Ted, which would have buried it, and I said "no soap."

The president and his aides kept pressing Healy to play down the story but he stood his ground. "So finally, Jack gave me access to the whole thing," Healy said.

On March 30, the *Globe* published the story. Ted immediately issued a statement accepting full blame. His *mea culpa* saddened his supporters and gladdened the hearts of political opponents. It read in part:

I made a mistake. I was having difficulty in one course, a foreign language. I became so apprehensive about it that I arranged for a fellow freshman of mine to take the examination for me in that course....

What I did was wrong. I have regretted it ever since. The unhappiness I caused my family and friends, even though eleven years ago, has been a bitter experience for me, but it has also been a valuable lesson. That is the story.

Surprisingly, the cheating episode caused hardly a ripple in the campaign. McCormack never mentioned it, and the polls showed that the voters couldn't have cared less.

Ted faced three hurdles: he had to win his party's nomination that June at its convention in Springfield; McCormack, at thirty-eight, was a bright, seasoned, aggressive campaigner. If Ted won, Ed could choose to run in the September primary without his party's backing. And the winner would face off against a Republican challenger, who would most likely be George Cabot Lodge. Lodge's political lineage was more distinguished than that of either the Kennedys or the McCormacks.

Henry Cabot Lodge, George's great-grandfather, was a revered name in national as well as Massachusetts politics, a U.S. Senator for thirty-two years and renowned as "the scholar of politics" for his many historical works. George's father, a two-term senator, the very model of a Boston Brahmin, had been defeated by John Kennedy in 1952.

Joe wasn't fazed by either opponent. "We're going to sell Ted like cornflakes," he said.

By April, the Kennedy machine was finely tuned—engine lubricated, some parts discarded and replaced by others for better operation, the best mechanics hired to run it.

At campaign headquarters, Steve Smith ordered his staff to put together a biographical file on each of the 1,719 delegates to the convention. "I want to know everything about each of them," he instructed. "How old he is, where he went to school and how far, the size of his family, where he lives, what he does for a living, how much money he's got, what his hobbies are." Most of all, Steve wanted to know how the delegates felt about the Kennedys.

Staff members fanned out across the state, visiting about 1,300 delegates personally, making the case for Ted. The machine was so sensitive that any derogatory remark a delegate might make about the candidate or the family would be overheard and relayed back to headquarters by a volunteer. An aide would then be dispatched at once to visit the delegate, to explain a situation or get him to change his mind.

Bobby Kennedy had said he would not go to Massachusetts, but he didn't mean that he would not help out in Washington whenever possible. When he was told that pretty Beverly Lynch of Lunenberg, at twenty-one the youngest delegate to the convention, was visiting the capital with her mother, Bobby invited both of them to lunch. They accepted happily.

Joan invited a delegate's wife to lunch with "a few of the girls." The woman reported back to her husband that she had had a wonderful time.

The delegate threw up his hands. "I can vote against the Kennedys, damn it, but I can't vote against my wife."

Ted used the telephone a great deal to woo delegates. Sometimes he had problems. When he called one woman delegate and introduced himself, she was suspicious. "If you're Ted Kennedy," she said, "tell me the date of the president's birthday."

Ted wasn't sure. "When was Jack born?" he whispered to an aide. "Was it the twenty-seventh or the twenty-ninth of May?" The aide didn't remember either. Ted took a stab. "It's May twenty-seventh," he told the delegate.

"No it's not. It's May twenty-ninth," she snapped as she slammed down the receiver.

When the Kennedy machine learned that a delegate's wife had taken her child to a doctor, Ted was informed. He called the woman to ask about the youngster. Of course, she was impressed, told her husband, and Ted had another vote.

Ted stumped all through March, April, May and early June under the slogan: "He can do more for Massachusetts."

On June 6, the Thursday before the convention opened, Ted Kennedy came to Springfield, his motorcade welcomed by a twenty-two-piece brass band, paid for by Joe. To a wildly cheering crowd, he predicted a runaway victory on the first ballot. It was not the usual empty rhetoric. Ted had 1,196 delegates in his camp, many more than he needed to win.

Win he did on Sunday, June 8, humiliating Ed McCormack by a two-to-one margin. When the vote reached 691 to 360, Ed McCormack threw in the towel. He entered the hall to resounding cheers, conceded defeat, thanked his supporters, and said this was only the opening round. He planned to run against Ted in the primary elections in September.

Steve Smith, who had expected Ed to continue to fight, threw the machine into high gear. He said that Ted would continue to make speeches, Kennedy women would be everywhere and, most important of all, hundreds of tea and coffee parties would be held all over the state.

Kennedy's staff would enlist a woman supporter in each neighborhood to sponsor an "afternoon with the Kennedys" party. She would invite friends and neighbors and supply the beverages, which would be served in cups with the Kennedy name, sent over by the organization. One of the Kennedys—often Rose, sometimes the candidate himself— would show up to mingle with the guests and make a brief speech. Sometimes even the candidate himself.

Patricia, Eunice, Jean, and Ethel didn't miss a county. They addressed rallies, spoke at women's clubs and, when no meeting was scheduled, rang doorbells. "Hi, I'm Ethel Kennedy. I hope you will vote for my brother-in-law."

And Joan. "I'll do anything to help Ted," she said, and the pros took her in hand for merchandising on an Olympian scale. Donald J. Dowd, then thirty-two, one of the five coordinators of Ted's campaign, was assigned the job of selling Joan. Gerard Doherty, Ted's campaign manager and friend, a sensitive and perceptive man, had qualms about enlisting Joan because, he said, as a novice campaigner she had literally no idea of what lay ahead and how she would react.

The other Kennedy women, Doherty said, were experienced and hardened, but as for Ted's wife: "We had to remember that Joan was a duck who had never been in water like this, and here she was being dropped into a very full lake."

Joan's day began shortly after 8:00 A.M. and didn't end until nearly midnight. Visits to the media had high priority, Don Dowd explained, "You have to start at the newspapers early in the morning so you can make the deadlines." Joan would tour a newspaper plant, smiling and shaking hands in all the departments, talk to the reporters and editors, pose for pictures and answer a wide variety of questions. Afterward, a television station might be on the schedule for an interview which could last about an hour. It would be followed by several coffee visits, which had been scheduled at staggered times. At each, she wandered among the guests for about an hour.

At lunch, Joan had no quiet time for herself, no chance to kick off her shoes and relax in a back room of some restaurant. Don Dowd took her to high-visibility places; a crowded coffee shop, a shopping mall or a main street. Women would recognize her, come over for a chat and, hopefully, tell friends and neighbors what a very nice wife Ted Kennedy had.

A visit to a children's hospital would be followed by a tour of an old-age community center. In the evening, she would address a meeting, remaining until almost twelve. Always, after each appearance, she would anxiously ask Don or his wife Phoebe, "How did I do? Was I all right? Did they like me?"

After midnight, she would finally go to a motel room and wake up to another grueling day.

Joan tired as the weeks went by, but Ted, fueled by the excitement, campaigned eighteen hours every day, speaking to as many as a half-dozen organizations, visiting at least one factory daily and shaking countless hands. He had all of Jack's mannerisms, from the flat Boston accent to the pistonlike right arm. One woman reporter, watching the women who jammed the rallies, put it bluntly: "Charisma, hell. It's just plain old sex appeal."

An awestruck McCormack aide said Ted went almost everywhere in Massachusetts. "He's been in places like Gill," he declared. "Who ever goes to Gill? This guy went to Gill to see one delegate they got there. Most people wouldn't know where Gill is. Well, Ted Kennedy went there." (Gill, population about 1,000, is in the north-central part of the state.)

Author and close family friend Joe McCarthy made this assessment of Ted: "He isn't very heavy mentally. He's a bright and capable guy but nothing like his brothers. In many ways he's a fathead, a little bit conceited, a little bit cocky, the kind of guy who'd never finish a sentence when you asked him a question. He simply didn't think things through, as Jack and Bob did.

"But Ted had something else the others didn't. He could go into a bar and put his arm around a guy and buy drinks for everybody in the house. Or he could get up on top of a sound truck in South Boston and sing 'Southie is My Home Town.' Written in the twenties by Benny Drohan, the song is practically South Boston's national anthem."

The high points of the campaign came on August 27 and September 5, when the two candidates faced each other in televised debates; the first in South Boston High School, the second in the War Memorial Building in Holyoke.

Before the opening encounter, Jack, Bobby, Ted Sorensen, Joe Gargan, Ted's assistant, Milton Gwirtzman, and a few other aides came to Hyannis Port. Bobby announced their arrival with a breezy, "Have no feah, we are heah!"

The brothers tossed a football on the lawn as they discussed the questions that might arise. One Ted had not thought through was why he wanted to become a senator. Gwirtzman recalled Bobby telling him: "If you get that question, tell them about public service. Tell them why you don't want to be sitting on your ass in some office in New York."

McCormack's blistering assault on Ted during the debate is a legend in Massachusetts politics. He called Kennedy's slogan—"He can do more for Massachusetts"—the "most insulting I have seen in Massachusetts politics." He asked Ted, "What are your qualifications?... You've never worked for a living. You have never run or held an elective office."

And, in the withering charge that has echoed down through the years, he turned to Ted, pointed, and declared, "I ask... if his name was Edward Moore, with his qualifications, with your qualifications, Teddy, if it was Edward Moore, your candidacy would be a joke. But nobody's laughing because his name is not Edward Moore. It's Edward Moore *Kennedy*."

Newspapers reported next day that Teddy was in a state of shock at the virulence of the attack. He was astounded but not confused or dazed at all. He was so furious that he had to hold his body rigid to control his rage. Later that night, he told Frank Saunders, the family chauffeur, he had come very close to rising from his chair and punching McCormack. "He was more upset about the attack on the Moore name than he was at McCormack's calling his candidacy a joke, Saunders said.

The media was impressed by Teddy's grasp of the large political and social issues, commenting that he could spin out facts and figures as readily as his brother Jack. Ted was tutored exhaustively by a Harvard professor of government on everything from the size of France's gross national product to how much money the Soviet Union was spending on armaments. According to Murray B. Levin, political science professor at Boston University, "The Kennedys had grasped that a... barrage of statistics contain[s] a latent and unspoken message: The candidate who can cite hundreds of figures... must be not only highly intelligent and educated, but also a man who cares, for he would not have mastered these data if he were not interested in using them to benefit the public."

McCormack's savage attack was overkill, and it boomeranged. He was the one who appeared unsenatorial, a throwback to the days of firebrand

Irish pols who never hesitated to dig up dirt and hurl it at opponents with abandon. Teddy, however, while he looked youthful, behaved in exemplary fashion; he was calm, well spoken, polite, gentlemanly. *He was the one who looked like a senator,* said Dr. Levin. While Joe Kennedy fumed at what he thought was an outrage, Teddy's staff reasoned that using a scalpel instead of a bludgeon would have been more effective for McCormack.

Nor did Ed's crack about "never working a day in your life" impress Massachusetts workers who, by and large, did not place great value on toiling in the mills and factories. Perhaps the funniest remark came from a factory hand who approached Ted a few mornings later when the candidate showed up at the gates of his plant.

"Teddy, me boy," he said, "I hear you never worked a day in your life. Well, let me tell you, you haven't missed a thing."

Kennedy won the primary handily, receiving 60 percent of the votes and defeating McCormack by 559,303 to 247,403.

The race against the dignified 6'5" Lodge was a romp. Never considering him a threat, Ted played it for laughs. At a Temple Israel meeting in Natick, the chairman introduced the president of the brotherhood as the initial speaker. Ted leaped to the rostrum. Straight-faced, he apologized, "I'm sorry. I'm awfully sorry. I thought he meant the brother of the president." It brought down the house, and Ted used the same gag many times.

The final tally was 1,162,611 votes for Kennedy, 877,669 for Lodge. Seven weeks before he turned thirty-one, Edward Moore Kennedy became the youngest senator in Washington and the only brother of a sitting chief executive to serve in the Upper House.

Even though he was convinced that Ted would win, Joe refused to go to bed until victory was assured. And, when it was, Ted called him first. Then he called the President of the United States.

He was Good Ted in the Senate. Aware, when he took office on January 9, 1963, that his every act and word would be scrutinized closely by his fellow senators, he told reporters he wanted only "to stay out of the headlines and out of the swimming pool." Journalists guffawed remembering Ted's exuberant leap into the water, fully clothed, at Hickory Hill, when pool dunking of guests was Bobby and Ethel's idea of great fun.

Then Ted set out to learn his job.

He told me; "There's no school for senators. You learn the job by listening to other senators, observing and studying the great institution and how to make a contribution to it."

But there are rules. Said Dr. Donald R. Matthews in his study, *United States Senators and Their World*, "many able men have wrecked their legislative careers because, through arrogance, stupidity or both, they did not conform to...unwritten rules of the game as displayed on Capitol Hill.

"The new Senator," wrote Dr. Matthews, "is expected to keep his mouth shut, not to take the lead in in floor fights, to listen.... Freshman are also expected to show respect for their elders and to seek their advice. They are encouraged to concentrate on developing an acquaintanceship in the Senate."

From an old friend of his father, Ted received similar advice. "You have made such a brilliant beginning," wrote Lord Beaverbrook, "that you must walk warily, so that the upward swing may continue through the years until you reach the summit."

Ted Kennedy, assigned a seat in the very last row of the chamber, followed the rules. He sought friends among both Democrats and Republicans. He was named to the Labor and Public Welfare Committee and the Judiciary Committee and served on their subcommittees, appearing at all meetings and studying carefully the bills and resolutions proposed. He rushed to answer every quorum call and took his turn sitting in for the vice president as president pro tem of the Senate during tedious debates.

He was a perfect target for jokes, which he realized, and he wisely added to the crop himself. On the *Tonight Show*, Johnny Carson said, "He was the only candidate who made his acceptance speech while wearing Dr. Dentons."

And Ted, speaking to a meeting of women journalists, told them, "There is no reason to think that I am emphasizing the fact that the president is my brother just because I had a rocker installed in my Senate seat this afternoon." The audience, aware that JFK had been advised to use a rocking chair to ease his back pain, guffawed.

Ted paid the obligatory courtesy calls on his older and more experienced colleagues. One of his first visits was to Democratic Senator James O. Eastland of Mississippi, who took Kennedy under his wing soon after he came to the Senate.

The seventy-four-year-old chairman of the Judiciary Committee, a glass of bourbon-and-branch in his hand, told Ted: "Boy, your brother never made it here because he used the Senate to run for president. You may want to run for president someday yourself, but you'll be happier here and make more friends if you do your homework.

"Don't try to avoid the ditch digging. It's part of the job."

When Ted stopped by the office of Senator Richard B. Russell of Georgia, he received similar advice. Kennedy reminded Russell that both of them had barely reached the constitutional age requirement when elected to the Congress.

"That's true, son," Russell responded testily, "but you see, son, I had already been governor of my state."

Kennedy turned down most invitations from organizations for speeches, was accessible only to newspapermen from Massachusetts, and even refused to appear on national television.

Intent on fulfilling his pledge to "do more for Massachusetts," he obtained $135 million in new federal contracts, grants and loans for his state, and promised more. When he went to New York, however, to win contracts for Massachusetts from the Grummann Corporation on Long Island, he offended New York Senator Kenneth Keating.

Kennedy told the Grummann people that some of the subcontracting work on the lunar excursion module "required the kind of special technology and skilled work force for which Massachusetts is especially well qualified." Keating denounced his action as piracy, but the *Boston Traveler* applauded.

"If making a pitch for new industry makes Teddy a pirate," the paper noted, "let's salute the Jolly Roger."

Former Democratic Senator John Tunney of California, who remained a close friend, recalled a long discussion about the Senate during a four-day weekend visit to Washington.

"He told me his career was really going to be there. He urged me to seek a Senate career. He enjoyed being in the Senate. He thought a person could get an awful lot done in the Senate."

After the election, Joan flew to Washington to hunt for a house. Jackie and Ethel counseled her to find a place in Georgetown, close to Capitol Hill, if she wanted to see her husband and have him see their children. She rented a furnished red-brick house at 1336 Thirty-first Street, for which they paid $600 a month.

In Boston, one veteran Irish pol made a prediction: "I knew Jack when he was thirty and a congressman, and he was nothin'," he said. "But Teddy's already way ahead. He is the Kennedy they're going to put in the history books."

Ted and Ed McCormack are good friends now. They joke about their acrimonious debate whenever they meet. At a retirement party for Garrett Byrnes, who was district attorney for Suffolk County (Boston) and Ted's first boss, Ted said in his address, "When Eddie McCormack and I had that debate, he said I had never worked a day in my life. When I went to Garrett and told him, he answered, 'He was right.'"

Ed began his talk by turning to Ted and saying, "There's one thing you've got to thank me for. I made your middle name famous."

McCormack believes that, from a standing start, Kennedy has done an "outstanding job" in the Senate. "Jack and Bob were very creative people who would make dramatic proposals and have a press conference, and that would be it," he said. On the other hand, Ted has not only come out with innovative programs for his constituency but also follows through. He works hard in the committees for his measures, establishes personal relationships with other senators, and lobbies hard to have them enacted. Senators now look to him as the bellwether of positions they should take if they want to be considered progressive or liberal.

"He's got himself screwed up in some personal peccadilloes, but it hasn't had the effect on his performance as a senator that a lot of people would like to see it have. I see a lot of people like that, lawyers who are outstanding attorneys by day and get smashed at night. They're different people once the day's work is done.

"You've got to say that Ted is a remarkable man who concerns himself with the problems of our day. He tries to come up with solutions. While they are problems he does not personally experience, he realizes that others do, and he is trying to solve them. I like him. I admire him. He's been a good senator."

On Friday, November 22, 1963, Ted Kennedy left his seat in the Senate chamber for the vice-president's chair, where he was scheduled to preside over the afternoon session. There were only eight senators on the floor and some fifty spectators in the galleries when the Associated Press ticker in the Senate lobby clicked out a bulletin at 1:42 P.M.

William Langham Riedel, the Senate press liaison officer, rushed to the machine and read:

"President Kennedy was shot as he rode in a motorcade in Dallas, Two shots, Blood was seen streaming from his head."

Riedel raced onto the Senate floor where he met senators Spessard Holland and Everett M. Dirksen and told them what had happened. He saw Ted looking over some papers at the rostrum and ran up to him.

"Senator Kennedy," he said, "your brother the president has been shot."

Stunned, Ted left the rostrum and ran to a nearby telephone to call the White House. Holland took his place in the chair. Kennedy was unable to get his call through and drove to his Georgetown home with Milton Gwirtzman and Claude Hooten, a personal friend from Houston, Texas. Gwirtzman, at the wheel, raced through red lights. Ted cautioned him to be careful.

At his house, he learned that Joan had gone to the Elizabeth Arden salon on Connecticut Avenue. He tried to call his parents at Hyannis Port, but the lines were overloaded by the surge of calls in and out of the area, and he couldn't get through. He remained at the house while Gwirtzman went to pick up Joan. Returning to McLean, Gwirtzman suggested they go to his home, but those phones weren't working, either. They raced out and drove to the White House.

"The police waved us right in the entrance on East Executive Avenue," Gwirtzman said. "No one had to tell Ted. Just from the look on people's faces, the women sobbing, you could tell the president was dead."

An open line was finally found in the office of Dr. Janet Travell, the White House physician. Eunice and her husband, R. Sargent Shriver, were there and listened as Ted spoke to his mother at Hyannis Port. Dr. Travell, noting Ted's white face and the quaver in his voice, offered him a sedative. Ted didn't want it.

He called Bobby, who had heard the news from J. Edgar Hoover at Hickory Hill. Gwirtzman recalled, "They were responding in the same way they would respond to a crisis in a campaign, dividing up the assignments."

Bobby would go at once to Jackie and her children. Shriver would handle the funeral arrangements. Ted and Eunice would fly to Hyannis Port to be with their parents.

ed's grandfathers were the sons
f Irish immigrants who fled the
evastating potato famine and
phus epidemic in the mid-1880s.
hn J. (Honey Fitz) Fitzgerald was
vice mayor of Boston and three
mes a congressman. (John F.
ennedy Library)

Patrick J. (P.J.) Kennedy, Ted's
paternal grandfather, was a
saloon keeper who also rose to
political prominence, serving
five years in the Massachusetts
legislature. (John F Kennedy
Library)

At twenty, black-haired, blue-eyed Rose Kennedy was one of the prettiest girls in Boston. She married Joseph P. Kennedy, Ted's father, in 1914, and in seventeen years bore him nine children. (John F. Kennedy Library)

Joe, Rose, and eight of their children on the grounds of the Hyannis Port estate in 1928. John is kneeling at left. Seated, left to right, are Bobby, Eunice, Jean, Joe and Rose, Pat, Kathleen (in front of Rose), Joe Jr., and Rosemary. Teddy had not yet arrived. (John F. Kennedy Library)

This famous picture of the Kennedy family has been published all over
the world. It was taken in London when Joe was U.S. ambassador to
Great Britain. At left is Joe, at far right Rose. John (left) and Bobby (right)
flank the fireplace, and young Ted, in sailor suit, is at right. Joe Jr. is
behind his mother, Rose. (John F. Kennedy Library)

Joe, the patriarch, many times a millionaire before he was thirty, bought an estate at Hyannis Port on Cape Cod, where he insisted that all his children follow a rigid athletic schedule. Here is Teddy, age seven, practicing his golf swing. (John F. Kennedy Library)

Joe resigned as U.S. ambassador to Britain in 1940 after making indiscreet remarks about the British war effort. Never again would he hold a government post. In 1941, back home in Hyannis Port, he is pictured with (left) Joe Jr. and Jack (both standing), and Bobby. (John F. Kennedy Library)

Joe Kennedy's dream of seeing his firstborn son in the White House
was shattered when Joe Jr. (left), a bomber pilot, was killed over the
English Channel during a mission in 1944. Jack, at right, won the Navy
and Marine Corps medal in 1943 for bravery when his PT-109 was
rammed by a Japanese destroyer in the Solomon Islands. (John F.
Kennedy Library)

In December 1946, Bobby (right) was assigned to duty aboard the
2,200-ton destroyer *U.S.S. Joseph P. Kennedy, Jr.,* named for his brother.
At the commissioning in Quincy, Massachusetts, Joe Sr. greets his son,
Seaman 2nd Class Robert F. Kennedy, who groused because he never
saw any action. (John F. Kennedy Library)

The athletic Kennedys vacationing at Hyannis Port in the summer of 1946. Jack (left) is a youthful-looking twenty-nine, Bobby (middle) is twenty, and Ted (right) a husky fourteen. They are standing on the lawn in front of the flagship of the compound. (John F. Kennedy Library)

Teddy is holding the football, Jean and Bobby are with him in the rear, Jack and Eunice in front. (John F. Kennedy Library)

Joe and Rose come out to greet the players after a touch football game. Left to right: Jack, Jean, Rose, Joe, Pat (the H is for Harvard), Bobby, and Eunice. Teddy holds the football. (John F. Kennedy Library)

Ted Kennedy's consuming passion at Harvard was football. As first string right end, he won the much-coveted Harvard letter, awarded also to Bobby but not to Joe Sr. or Jack. (John F. Kennedy Library)

Eight

A Grand Wake

$\mathbf{T}$ed Kennedy was drunk. Gloriously, boisterously soused in the second-floor living quarters of the White House, along with a dozen or more equally loaded guests.

He did his imitations of political notables. He put his arms around the shoulders of friends and sang Irish songs. He doubled up with laughter when a member of his brother's cabinet found one of Ethel Kennedy's wigs and stuck it on his head.

Sometime during the evening, Ted and several others went outside, got into automobiles, and raced down Pennsylvania Avenue. Aristotle Onassis, the billionaire shipping magnate, waiting at the gates to be admitted after presenting his credentials to the guards, stared in amazement.

The cars sped across the Memorial Bridge to Arlington National Cemetery where, a few hours before, John F. Kennedy had been buried on a slope below the Custis-Lee mansion. They stood at the newly covered grave as the Eternal Light glowed brightly, then he returned to the White House. The party resumed. Stories were told about the fallen president's life. More songs were sung. More drinks consumed.

It was an Irish wake to be remembered, a grand send-off for the assassinated president.

The revelry, which continued until dawn, was a catharsis for Ted, family members, and Jack's close associates who were there. A number of parties were in full swing that Monday night, November 25, after the state funeral which had been viewed by an estimated 100 million persons on television. There had been yet another that morning. The third birthday of John, Jr., was celebrated at a small party in the family kitchen where the little boy clapped his hands in delight as Caroline and the children's nurse, Maude Shaw, sang "Happy Birthday," and he ripped open his presents.

Afterward, young John and Caroline, who was six, dressed in identical powder-blue coats, were taken to the Capitol Rotunda, where Jackie, Bobby, and the children had a few private moments at the bier of the president, then to St. Matthew's Cathedral near Connecticut Avenue for the requiem mass. On the steps, as the coffin was being lashed to the caisson, Jackie whispered to her son, "John, you can salute daddy now, and say goodbye to him."

The unforgettable picture of young John, his hand raised in a smart salute, wrenched hearts all over the world. Richard Cardinal Cushing, the tall, craggy-faced prelate who had officiated at the mass, said, "Oh, God, I almost died."

When Ted called his mother at Hyannis Port that terrible Friday afternoon, Rose already knew. Frank, the chauffeur, and other household help had heard the news on television; the sobbing women had turned up the volume and aroused Rose from her afternoon nap. When she snapped at them to switch off the TV, Frank blurted, "Mrs. Kennedy, the president has been shot."

Rose seemed about to faint. In a daze, she held onto the wall to steady herself, standing there, eyes closed, for a full minute. Gaining control, she asked if her son had been killed. When Frank said no, she returned to her bedroom and paced the floor as she listened to the television. When the announcement came from Parkland Memorial Hospital that Jack was dead, she told Ann Gargan, sister of her nephew Joey, who was in the house, "I've got to keep moving, keep moving." She continued to pace the floor.

Then, donning a long black cloak and wrapping a scarf around her head, she walked up and down the lawn, praying as the icy winds from Nantucket Sound stung her face.

When she reentered the house, Ted was on the phone. "I'm worried about your father," Rose told him. Ted said he and Eunice would fly to Hyannis Port and tell Joe. At Washington's National Airport, a military transport plane was waiting. Ted and his sister reached the Big House shortly after 5:30 P.M.

The delicate task of keeping the news from Joe until Ted and Eunice arrived had begun. Rita Dallas, his special nurse, had reported that the old man sensed something was up because the telephone installed in the house for the president did not stop ringing. The chauffeur took Joe downstairs in the elevator to watch a movie, a daily routine. But the phones kept ringing, and Joe became increasingly upset. He said he wanted to watch television, but Ham Brown, a Secret Service agent assigned by Jack to the Big House, had yanked out the wires in all the sets.

Ted and Eunice climbed the stairs to their father's room. Dr. Russell S. Boles, Jr., a Boston neurologist, was down the hall, alert to help if he was needed.

Ted, tears streaming down his face, told his father that his son, the president, had been shot in Dallas and was dead. "Teddy dropped to his knees and buried his face in his hands," a nurse recalled. "I saw his shoulders sag and Eunice, her face twisted with grief, said, 'He's dead, Daddy, he's dead.'"

Joe stared at them, not comprehending. Then tears coursed down his face.

Rose, Eunice, and Ted wept with him.

Ted remained at Hyannis Port until Sunday, the day before Jack's state funeral. He went directly to the White House, his face haggard, looking as though he had not slept for days. "Let's go up," he told Joe Gargan and several other aides. "Up" was to Capitol Hill, where the president's body was lying in the center of the Great Rotunda.

At the Capitol, two long lines of quiet mourners were moving up the marble steps to the rotunda, velvet ropes and twenty-five feet of stone floor separating them from the catafalque upon which rested the president's coffin. Ted and the aides entered the building at the East Front. Guards led them through the lines of shuffling people who, recognizing Ted, moved aside. At the coffin, Ted kneeled and prayed. Gwirtzman recalled, "The entire incident, in the night light, the utter silence, and the atmosphere of the time was eerie."

Nurse Luella Hennessey, again with the Kennedys at a time of crisis, had come to the Georgetown house to be with Jackie and the children. "Ted's marvelous disposition was gone," she told me. "He could hardly speak. He came to me, kissed me, thanked me for coming. But his face was so white and drawn. I got the feeling that any moment he would break down and cry."

Nine

Joan on the Rocks

"**I**t was a mismatch from the start," said Harry Bennett, Joan's father. "She wasn't the first girl to marry the wrong man, and she won't be the last. But when it's your daughter, it hurts like hell." He cited all the differences between the two: that he loved people and parties, while she was shy and withdrawn; that he was athletic, she was artistic; that he was deep into politics and she was steeped in Bach and Beethoven.

Bennett told me this in 1978, after he had retired from advertising and was living in Metairie, a suburb west of New Orleans, with his second wife Kurk. He and Joan's mother, Virginia, were divorced in 1970.

"I didn't know it back then," Harry said. Neither, of course, did Joan, who came to Washington starry-eyed. "How glamorous life can be!" she exclaimed as she was introduced to the glittering world of Camelot.

The fun of political life, which she enjoyed the first year, soon faded as the pressures began tightening. Submerging her own preference for a quieter lifestyle, Joan raced to airports to meet Ted, dutifully performed the countless hostess chores for streams of guests, and uncomplainingly allowed her home to be used at all hours for political meetings. Often Ted would call close to dinnertime to say he was bringing guests—six, ten, sometimes more. Joan and her two domestic servants would be frantic at first, but they learned to cope.

Wherever she went, Joan was under public scrutiny. She could not longer walk into a store to buy a robe, a handbag, or new pillows without being stared at, asked for an autograph, or questioned. Mealtimes were chaotic; the phone rang at all hours, people she didn't know came into her home, which always reeked of cigar smoke, but she smiled pleasantly and managed.

She joined the Senate Ladies, a tight little club of senator's wives, hoping to find kindred souls, but most were old enough to be her mother. She felt awkward at the Tuesday luncheon meetings, sewing and rolling bandages with them and peering at photos of their grandchildren. she had little to say to them, nor they to her.

When Ted's constituents came to the capital, Joan served as tour guide. She joined charitable organizations and spent several hours weekly at the Joseph P. Kennedy, Jr., Foundation, set up by the patriarch to support research into mental retardation.

Joan's gaffes were inevitable. Soon after her arrival in Washington, she was asked by a journalist: Who designs your clothes? Oleg Cassini, she replied, adding ingenuously that he gave her a 50 percent discount on every dress. Ted winced when he read the interview; other Senate wives snickered, and Mr. Cassini was not pleased by the disclosure.

Through Joan the nation learned, probably for the first time, that the president's back pains were so severe that he could not pick up his small children. The story made headlines; everyone in the White House from the president down groaned in dismay. Ted cautioned her not to be so forthcoming in interviews, but Joan kept chattering away. Soon she pulled aside another curtain, this time revealing a secret about Jackie.

The First Lady, often asked if she ever wore a wig, had stonewalled each time. But Joan gave it all away. Jackie, she said, had tried to convince her to wear one because it saved hairdressing time, especially when traveling. "She has three wigs and wears them a lot," Joan said. "I tried one once but I felt silly." Joan apologized to Jackie, who told her to forget it. She blundered again when she was asked if she was pregnant. "I don't know for sure," she replied.

Kennedy nurse Luella Hennessey, now a friend and frequent visitor, tried to convince Joan to accept the obvious fact that she wasn't one of the Kennedy girls and never would be. In Joan's upstairs bedroom in the summer home on Squaw Island, the older woman told me she had several intimate conversations with Joan.

"I told her that I had known the Kennedys since 1930," Luella said, "and that nobody knows better than I that they have many outstanding qualities. But so do you, I said to her. Yours are just as outstanding and they are very special. Together they make up you. There's no point at all in being a bad imitation of Ethel or Eunice or any of them. The one thing you can do—the *only* thing you *should* do—is be yourself."

Joan was staring out the window at the calm waters of Nantucket Sound as Luella offered this sage advice.

Had she accepted it, much heartbreak could have been avoided. But she did not. Rooted too deep was the feeling, as she said to me later, that "in this family you follow the crowd." She redoubled her efforts to match the "crowd." And, of course, she failed.

Her tensions increased. When she felt especially discouraged or had anxieties about an event, she fixed herself a martini. She found that it lifted her spirits.

On a freezing afternoon in January 1972, I visited Joan in her new home at 636 Chain Bridge Road in McLean. The rambling 130-foot house on six acres of rolling land on the banks of the Potomac River took a year to build and cost over $500,000.

The house is only a fifteen-minute drive from the center of the capital. Motorists pass it by without realizing who lives there because the Kennedy name does not appear outside, nor indeed does the house itself appear imposing from the road. Inside, it is magnificent. There is a 25-foot pink, green, and white bedroom with two bathrooms. The two-story, 32-by-21-foot living room has open ceiling beams and matching-grain oak floors secured by wooden pegs instead of nails. A piano stands in a corner, and there are five sofas upholstered in yellow-and-white English chintz, plus a dozen chairs and another dozen tables, grouped for intimate conversation.

On one wall is a breakfront filled with fine antique glassware Joan herself collected. The fireplace, faced with white marble, has an eighteenth-century English mantel of hand-carved wood. As in all the Kennedy homes, pictures of the family are everywhere.

Over tea in the living room, Joan told me, "I lost my self-confidence," she said, "a very easy thing to do when you suddenly marry into a very famous, bright, intelligent family. Please, I want you to know that the Kennedy women hadn't gotten to me. They were not responsible for deflating my confidence.

"No, I let it happen. I let myself be pulled into the Kennedy lifestyle, and I judged myself by their values."

Joan was being kind. Because she didn't fit into the clan, the Kennedy women teased her at every opportunity, and they came often. When she turned an ankle during a tennis game, Ethel jibed, "C'mon, you're not hurt. Get going."

Joan was an outsider at the Kennedy functions. At a dinner in Eunice and Sargent Shriver's home in Rockville, Maryland, the guests, many of them family members, joked with one another, laughed at Teddy's sallies, and conversed briskly about current affairs. They ignored Joan completely. She was silent all evening.

Another time, a day of sailing was scheduled for the family at Hyannis Port. All the women at the dock were dressed in faded jeans and old shirts. When Joan came down in a leopard-print bathing suit, Ethel remarked, "Really, Joan, did you expect the photographers?" Everyone laughed. Joan, unable to think of a snappy retort, quietly stepped aboard, embarrassed. The woman who told the story to Myra MacPherson, a Washington journalist, said, "That's what you had to do [quip back]. I got along because I didn't give a damn, was not in awe of [the Kennedy women] and wouldn't play a lady-in-waiting to Ethel."

Joan could not be as rah-rah politically, as athletic, or as fertile. Ethel, as much a Kennedy as though she had been born into the family, was having a baby almost every year. Joan, who had several miscarriages, had only three, though she had wanted more.

Her inability to bear more children probably heightened her feelings of inadequacy, especially since Ted had made the proud announcement, following their marriage, that he wanted at least ten. Said Nurse Hennessey, "It was discouraging and depressing for Joan not to be able to see her way through her pregnancies like Ethel did. Joan felt she wasn't as healthy as the others because she was unable to carry full term. The problem lay elsewhere, but there was no impairment whatever of physical health."

Joan needed to be needed. When she felt that she was, her confidence zoomed and she blossomed. When she thought she was not, her self-esteem plummeted. Then, her friends confided to me, the depressing thought that she was playing only a subsidiary role in her husband's life overcame her. "Joan," one friend said, "never thought nor read much about the rise of feminism, yet she was, at heart, a feminist. She didn't want to be an appendage to the man she married, keeping his home comfortable, serving as a dutiful political wife, making sure his clothing was pressed and his laundry done. She wanted to be respected for her own achievements."

After the murder of the president, Ted, in a period of emotional crisis, showed his need for her support, and she responded. She told me, "I began to realize that I, Joan Kennedy, had something important to contribute." What she had was the strength to help Ted overcome the catastrophe that had struck so swiftly and unexpectedly.

But when Ted resumed his political life and the pressures began anew, she found herself caught up again in the same whirl.

Jackie, who liked Joan a good deal more than the other Kennedy women did, became aware of her distress and took her under her wing. They had many conversations in person and by telephone about entertaining, on how to get along with politicians (all of whom Jackie despised), on celebrated writers, artists, and musicians.

Later, Jackie regretted that she had not counseled Joan about the deeper pitfalls. "If only she had realized her own strengths instead of looking at herself in comparison with the Kennedys," Jackie said. "Why worry if you're not as good at tennis as Eunice or Ethel when men are attracted by the feminine way you play tennis? Why court Ethel's tennis elbow?"

Early in her marriage, Jackie herself had felt pressured to be a Kennedy in all things, but decided it was silly—if not stupid—to try to match them. She refused to worry if her tennis game wasn't good enough, as long as she enjoyed the game. And she had the good sense to keep out of all touch-football games after she injured an ankle.

Even though Jackie was her friend, Joan felt overshadowed by her. "Can you imagine what it's like being the sister-in-law of a woman like Jackie?" she told a journalist. "The gorgeous clothes she buys—they all look so perfect on her. She's so perfect in every way, so utterly beautiful, nothing out of place. She's a woman who is idolized everywhere she goes, who sets the style for women. Everything she says gets quoted; her every movement is followed. Young girls want to be like her. Can you imagine what it's like in her shadow?"

Joan did not follow Jackie's example. Instead of accepting her inability to compete, she made a disastrous mistake. She went off in a radically different direction in order to be noticed, choosing a path that earned her scathing denunciation from the media.

Joan's lovely blond hair became blonder, longer, and looser. She acquired a wardrobe in the "mod" style, all in riotous patterns and hues. Her skirts became shorter. *Women's Wear Daily*, the leading trade journal of the fashion industry, criticized her taste sharply.

Once Joan arrived at a reception in a see-through chiffon blouse which revealed a blue bra, a wet-look skirt, and black boots. She appeared at one of the Tuesday Senate Ladies luncheons in gaucho pants, bolero jacket, a tight sweater, and suede boots.

The low point came several years later, on March 12, 1969, at the First Lady's annual reception for members of Congress at the White House. All of the other women wore afternoon dresses, well below the knee. Pat Nixon, who stood next to a tuxedoed President Richard Nixon on the receiving line, was dressed in a floor-length formal dress, with a high neck and wore long white gloves.

Joan appeared in a low-cut cocktail dress, shimmering with silver sequins, which ended six inches above the knee. "Wow!" exclaimed one cabinet member. Many of the guests were shocked, and when the photographs were published around the country, sacks of mail tumbled into Ted's office, most denouncing Joan.

The other Kennedy women snickered but said nothing to Joan. Neither did Ted, who didn't like it much, but was too kind to tell her. Later she told me, "I wish I had never done that. I didn't do it with a great deal of forethought. I feel a little ridiculous that I didn't see the stir it could cause. That was pretty naïve of me."

Ironically, the airplane accident that almost killed Ted Kennedy had given Joan's self-confidence another charge, this time a powerful one.

At 7:40 P.M. on Friday, June 19, 1964, Kennedy cast his vote for the civil rights bill his brother had sought and which Lyndon Johnson championed. It passed, 73 to 27, and Ted left immediately for National Airport, where an Aero Commander 680, a twin-engine plane, waited to take him to West Springfield, where he would be nominated for a full Senate term at the Democratic state convention.

With Kennedy was Senator Birch Bayh of Indiana, who was to deliver the keynote address, his wife Marvella, and Edward S. Moss of North Andover, Ted's administrative aide. The Aero Commander took off, headed for Westfield, a short drive from the Coliseum, where the delegates awaited them.

As the plane neared Barnes Airport, a heavy fog and a drizzling rain had soaked the runways. At the controls, 48-year-old veteran pilot Edwin T. Zimny of Lawrence peered into the blackness and could see nothing. Losing radar and control-tower contacts, Zimny relied on his instruments to guide him. When he finally burst through the fog, Zimny was grazing the tops of apple trees in an orchard three miles from the airport. It was too late to soar upward. The plane crashed into a hillside.

Birch Bayh and Marvella were thrown clear and—miraculously— escaped serious injury. The pilot was killed. Ed Moss, suffering massive brain injuries, died within hours.

At Cooley Dickinson Hospital in Northampton, doctors found Ted Kennedy in deep shock. The second, third, and fourth vertebrae of his lumbar spine (lower back), and the transverse processes which support the spine were fractured, his left lung was partially collapsed, two ribs on his left side were broken, his pulse was erratic, and his blood pressure was dangerously low.

In the emergency room he was given several transfusions, and antishock treatment was begun. Fluid and air were removed from his chest cavity, and he was placed in an oxygen tent. Fortunately, his spinal cord was not severed, which eliminated the threat of paralysis and none of his internal organs was ruptured. If they were, he would have had to undergo emergency surgery which, in his weakened condition, was extremely risky.

Doctors said he would make a complete recovery, but that it would take many months and that he would have back pain for the rest of his life. Transferred after three weeks to New England Baptist Hospital in Roxbury, a Boston suburb, he was strapped into an orthopedic frame, unable to move, his spine held rigid while it healed. He was rotated several times daily—"like a human rotisserie," he joked—and had to have his meals lying facedown. He had frequent visitors: family members, including Bobby, Rose, and his father; Cardinal Cushing, and Joan and their two children, Kara and Ted, Jr. One midnight, a special visitor was announced: President Johnson. Dave Powers came and said, "He [Ted] cheered me up."

Ted received more than eighty thousand letters and spent his time constructively. He invited leading economic and political experts to conduct thrice-weekly seminars at his bedside on industrial problems, foreign affairs, and human relations.

Bobby acted cheerful on his visits, but he wasn't. Once, after seeing Ted, he walked in a park near the hospital with a special assistant, Edwin O. Guthman, and, head down, wondered whether he should get out of politics. "How much do they [his parents] have to take? I just don't see how I can do anything now. I think I should just get out of it all. Somebody up there doesn't like us."

In addition to editing *The Fruitful Bough*, the book of reminiscences he compiled about his father, Ted discovered to everyone's surprise, including his own, that he had some talent as a painter. Working two nights a week, he completed seven oil paintings before he was discharged from the hospital. It wasn't easy. He painted with his right hand while his left held the canvas. "Just like Michelangelo," said Bobby, to whom he presented a seascape of Pemaquid Point on the southeast coast of Maine. Bobby added, "The only similarity between them was that they both painted on their backs."

A winter landscape was presented to Joan; Jackie received a Cape Cod scene with a bright blue sky and sea, a red cottage and a sailboat; to his parents he gave a picture of two fishing boats at a pier. All but one—a reproduction of a painting on the wall of his room—were done from memory.

In his absence, Ted had been nominated on June 22, 1964, for a full term at the West Springfield convention. And now, at the age of thirty-two, there was a race to be run. Joan ran it—all of it—between visits to the hospital. She was needed, and she became inspired. Her self-confidence surged.

Less than a month after a second miscarriage, she was on the hustings under the guidance of Ted's political planners Gerard Doherty and Eddie Martin, who had put together an arduous schedule. Each day, Tommy Joyce, a former marine, would be at the Squaw Island home soon after daybreak to drive her seventy-five miles to the hospital. In a small suite next to Ted's room, Joan set up an office, complete with files and a secretary. She discussed the speeches she was to make that day with Ted, and then took off.

Joan was not a polished performer. Before each address she would still be nervously studying her speech cards until she was introduced. At the start of each talk, her voice trembled and she clenched and unclenched her hands. Despite occasional stammering and stuttering, she won over audiences because she came across as natural and unaffected. She giggled at times, and people loved her for it.

When Joan forgot something important, she would clap her hands to her mouth like a schoolgirl and say that she was sorry, so sorry. Often she would say, "You'll have to bear with me. I'm a bit nervous." And they did. To reporters, she said, "I'm used to girly chats over coffee." She charmed them, too. Microphones often presented a problem. She had to bend over to speak into them until they were adjusted to her height. "I don't guess there are many of you who are twelve years old," she would say, "but I was this tall when I was twelve, and it wasn't fun then either."

Doherty and Martin kept count. She went to 351 towns and cities, in each of which she attended breakfast meetings, luncheons, tea and garden parties, parades, and dinners. At the larger affairs, the orchestra heralded her appearance with "A Pretty Girl Is Like a Melody" and "Hey, Look Me Over."

She drew huge throngs everywhere, the largest at Worcester, where people began lining up at 5:00 A.M. at the door of the auditorium. About 5,500 persons—the most in the city's history—attended the indoor event. Gushed the *Worcester Telegram:* "As dazzling as a movie star, blessed with the simple elegance of a queen and the friendliness of the girl next door, Mrs. Kennedy drew a standing ovation." Afterward, she stood for hours shaking hands in a receiving line. All this time, Ted had been unable to do any campaigning at all.

And it worked. On Election Day, Ted won by the largest majority ever recorded to that time in Massachusetts. He got 1,716,908 votes— 74.4 percent of the total—swamping his fifty-nine-year-old Republican opponent, Howard Whitmore, Jr., a former Massachusetts state representative, who received 587,663.

Bobby needled Ted, "Joan won the election for you."

So did Jim King, the campaign leader in Boston, who reminded Ted for years, "You didn't win in 1964, *Joan* won in 1964."

On December 16, Ted Kennedy left the hospital to recuperate in Palm Beach, where he remained for several weeks.

Joan's exhilaration at her campaign accomplishments did not last long. Ted, healing rapidly, resumed his active political life and Joan returned to her official role, which was social and not much more. Ted was no longer the attentive suitor and young husband. He became the aggressive Kennedy male, expecting her to go wherever he wanted her to go and be wherever he told her to be. Joan obeyed dutifully. At parties, he often ignored her all evening while he danced with other women, humiliating her and infuriating her friends.

Fears about her husband's safety haunted her constantly. The absence of identification at their home was little defense against attack; anyone who wanted to could find where they lived. "We're wide open here," she told me. She was especially fearful that if Ted ran for president, something terrible might happen.

Reports of Teddy's incessant skirt chasing, which he made no effort to conceal, upset her. She was unlike Rose, who chose to ignore her husband's infidelities and totally unlike Jackie, who was aware of Jack's escapades but never spoke about or confronted him about his affairs. (Only one incident of her confrontation has been reported, and it showed true class. Once she discovered a woman's undergarment beneath a pillow in the president's bedroom. Holding it between thumb and forefinger, she brought it to him and said, "Would you please shop around and see who this belongs to? It's not my size.")

Jackie had been hardened to marital discord in her youth; Joan was not. Jackie's father, John V. (Black Jack) Bouvier had a reputation as one of the most notorious philanderers of high society. When she was twelve, she had seen her father and mother go through a messy divorce. Later, her mother Janet told Jackie that on her honeymoon cruise with her new husband, he had an affair with a passenger which lasted until the ship docked. Janet's reason for telling her was to underscore the fickleness of some men, but Jackie found the story hilarious. She related it with delight to her friends.

Joan could not escape into child rearing, as Rose did; she could not look the other way, as Rose and Jackie did. She might have filled her life with music and her children, charity work, friends, and her home, but she didn't. She was a sheltered, rich girl who had never come up against Kennedy-type mores. And she was shattered.

She drank more martinis to blunt the pain and began seeing a psychiatrist, who prescribed tranquilizers. Unfortunately, they exacerbated the effects of her drinking.

By 1966 Joan's distress was beginning to become apparent in public. Senate wives and Ted's colleagues looked at her curiously as she stumbled and weaved while walking. Reports that Joan was hitting the bottle heavily began to spread. Kennedy family friends tried, with little success, to deny that she was in trouble and to keep alive the image of the "golden couple."

Lem Billings, who had an apartment on upper Fifth Avenue, a few blocks from the eleven-room coop Jackie had bought at 1040 Fifth Avenue, said, "Joan is terribly in love with her husband and I think anybody in love as she is and who enjoys her children as much as she does—how can she be unhappy?"

But even lanky, craggy-faced Lem, a heavy drinker himself, and chief sanitizer of the Kennedy family's reputations and activities, could not say that Ted was in love with Joan as much as she was with him. "Joan would like to have Teddy more to herself, but she married a politician, and she's got to live with it. Joan won't ever adjust to the fact that she's got to share Ted," Lem told me.

Ted kept distancing himself from Joan as the sixties drew to a close. After Bobby died, Joan reached out to her husband, but Ted grieved alone on his solitary sails. The tragedy at Chappaquiddick the next year let loose a new wave of gossip about Teddy and women. Joan, three months pregnant, was humiliated.

Now, for the first time, the story that their marriage was in trouble appeared in the newspapers and was voiced on television. A month after the accident, Joan suffered her third miscarriage.

In October 1970 Joan made her concert debut as a pianist at the Academy of Music in Philadelphia with members of the Philadelphia Orchestra. (Because the concert was a fund-raiser for Pennsylvania's Governor Milton Shapp, the event was not officially part of the orchestra's season but sixty members, playing as individuals, took part.) Joan rehearsed for weeks, intent on being a success in what she knew best. She played the second movement of Mozart's Piano Concerto no. 21 in C, and Debussy's Arabesque no. 1 in G, and she was good. She received a standing ovation and, the next day, excellent reviews from music critics.

Ted, who arrived only a half-hour before she appeared, went backstage afterward. "Well done, mommy, well done," he told her. This from the one person whose admiration Joan wanted above all others. A reporter, watching, was disgusted. "Well done, mommy, for God's sake!" he wrote, comparing Ted's tepid praise to Governor Shapp's enthusiastic response after his twenty-two-year-old son Richard sang a duet with Jan Peerce. The governor leaped onstage, embraced his son, and kissed him, to wild applause.

Joan drank more and more martinis. "How many?" I asked her.

"Too many," she replied. "I never kept count."

The martinis gave her courage but turned her into a falling-down drunk.

"I was a very sick lady, then," she admitted to me. So sick that she would fly regularly to the homes of friends in Santa Monica, California, to dry out. So sick that she neglected her personal appearance. Her face became gaunt, her cheeks hollow, her hair straggly.

One reporter's blunt comment to me was "She looked like she had been dragged through a rathole. She doesn't seem to give a shit anymore."

Ten

More Wenching and Drinking

Even as Ted Kennedy's political star was ascending, he could not stop boozing and chasing women. It was done openly, with little regard for public opinion. His behavior was as circumspect as that of fraternity boys cavorting around the center of town on Saturday nights, and at the same level of rowdiness.

Usually men with a broad streak of unbridled behavior will, in the time-honored phrase, sow their wild oats in their youth, then settle down to a more acceptable lifestyle. Astonishingly, Teddy never settled down. Even as he approached his sixtieth birthday in 1992, he worsened.

He came on to every attractive woman who struck his fancy. His approach is crude, unsophisticated, like a teenage boy with raging hormones who wants to have sex. Once, when he called a young woman for a date, she turned him down and said later, "It was pathetic, very high school, a lot of giggling and heavy breathing."

During the Senate Judiciary Committee hearings on the confirmation of Judge Robert Bork for the Supreme Court, Ted entered the Senate elevator with a pretty network television producer. Before the doors closed, Ted was asking about her plans for the weekend and tried to make a date. The producer declined, saying she was expecting a visit from her sister. "*She's* the wild one," the producer said, in an attempt to blunt the senator's attentions. The effort boomeranged. "Bring her along!" Ted bellowed. Neither sister accepted.

Early in 1992, I went to the Cape Cod waterfront, where Ted vacations, and heard many stories from boatmen, marina personnel, and residents about his aggressive girl chasing and hard drinking. Said the owner of the marina, "Every time that man comes in with his boat—and this has been going on for a lot of years—it's with a different young woman less than half his age and a galley stocked with wine and liquor. One time he brought his boat in, and the combination of liquor and something he ate hit him and he made a disgusting mess."

"Almost every weekend..." wrote Norma Nathan in the *Boston Herald*, "There is the Senator schlepping into Hyannis Port with a fresh blonde in tow. You've heard of the Book-of-the-Month Club; Kennedy has a Blonde-of-the-Week Club." Ms. Nathan said that on one outing, when his boat was wedged on rocks in Wood's Hole, on the south-western tip of Cape Cod, he had a pair of blondes aboard. He was the only male. The following weekend, Nathan reported that he was more generous—there were two other blondes aboard ship—one for himself, and the other for a fellow senator.

In 1989, a lobbyist took a delegation from one of the African republics to meet Kennedy. He found the senator "drunk...stumbling and slurring his words and red in the face and smelling of alcohol." One of the Africans, a high-ranking official, gave Ted a necklace to present to Rose, who would be celebrating her ninety-ninth birthday that July. Kennedy took the package and, when he left with the Africans, tossed it on a desk. His rude behavior astounded his visitors.

In 1991, Ted came into the editorial offices of a newspaper in response to a request for an interview. The reporter who spoke with him told me, "He was absolutely hung over. He looked barely pulled together after a hard night. His hands were shaking, his face was bloated, his eyes bloodshot. He was able to answer the simpler questions—routine questions about legislation he was sponsoring or backing because he had talked about them so often they came out automatically.

"But when the questions strayed into other areas, he looked totally confused, stammering incoherent replies. An aide, who accompanied him, prompted him and, robotlike, he repeated the words.

"It was sad. Very sad."

Kennedy has denied several times, on television and in newspaper interviews, that he has an alcohol problem. He could be the last one to know. The thousands of studies on the causes and treatment of alcoholism in the past half-century have not changed one of the basic certainties about the disease: that sooner or later, victims deny they are sick. "Denial is the mechanism that allows the drinker to keep drinking: it says that he or she is not an alcoholic," said Eric Josephson, Ph.D., of the Columbia University School of Public Health.

There is no litmus test for alcoholism, no smears, blood examination, urinalysis, or scans. There are only definitions. Dr. Robert J. Campbell, medical director of Gracie Square Hospital, an alcohol treatment expert, asserted:

"Alcoholism disease takes several different forms. It is defined as any use of alcohol that causes trouble with an individual's job, personal relationships, or health. The person is unable to recognize that alcoholism is a major factor in his problem, and he is unable to handle drinking physically, emotionally, or socially."

Dr. Campbell pointed out that some alcoholics are "binge drinkers." "They can abstain for a length of time, and then may decide to drink on a holiday, an anniversary or when a problem strikes. When that drink is taken, the person is out of control."

Could such a person function well at his job? "Certainly," said Dr. Campbell. "He can seem to handle it normally as long as he doesn't drink. But if he drinks, he generally loses control over his intake."

Ted Kennedy is not a morning-to-night drinker; he can and does go without alcohol for days, even weeks, which could explain why he can work so hard and effectively as a legislator. Each year he stops drinking on January 1 and abstains for seven and one-half weeks until his birthday on February 22. Friends such as John Seigenthaler have been at parties with him when he sips only wine, and not much of that.

Increasingly, over the years, reports of Teddy's playboy conduct and compulsive womanizing have made news, not only in the tabloids but the mainstream media.

His amatory experiences appear to be endless. "What I don't understand," said Truman Capote, "is why everybody said the Kennedys were so sexy." He explained:

"I know a lot about cocks—I've seen an awful lot of them—and if you put all the Kennedy's together, you wouldn't have a good one. I used to see Jack in Palm Beach. I had a little guest cottage with its own private beach, and he would come down so he could swim in the nude. He had absolutely nuthin'! Bobby was the same way; I don't know how he had all those children. As for Teddy—forget it."

If we can take Capote's assessment of the size of Ted's genitalia, one can only wonder how one man could do so much with so little.

Teddy would establish romantic relationships with women, some of which would last a few years, one more than a decade. One of his longer relationships was with beautiful Helga Wagner, the Viennese jewelry designer, whom he met in the late 1960s. They remained close for more than ten years, before and after Chappaquiddick, and stayed good friends long after their romance cooled.

But just before the accident at Dike Bridge, Teddy was also having an affair with Llana Campbell, an attractive member of European nobility who was frequently his guest at Martha's Vineyard.

Another long relationship involved the wealthy twenty-eight-year-old socialite Amanda Burden, whom Ted met in 1972. Amanda, the step-daughter of William S. Paley, then chairman of the board of the Columbia Broadcasting System, had separated from her husband, Carter Burden, a New York socialite and Democratic New York City councilman. She had gone to Sun Valley, Idaho to obtain a divorce. The Kennedy-Burden relationship had been chronicled extensively in many reputable publications, including *Newsweek*, the *Washington Post*, and *Women's Wear Daily*, but Ted denied any romantic interest in Amanda.

On September 3, 1972, Arthur C. Egan, a tough investigative reporter, prowling around the waterfront during the Labor Day holiday at Rockland, Maine, filed an explosive story to his newspaper, the *New Hampshire Sunday News*:

"Two high-stepping playboy U.S. senators, taking advantage of a Congressional recess, spent a pre–Labor Day holiday sailing around Penobscot Bay with 'two lovely females' who were definitely not their wives," it began.

The senators, Egan wrote, were Edward M. Kennedy of Massachusetts and John V. Tunney of California.* The quartet sailed for at least four days aboard Kennedy's power sloop, the *Curragh*. The only other person aboard was a crewman who acted as captain.

---

*Tunney's wife, Mieke, had filed for divorce the preceding May.

Kennedy and Tunney issued denials, asserting that the sail was a "family affair." According to Ted, Joan had joined him for several days and then left, adding somewhat ungallantly, "The rest of the time I was stuck with my two sisters-[Pat Lawford and Jean Smith]. Can you imagine anything worse than being stuck off the coast of Maine with those two?"

However, Arthur Egan told me, "I stake my life and my reputation on the accuracy of that story. I've been in this business a long time, and I would rather kill a story than write one I wasn't sure was true."

Stories of Ted's loutish behavior have been reported from all over the world, from the elegant Claridge's in London to Paris, from Palm Beach to New York's Fifth Avenue. Here, at a debutante party in the home of a friend, said Dominick Dunne, the young guests were appalled by Ted's "tit-and-fanny pinching" and his out-of-control drinking.

A chronicle of the other women to whom he has been romantically linked before and after his December 1982 divorce from Joan follows. It is by no means complete.

1969. In April, three months before Chappaquiddick, according to one account, Ted visited Las Vegas, worrying the local sheriff, who was so apprehensive about possible assassination attempts that he assigned eight deputies to the sole task of keeping Ted under watch night and day. "One evening," the story recounts, "Ted said goodnight to his guards, telling them that he was turning in. But instead of going to bed, he slipped out of his room at the Sahara Hotel and went to the Sands. Two of the deputies, following him secretly, saw him enter a room on the 18th floor. Shortly thereafter, they saw a blond showgirl enter the room. The deputies maintained an all-night vigil, staying at their post despite pleas from Ted's cousin, Joe Gargan, that they leave Ted in peace. Nobody, they say, emerged from the room until morning."

1970. Ted went to Paris for the funeral of Charles de Gaulle, the former president of France. Newspapers throughout the world reported that he danced until 5:00 A.M. in Il Club Privato on the Champs-Élysées, with thirty-five-year-old Princess Maria Pia de Savoy of Italy, eldest daughter of former King Humbert. Reports said he jumped up and down, froglike, on the dance floor, then showed up a few hours later for the rites in Notre Dame Cathedral.

1973. Ted is linked romantically with Suzy Chaffee, a thirty-two-year-old blond, three-time world freestyle ski champion. Chaffee, the "Suzy Chapstick" of television commercials, met Ted the year before. Suzy, however, denied any romantic attachment to the senator.

1975. Ted began dating Page Lee Hufty, twenty-seven-years-old and blond, whose family inherited a portion of the Standard Oil fortune.

1982. Ted met Lacey Thompson Neuhaus, former actress and fashion model, daughter of a wealthy Houston investment banker. Lacey, blond and about thirty years old, reportedly had a year-long relationship with Pierre Trudeau, then prime minister of Canada. Ted and Lacey continued to date for the next few years.

1983. Ted is seen hugging and kissing a new lady friend, Helena Lehane, at the Heartbreak Disco in lower Manhattan. At times, Helena sat on his lap. Teddy is reported to be romancing television actress Cynthia Sikes, who plays a doctor on the *St. Elsewhere* series. Cynthia is twenty-nine.

1984. Ted reportedly falls in love with Beverly Sassoon, divorced wife of Vidal Sassoon. Beverly is thirty-eight, Ted fifty-two.

1985. Ted dated Cindy Pace, a Joan look-alike. Cindy was twenty-six. Ted's daughter Kara was two years younger. Ted and Senator Christopher Dodd of Connecticut were having dinner with their dates in a private dining room at La Brasserie, a chic Washington restaurant. When the women retired to the restroom, Ted called a waitress. When she entered, he lifted her up and threw her atop the food-laden table. Startled, the waitress began to get up, but Ted grabbed her again and deposited her in Dodd's lap. With Dodd holding her, Ted rested his weight on her, leaping off when another restaurant employee entered. Ted said, correctly, "Makes you wonder about the leaders of the country."

1987. Ted was caught literally with his pants down. A pretty young blond was on the floor of the same private dining room, her skirt above her waist. It was not the most opportune moment for a waitress to come in, but one did. Teddy jumped up, the young woman rearranged her clothes, and they resumed dinner. Two young female Senate pages were descending the Capitol steps late one afternoon when Ted's car passed by. Opening the door, Kennedy asked if one would have dinner with him. When one girl shook her head, he turned to the other, who also refused his invitation. Both pages were only sixteen years old. (Congressional pages are protected by Congress. Perhaps Ted did not know they were teenagers; and, the girl reported, he said nothing that could be interpreted as a sexual advance.)

1988–1991. Ted's relationship with Dragana Lickle, divorced wife of Gary du Pont Lickle, ended. Joseph Farish, a Palm Beach attorney, represented the du Pont heir in a suit over visitation rights to their two small children and additional support. Dragana, who had custody of the children, would take them to the Kennedy mansion, which annoyed du Pont because, Farish said, "He thought Ted was a bad influence." Farish said that Ted and Dragana had a "slap and tickle relationship for quite a while." Susan Kennedy (no relation), editor of the *Palm Beach Social Register*, said Dragana was the only woman Ted had taken home to meet his mother. Ms. Kennedy reported that Dragana dumped Ted in April.

1989. Ted got into a hassle at American Trash, a bar on Manhattan's Upper East Side. Bouncer David Shapp said that Ted came in at 1:00 A.M., "absolutely inebriated," and engaged in a political discussion with a group of young people. A patron, interrupted by the discussion, shouted, "Why don't politicians do something about drugs?"

Kennedy replied, "Get out of my face."

Angered, the patron told the senator, "You're nothing like your two brothers." Kennedy responded by throwing a drink in the man's face. At 4:30 A.M., friends put Ted in a cab and sent him home. The next day, Kennedy's office issued a statement saying that the senator had stopped at the bar after dropping friends off and before going to his sister Pat's apartment. The incident "was of no consequence," the statement said, "and the Senator regretted it had occurred."

1991. Ted's new girlfriend was a college student, twenty-two—thirty-seven years his junior. The *Boston Herald* reported that she was a graduate of Marymount University. The "romance" would have been placed in the "hot rumor" bin, were it not for a photograph of the couple, snapped by a cameraman off St. Tropez. Ted is shown atop a young woman aboard a speedboat. A colleague, examining the photo-graph, quipped to Ted, "Well, I see you've changed your position on offshore drilling."

Although Ted Kennedy has swung more than most politicians, he is by no means the only swinger in Washington. Former Secretary of State Henry Kissinger once said, "Power is the greatest aphrodisiac."* Capital dignitaries of all ranks have taken full advantage of the erogenous appeal of their positions.

Thousands of young women come to Washington each year, starry-eyed, dedicated to public service and, of course, awed by the political officials for whom they work. They are easy prey for libidinous politicians. "It's like picking apples from a tree," one representative told me. Warren Weaver, former Washington correspondent for the *New York Times*, once said, "Congress swings like no other part of the federal establishment."

Lobbyists do more than try to sway legislators. They offer the call girls as added inducements to vote for measures they are pushing. Senators and representatives boast of their conquests like fraternity boys at college.

When Donald W. Riegle, now senator from Michigan, was a young representative he wrote a book, *O Congress*, in 1972, chronicling his life in Congress. He recalled: "On the floor of the House this afternoon I talked with a colleague who has just returned from a long, busy weekend out of town. He was exhausted but he still had strength enough to give me a running account of his sexual exploits. Over the weekend he had 'scored' with four different girls—and almost 'scored' with two more. Congressmen on the make around here usually lead active lives. The fact that a member might be married makes no difference at all."

Apparently age does not slow them down. Once Senator Carl Hayden of Arizona, nearing ninety and barely able to shuffle to his seat, was asked by Senator Thomas Kuchel of California, "Hey Don Carlos, did you get laid last night?" Hayden turned, slowly, and replied with a long wink.

The American public, now skeptical that Congress is working on its behalf, should add to its skepticism the fact that the men they chose to ·

---

*Although Kissinger dated a number of attractive women, he himself never committed any improprieties.

represent them spend a fair amount of time observing women who watch their deliberations from the visitors' gallery above the chambers. This sport is called thigh watching. Young women become entranced by the spectacle of lawmakers in the process of debating measures. As they lean forward, they innocently spread their thighs apart. Legislators are quick to spot the most enthusiastic of the observers, pass the word, and, by twos and threes, move to the best vantage point. In summer, they often catch a few female visitors not wearing undergarments.

Senator Estes Kefauver, the Tennessee Democrat who was Adlai Stevenson's 1956 running mate, grabbed at every woman who came near him. Once, when a pretty newspaperwoman was shown into his office for an interview, Kefauver disrobed her deftly and was atop her in less than a minute. The interview followed. Another time he got into the "Senators only" elevator in his office building. When the doors opened on the main floor, senators waiting for the elevator were startled to see Estes in vertical *flagrante delicto.*

If Jack Kennedy's political career was not harmed by his extremely lively sex life, why couldn't Teddy get away with his peccadilloes as his brother did? What Ted did not fully grasp—until finally his eyes were opened after the sordid Palm Beach episode in 1991—is that times have changed.

If John Kennedy were running for president today, neither his wit, nor his charm, nor his movie-star looks could overcome the negative effects of his tarnished character. When he won the presidency, a politician's girl chasing was not considered news important enough to print. One anecdote is telling. After Kennedy's election, a young reporter for the *New York Times* was assigned to sit in the lobby of the Hotel Carlyle in Manhattan to check the notables coming to visit him. His assignment was to look for clues to possible cabinet appointments. Late that evening, the reporter called his editor. "Nobody of any importance went up to the president's suite," he said. "The only visitors he had were Hollywood starlets every few hours."

No story, the editor agreed. The reporter went home.

But, after Chappaquiddick, the nation learned for the first time that their political leaders had active social lives outside of governing, and they didn't like what they were hearing.

Former Texas senator John Tower failed in his bid to become secretary of defense because questions arose about his drinking and womanizing. When Governor Bill Clinton campaigned for the nomination and presidency in 1992, he had to deal almost constantly with the story, published by *Star* tabloid magazine, that he had a twelve-year relationship with blond Gennifer Flowers. The highly rated TV show *60 Minutes* questioned him about the alleged affair. Pundits such as syndicated columnist David Broder lamented that the lively debate was "an unbelievably weird way to choose a potential president of a nation with the world's largest nuclear stockpile, its biggest but badly sputtering economy, and most serious international responsibilities." But the realistic fact is that many voters, doubtless influenced by the media barrage, think that womanizing *does* matter, as shown by exit polls during the 1992 primaries. One in four, according to a *New York Times/CBS* poll, said they would not vote for a candidate who had been unfaithful to his wife; this percentage is enough to swing an election.

Also in 1992, Senator Brock Adams of Washington announced that he would not seek reelection following accusations of sexual misconduct with eight women. The *Seattle Times* quoted the women, who were not identified, saying that he had sexually harassed them for about fifteen years, kissing and fondling them over their objections. Four said he had either used or tried to use drugs to render them unconscious. One asserted he had tried unsuccessfully to rape her. According to the newspaper, seven had signed statements attesting to the veracity of the charges and said they knew they could be subpoenaed to defend their charges in court if the senator decided to bring legal action. The eighth, the paper said, expressed willingness to sign the statement. Adams denied the charges, but said he decided to end his Senate career to avoid further damage to his family and backers.

Until Chappaquiddick, Ted's drunken escapades were observed but not reported by the mainstream media. A case in point:

In April 1969, Teddy went on a spree that shocked and saddened those who watched him. As head of a Senate subcommittee on Indian education, he led a group of senators on a three-day inspection of Alaska's small Indian population. On the way home, the party, which included staff members and media representatives, landed in Fairbanks from three C-130s in which they had conducted their inspections. The group then transferred to a large commercial jet which also carried other passengers.

Kennedy began drinking from a flask he carried before boarding the aircraft and continued throughout the flight. He staggered drunkenly up and down the aisle, taking pillows from the overhead storage bins and throwing them at the media and the other passengers, all the while bellowing, "Eskimo Power—Eskimo Power." At one point, an aide brought him a cup of hot coffee which Kennedy took, then stumbled down the aisle, stopping at the seat of a woman who was holding a baby in her arms. He held the cup only a foot or so above the baby's head. Spotting the danger, a reporter moved him quickly away.

Time, Newsweek, and *Life* magazines, informed by their correspondents of the incident, decided against running the story. The *Life* reporter, Sylvia Wright, memoed her editors: "He's living by his gut; something bad is going to happen."

Three months later, something very bad did indeed happen on Cape Cod.

Eleven

The Senators Kennedy

On January 4, 1965, a cold but clear Monday, Joe Kennedy was in a state of high excitement. Telephone calls came to Hyannis Port every quarter hour and were relayed at once to Joe in his bedroom. Shortly after noon, he received the news he was waiting for. Bobby and Teddy were sworn in as senators at the opening of the 89th Congress in the capital.

Bobby stood aside as Ted, encased in a stiff leather back brace and leaning on a cane, hobbled down the aisle to thunderous applause from his colleagues. Bobby's appearance, said Arthur Schlesinger, Jr., was greeted with "visible skepticism"—presumably because his experience was with law enforcement, not lawmaking. In the visitors' gallery were a couple of dozen Kennedys: Joan , a very pregnant Ethel (with her ninth child), Pat Lawford, Eunice, Jean, and a flock of children.

While Ted's back healed the previous year, Bobby had taken a heavy blow from President Johnson, who had hated him ever since the 1961 primaries. Bobby had blamed Johnson, who had sought the nomination, for charges by his backers that Jack suffered from Addison's disease and had tried to convince Jack not to name him as his running mate.

Jack's family and friends denied repeatedly that he had Addison's disease. Bobby claimed his brother suffered only from a "mild adrenal insufficiency." However, subsequent research, particularly by Joan and Clay Blair, Jr., had shown that JFK did indeed suffer from Addison's; the diagnosis was finally confirmed twenty-nine years later by the two principal pathologists who performed the autopsy on Kennedy at Parkland Memorial Hospital. They found that JFK's adrenal glands, which sit atop the kidneys, were shriveled and virtually destroyed. The pathologists, Drs. J. T. Boswell and James J. Humes, discussed their findings in the October 7, 1992 issue of the *Journal of the American Medical Association*, with George D. Lundberg, the *Journal's* editor. Wrote Lundberg in an editorial: "Based on published and verified clinical information and verified autopsy findings, we may now make a firm diagnosis of chronic Addison's disease, probably idiopathic [arising from an unknown source] in John Fitzgerald Kennedy."

Bobby never cared much for LBJ, but he began to despise Johnson after he had made the claim which could have hurt Jack's chances. Bobby vigorously opposed Johnson as vice-president, conceding reluctantly only after Jack pointed out his value as a vote getter in the South. Knowing this, Johnson thereafter hated Bobby, referring to him as "that little shit-ass," "that little bastard," and a "son of a bitch."

In 1964 Bobby set his sights on the vice-presidency, with LBJ heading the ticket for a full term. Johnson was opposed to the idea, but groused only to his brother, Sam Houston Johnson, and a few other intimates. In June, however, polls showed that Johnson could win easily without Kennedy on the ticket. Gleefully, he told Sam, "I don't need that little runt to win. I can take anybody I damn please."

On July 27, three weeks before the convention, Johnson called Bobby to the White House and told Bobby that he wouldn't choose him as his running mate. Aware that an unceremonious dumping would lose him the support of Bobby's backers in the party, Johnson softened the blow with a promise to name him to any cabinet post or ambassadorship he wished.

After mulling over the offer for several weeks, Bobby said no, resigned as attorney general, and ran for the Senate from New York, opposing Kenneth Keating, the popular Republican incumbent. Bobby was assailed as the carpetbagger, which he was, answering the charge with the weak claim that he once had lived in Bronxville and Riverdale. Still, despite his near-total ignorance of the problems and geography of New York, not to mention its colorful landmarks he defeated Keating 3,823,749 to 3,104,056. (He had never heard of Nathan's popular hot-dog stand in Coney Island, a required stop for all office seekers, and called its founder Nathan Handwerker "Hamburger.")

Senatorial brothers have been a rarity in America's history. Dwight Foster of Massachusetts and his brother Theodore of Rhode Island served at the same time from 1800 to 1803. Three Washburn brothers— Israel of Massachusetts, E. B. of Illinois, and C. C. of Washington served in the Senate from 1855 to 1861. A fourth brother, W. D. Washburn of Minnesota, served one term from 1889 to 1895.

Lost to history is any comparison between the Fosters and the Washburns; very closely watched were the Kennedy brothers. They were as different in their roles as legislators as they were in character and personality.

Bobby was an ideologue, Ted, a pragmatist. Bobby was bored by the glacial pace of the Senate, Teddy, having learned quickly how to work within the system, understood the need for patience. Bobby was less a lawmaker than a tourist attraction, pointed to by visitors in the gallery and squealed at by people who recognized him on the street; Teddy was in the supporting cast of Kennedy stars. ("Oh, and there's Teddy, too!")

Bobby's legislative accomplishments were negligible; Teddy had a respectable number of measures passed and amendments added to bills. Bobby wasn't popular with the other senators. "He never went to charm school," observed Senator Richard Russell of Georgia, then dean of the Senate. Teddy, a team player, was well liked. He had conquered the early antipathy of fellow members, one of whom had expressed the views of many when he suggested the creation of an Edward M. Kennedy Foundation whose sole purpose was to help wealthy, unworthy young politicians begin their careers at the top.

Bobby's staff was as undisciplined in the ways of the Senate as their boss. There would be constant battles, often in loud voices, in the small rooms they occupied in the Old Senate Office Building, and equally cramped rooms later in the new building. Bobby could not—or would not—discipline them. Ted's staff functioned smoothly and was better coordinated. He encouraged them constantly by writing little notes expressing his gratitude for jobs well done. Bobby rarely did. Oddly, while Bobby was often unprepared himself, he would lash out at incompetence and lack of preparation on the part of staff members.

Bobby chafed at having to master the details of measures under consideration; Teddy spent hours in the evening and rose at 6:30 A.M. to read all the newspapers and the documents in his briefcase. David

Burke, Ted's administrative aide, said, "Clearly, young Kennedy knew more about the hearings and enjoyed the procedure more than Robert Kennedy did."

At hearings of the Labor and Public Welfare Committee, to which he and Ted were assigned, Bobby would introduce amendments, about whose details he obviously remained unfamiliar. Burke and Adam Walinsky, then one of Bobby's aides, would bite their lips as Kennedy would stumble through explanations of changes he wanted to make. Said Burke, "When the chairman or some other senator would ask him, 'What does this mean, and what are you trying to do?' Bobby would say something like 'I haven't the slightest idea, but I know it's a good idea, so let's do it anyway.'"

Senators, who didn't legislate by instinct, would continue to press Bobby to explain his points in greater detail. "He'd bumble and fumble, and his staff guys would be having a nervous breakdown behind him," Burke said. Ted, half-compassionate, half-happy at the chance to needle his brother, once sent him a note: "I don't care about the other fellows. I understand it." Bobby laughed so hard that he could not regain his composure for a full minute.

"In the Senate committees and on the floor, you always had that feeling that Bobby was about to explode," said Dun Gifford, Bobby's campaign aide during his presidential campaign, and later Ted's legislative assistant. Explode he did at a committee hearing one afternoon as the debate droned on and his patience wore thinner and thinner. Finally Bobby tossed all the documents on his desk into the air and bolted from the room. Ted was acutely embarrassed.

Bobby rarely stayed in the Senate chamber longer than an hour. Ted remained at his desk for hours most days. Bobby would come into the chamber from the door nearest the elevator and slink into his seat without talking to anyone. Ted made a grand entrance, booming "hi's" to everyone he saw. Teddy waited fourteen months before making his maiden speech; Bobby made his, a powerful condemnation of nuclear-weapons proliferation, a little more than five months after he was sworn in, earning grumbles from "the club" that it was too soon.

Because of his dedication to liberal causes, Bobby developed a cult following. Said Tip O'Neill, "He brought many young people into politics, like his brother Jack." Ted did not magnetize the nation's youth.

The brothers jibed at each other on and off the floor. Bobby told the

Democratic state convention in Massachusetts, "My brother Ted favors an open convention, one where the delegates fully consider all the possibilities, debate their merits, and then pick whomever Ted selects."

Ted got the big laughs with "Bobby is house hunting. There's a house he's interested in on Pennsylvania Avenue, but it is already occupied, and the present owners give no intention of wanting to move out."

Ted's joke was not a joke at all, and the brothers knew it. "The Senate was a stepping-stone to the White House for Bobby, just as it was for Jack," Kenny O'Donnell told me. It was a view expressed by the *New York Times* when Bobby announced that he would run for the Senate, and it was widely believed inside the Beltway. John Davis, Jackie's cousin, said that by the middle 1960s Bobby's ambition to lead the country "had developed into an all-consuming passion." Max Lerner said, "He [Bobby] used the Senate largely as a staging ground for the presidency and he was in a hurry."

By midsummer of 1965, many in Washington assumed that the brothers Kennedy were spirited rivals, not only in the Senate, but for what lay beyond. In October, Adlai Stevenson III, then candidate for Illinois state treasurer, said at Elmhurst College, sixteen miles from Chicago:

"It's well known that President Johnson is watching with interest the political activities of Senator Robert Kennedy. But perhaps it's not so well known that Senator Robert Kennedy is watching with more than passing interest the political activities of Senator Edward Kennedy."

The audience laughed because commentators were buzzing about the question; "Whose turn comes first, Bobby or Teddy?" But after the elections, the spotlight moved away from Teddy and shone brilliantly on Bobby. Teddy seemed to be laying his groundwork slowly, accepting many of the hundreds of requests he received each week for speeches around the country, enthralling audiences, especially the women, by his good looks, easy smile, and simple friendliness. As the brothers fanned out on campaign appearances on behalf of Democratic candidates in the 1966 race, jokes about the presidency spiced their speeches. In California, Bobby told audiences he had received a telegram from Ted reading: "Lyndon is in Manila. Hubert [Vice-President Humphrey] is out campaigning. Congress has gone home. Have seized power. Teddy."

Ted told his audiences: "That's silly. Everyone knows that if I ever did seize power, the last person I'd notify is my brother."

Wrote the *Wall Street Journal*: "Everyone simply assumes that Bobby, six years older and more aggressive, gets first crack at the Presidential nomination in 1972 or whenever."

Perhaps the most perceptive comment came from a senator who asked the chairman of a committee if Bobby was being accorded special consideration, inasmuch as he was only a freshman senator. The committee chairman replied, "Oh, no. I treat him the same way I'd treat any future president."

Kenny O'Donnell knew Bobby was aiming for the Oval Office. "Are you kidding?" he told me in Boston. "You can bet the store he is."

But was Teddy? "Who the hell knows!" Kenny exclaimed. "Right now, he's found a home in the Senate."

On April 8, 1964, just four-and-one-half months after Jack was killed, Joan helped Kara, then four, into a new dress and Ted, Jr., two-and-a-half, into a brand-new suit and took them to the visitors' gallery of the Senate chamber to watch Ted deliver his maiden speech. (Patrick had not yet been born.) Already there were Ethel and Jean Smith with some of their children.

In his address, Ted made a powerful statement of his stand on civil rights, to which Jack had finally become deeply committed during his last months.

"My brother," he said, "was the first president of the United States to state publicly that segregation was morally wrong. . . . If his life and death had a meaning, it was that we should not hate but love one another; we should use our powers not to create conditions of oppression that lead to violence but conditions of freedom that lead to peace. . . ."

Ted pointed out that America must adjust to "realities": "Negroes," he said, "are going to be members of the community of American citizens with the same rights and responsibilities as every one of us." The country, he said, has made similar adjustments for three centuries as it absorbed ethnic groups from all over the world, and "we have not suffered from the effort."

Ted Kennedy was convinced that the battle for racial justice would continue for many decades; he was equally certain that health care, a dominant issue in the sixties and seventies, would still be an overarching one in the nineties.

In 1965, when he was named to the Health Subcommittee of the Labor and Public Welfare Committee, he embraced the issue of government-supported medical care and made it his own. He became the country's foremost champion of national health insurance, battling the combined lobbying power of doctors' organizations, medical schools, and drug companies. "On no other set of issues was Kennedy so far out front on that cutting edge of social change," said Theo Lippman, Jr. in his book on Ted's career.

While some of Edward Kennedy's domestic and foreign programs were derived from his brothers, many were his own, formed by his own growing experiences and the idealism that captured American youth in the turbulent sixties.

In 1970, in a memorandum sent from his office, Teddy stated:

> "If one thing is clear in the United States of 1970, it is that health care is the fastest-growing failing business in the nation—a $63 billion dollar industry that fails to meet the needs of our people. Today, more than ever before, we are spending more on health care and enjoying it less.
>
> "Our current health crisis cuts across all political, social, economic and geographic lines. It affects rich and poor, black and white, old and young, urban and rural alike."

Ted's efforts to create a system of national health insurance began in 1971, when he and Rep. Martha Griffiths of Michigan introduced companion bills—S-3 in the Senate, HR-22 in the House—to provide mandatory universal coverage for all workers. Premiums would be deducted from paychecks, as in Social Security. Employers would contribute $3\frac{1}{2}$ percent, employees 1 percent, and the remainder of the funding would come from general revenues. Doctors' fees, hospital costs, X rays, medical appliances and equipment, and basic dental care for children under fifteen would be covered completely. Limits would be placed on nursing-home care and psychiatric services.

Ted was also one of the earliest lawmakers to seek a solution for crime in the streets—bad then, but not as rampant as it would become. Declaring that "we cannot call ourselves free men if we cannot walk our streets in safety, Kennedy understood that the seeds of crime were nurtured by poverty, illiteracy, deprivation, and unemployment. At the same time, he was mindful of the need to enhance the effectiveness of the police forces. "We must give them the kind of public respect, personal dignity, income, working conditions, and fringe benefits that we give other kinds of professionals in the community," he said.

With both brothers murdered by bullets, it is little wonder that gun-control legislation and a crusade against violence in the streets have been on the top of Ted's legislative agenda. Since the assassination, he shudders at any loud noise that may sound like a gunshot. Ethel still cannot watch a move or television show in which guns blaze. Her friends vet all films shown in the large cabana near the pool. On the rare occasions when they miss a shooting scene, she will rush out of the cabana.

Kennedy has introduced gun-control measures regularly, one each year, but none has even emerged from the committee stage. In 1967, before Bobby was killed, he had taken his case to the powerful National Rifle Association, telling them that sportsmen would encounter only limited problems if control laws were passed. "Is it not worth these minor inconveniences," he asked, "if we can avoid one murder, one suicide, one accident, or ten, or a hundred, or a thousand?" But the NRA was not moved.

After May 15, 1972, Kennedy felt that the country was ready for a ban on handguns. On that day, Governor George C. Wallace of Alabama, at the height of his primary campaign for the presidential nomination, was paralyzed by a bullet fired by gunman Arthur Bremer while speaking at a shopping mall in Laurel, Maryland. But Ted failed again.

Out of loyalty to his brother, Ted at first supported JFK on the Vietnam War, although Jack had increased the number of "military advisers" from 685 at the start of his administration to 16,500 at its end. Soon, however, Ted began doubting the wisdom of increasing U.S. involvement which had accelerated rapidly under LBJ.

In 1966 Ted returned from a trip to Vietnam questioning what we were accomplishing in the light of the suffering he saw. Shortly after the visit, he introduced an amendment to the Foreign Assistance Act to add $10 million for humanitarian purposes in Vietnam.

In 1968 Ted said that the kind of war we are fighting in Vietnam will only make it more difficult for that country to create a workable political future because of the widespread destruction the war had wrought. He further questioned whether the government of South Vietnam was worthy of the sacrifice of thousands of American lives: "The government we are supporting does not have its heart in the cause of the people and offers no indication that it can win their lasting confidence.... We should make it clear [to the Saigon rulers] that we cannot continue year after year picking up the pieces of their own failures."

"The quicker we get out, the better off we're going to be," he said in 1970.

That year, in a speech that started on an impassioned note and remained impassioned to the end, he told the National Convocation of Lawyers on June 7, 1971, that the slaughter in Southeast Asia must end.

It was Kennedy's most memorable speech, although it was little publicized at the time because of the dramatic news and pictures coming out of Vietnam, and it is hardly remembered today.

Yet it ranks with JFK's inaugural address, his watershed speech to the Houston Ministers Conference in which he cleared the air of the thorny issue of his Catholicism, and his *Ich Bin Ein Berliner* speech. It can stand alongside Bobby's moving extemporaneous two-minute talk from a flatbed truck in an Indianapolis athletic field, where he told a large crowd that King had been slain and pleaded for racial harmony.*

The Vietnam conflict had been intensified in 1965 by Johnson, and now, in the Nixon administration, it was an issue tearing the nation apart. Because it reflects Ted Kennedy's innermost feelings about the war, it is important to quote a portion of what he said:

"We are the vanguard of a growing people's army to end the war and cleanse the conscience of America. . . .

"We come representing the people. We come as advocates of a restless, yearning spirit of America, a spirit that prays for peace and a final ending to the war.

"What is this game that others play with us? Why is the will of the people so thwarted, the hope for peace denied? What is it about the immoral act of war in Vietnam that gives it a life and license of its own? There is no answer, except to say that because Congress slept, the Constitution failed to function and America lost its way

"But is more than that today. It is fear that perpetuates this war. Men in high places fear the conclusions staring them in the face. The war in Vietnam is only about who shall control the government of Saigon—no more, no less. Yet fear precludes the only answer that means peace. . . .

"How many more American soldiers must die, how many

---

*Following King's murder, riots flared in New York, Chicago, Washington, Baltimore, Philadelphia, and more than 150 cities. Indianapolis, where Bobby that night asked for prayer, compassion, and an end to hatred, was the only large city where no major riot erupted.

innocent Vietnamese civilians must be killed, so that the final end to the war may be announced in 1972 instead of 1971?

"We must destroy the cancer that has been transforming the noble spirit of our nation in the eyes of our own citizens and in the eyes of freedom-loving peoples throughout the world. We must spread the truth that our present policy is a policy of war, not of peace; a policy of violence, not of love; a policy of despair, not of hope—a policy that can only drag us further down into the abyss of death and immorality into which we have been descending for so long. . . .

"And some day, when the war is over, and its horror is no longer a headline but a memory . . . let us at least be able to say it ended because Congress at last awakened, and the Constitution began to function, and America found its way."

Ever since he entered the Senate, Kennedy was convinced that America's young people were often ahead of the politicians on key issues and should not be barred from participating in the voting process until the age of twenty-one. He pointed out that young people, both black and white, were in the forefront of the civil-rights struggle, illustrating this with a dramatic story.

Early in 1960, he said, four students from a black college in Greensboro, North Carolina, were denied service at a lunch counter and refused to leave. The sit-in, daring at the time, was big news. "My college generation," Kennedy said, "would have shrugged and gone on to the sports page. But this time it was different. Students throughout the North identified with the young idealists sitting in at the lunch counter. Before long, many thousands were demonstrating in sympathy in some way."

Students, Kennedy said, have become our national conscience. Repeating constantly that "if they're old enough to fight, they're old enough to vote," Ted was a leader in the fight to reduce the voting age to eighteen. His name was attached to a Senate bill, along with senators Mike Mansfield of Montana and Warren G. Magnuson of Washington, which was passed in 1970 by a vote of 64-17. Speedy passage in the House followed, and President Nixon's signature made it into law.

Because the law applied only to federal elections, a constitutional amendment was necessary to eliminate state restrictions. The Senate passed the Twenty-sixth Amendment* unanimously; it whizzed through the House thirteen days later and, by June 30, had been ratified by the required two-thirds of the states. Nearly 12 million young people thus became eligible to cast ballots in all elections.

"It is not too much to say," wrote Theo Lippman, "that if Kennedy had not lobbied in the House and Senate for the bill, eighteen-year-olds would not be voting today."

In 1968, after the assassination of his brother, Ted Kennedy could have had it all. He could have been the second Kennedy to sit in the Oval Office.

Pierre Salinger was convinced that Teddy could win; so were David Burke, Steve Smith, Burke Marshall, and Kenny O'Donnell. So, too, were many members of the media. "There was one man capable of pulling off such a staggering political coup and his name was already on everyone's mind: Senator Edward Kennedy," said David English of the *London Daily Express* who covered the entire campaign with his staff.

Teddy was the only Democrat who could defeat Nixon in 1968. Senators George McGovern and Eugene McCarthy had burned out and Hubert Humphrey seemed headed for the nomination, but visionaries like Allard Lowenstein, the antiwar activist from New York who had helped persuade Bobby to run, were certain that the August convention could be stampeded by Teddy, the true inheritor.

But Teddy was cruising the seas in lonely bereavement over Bobby's death that tragic June in California. On August 19, a week before the convention was to open, Mayor Richard J. Daley of Chicago sent Ted an urgent message which was transmitted by radio. He was to call Daley at once. Anchoring his boat, Ted rowed the dinghy ashore, wondering what the nation's most powerful political boss wanted.

Daley had decided that Humphrey couldn't defeat Nixon. "But you," he told Ted, "are a winner. You can carry the convention; you can carry Illinois; you can carry the country."

---

*The amendment stated: "The right of citizens of the United States, who are eighteen years of age or older, to vote shall not be denied or abridged by the United States or by any State on account of age."

One of Daley's chief concerns was that if Humphrey lost Illinois, he would drag Daley's entire slate down with him. Ted said he'd think about it. He thought about it all next day, then called Daley and refused.

But that didn't end the matter. Steve Smith, a delegate from New York, was buttonholed by Daley and asked to fly back to Hyannis Port to persuade Teddy. Smith went, but he was careful not to push Ted too hard. He wasn't sure that Ted had healed enough to undertake the rigors of a presidential campaign. And he wondered whether this was the time for Ted to relinquish the heavy family obligations he had taken upon himself.

Daley telephoned each day, often twice. By then the media also called Ted the savior of his party. Moreover, it was no secret that thousands of protesters of the Vietnam War were, by 1968, 25,000 Americans had already lost their lives (a toll that eventually would be doubled), were planning to turn Chicago and the convention into a battleground. Ted was the martyred brother, the head of the clan, attractive, galvanic, fully sympathetic to their cause. Only he could avert chaos.

The rivulet that had begun flowing only a few weeks before became a torrent. But Ted's spirits were still low. When he was told in Hyannis Port that his name would be placed in nomination by Governor Michael DiSalle of Ohio, he turned in his porch chair, said, "Isn't that something?" with little enthusiasm, and fell back to brooding.

Once Daley asked, "Would Ted take the number-two spot on the ticket?" but Teddy still said no.

By this time the question had been debated publicly so often that Kennedy was forced to issue a statement: "I have informed the Democratic candidates for the presidency* and the chairman of the convention that I will not be able to accept the presidential nomination if offered, and that my decision is final, firm, and not subject to further consideration."

But Ted's supporters still wouldn't give up. "We want Ted" banners appeared at the convention. On the floor, Pierre Salinger said they were all primed to go and "all we need now is Ted's word." While Ted

---

*Senators Hubert Humphrey and Eugene McCarthy of Minnesota and Alabama Governor George Wallace.

hadn't gone through the primary process, his supporters were sure that he cold stampede the convention.

In Chicago, the fuse for an explosion was already lit. Some eighty organizations calling for an end to the Vietnam War had converged on the city; about 25,000 activists were there, gathering in the parks and streets surrounding the International Amphitheater, where the convention was being held, sneering, jeering, catcalling at the police. Dick Daley had taken no chances. A seven-foot chain-link fence topped with barbed wire surrounded the entire hall, all of the city's 11,500 police were ordered on duty twelve hours each day, and 5,500 National Guard troops were placed on alert.

Before the convention opened, the fuse reached the powder and the city exploded. For days cops waded into the demonstrators, whaling away with clubs and lobbing tear gas into their midst, beating and gassing innocent spectators who were unlucky enough to get in their way. Inside the amphitheather, Senator Abe Ribicoff of Connecticut assailed the "Gestapo tactics" in the city. Daley, on the national television, mouthed obscenities that could easily be lip-read by viewers. For added emphasis, he gave Ribicoff "the finger."

Still deep in mourning, Ted Kennedy didn't see much of the mayhem, nor did he watch the proceedings in Chicago. Call after call came to Hyannis Port; Ted was either out on his boat, unavailable, or sometimes he would mumble some kind of reply, none of which encouraged his supporters.

Finally they gave up and the Democrats nominated Hubert Humphrey for president and Edmund Muskie for vice-president on the first ballot. Nixon defeated Humphrey in a close race: 31,770,237 to 31,270,222 votes. Wallace, the spoiler, received 9,897,141 votes. Later Kenny O'Donnell told me, "We were stupid. Shit, the guy was sick with grief, but we were all so carried away that we didn't look at it through his eyes."

Toward the close of 1968, Ted, having recovered in some measure from his grief, made a move that was widely interpreted as positioning himself as a leading candidate for the 1972 nomination. It was a sudden decision, made in December while skiing at Sun Valley, Idaho. For weeks he had been weighing the possibility of battling the redoubtable Russell B. Long of Louisiana, son of "Kingfish" Huey Long, for the job of assistant majority leader, or Democratic whip. Senators choose the whip at a party caucus at the start of a new session.

From Sun Valley, Ted called dozens of senators and got the support of many, including Vice-President Humphrey and Majority Leader Mike Mansfield. When he returned to Virginia, he and his aides continued their telephone lobbying. At the caucus of the senators on January 3, 1969, Kennedy beat Long 31 to 26.

The job was donkeywork: keeping track of how the senators voted, helping to schedule legislation, and organizing interminable conferences on party policy, but it was good therapy for Ted and established him as one of the party's leaders. Ted was not unmindful of the fact that LBJ, in his first term as senator, had been elected majority whip in 1951, and before long had become majority leader. Mike Mansfield, too, had begun as minority whip.

Many editorial cartoonists were convinced that Ted was already running. Oliphant, in the *Washington Star*, pictured Richard Nixon at the White House gates, two suitcases behind him. Sitting on the stone base a few feet away was Ted Kennedy, also with two suitcases. Ted told writer Theo Lipman, Jr., that he saw the whip job as an "opportunity to learn more about the range of issues that was coming up, to become more of a specialist."

Ted Kennedy was positioning himself on the track to Senate leadership. But the presidency? That remained to be seen.

Twelve

The Drowning of Mary Jo

Over the years countless myths have lodged tenaciously in many minds about the events that occurred on a pencil-shaped island east of Martha's Vineyard in the summer of 1969. Numerous theories have been advanced, most unproven and unprovable; hundreds of biased accounts by both Kennedy haters and Kennedy idolaters have been published.

The complete truth about that night and early morning on Chappaquiddick will probably never be revealed. Only two people know: one is dead, and the other has said repeatedly that he has told all and nothing remains to be said.

As others have, I visited the area where Kennedy's black Oldsmobile plunged into the cold waters of Poucha Pond, interviewed scores of persons about the tragedy, scoured vast amounts of material written about it and heard the senator himself, without prompting, talk about how it has affected his life.

Some stunning surprises came to light as I attempted to sift conjecture from fact.

First a recapitulation of the facts:

Ever since Bobby's death, the "boiler-room girls," who had manned the telephones in his 1968 presidential campaign to keep tabs on the convention delegates, had remained in touch with each other and with the Kennedys. That weekend a reunion had been planned to coincide with the Edgartown Yacht Club Regatta, July 18 and 19, in which both Ted Kennedy and Bobby, Jr., would compete.

Joey Gargan made the arrangements, reserving rooms for the women at the Katama Shores Inn near Edgartown on Martha's Vineyard. Kennedy and the other men who would make up the party would be put up at the Shiretown Inn in Edgartown. Gargan also rented a small cottage on Chappaquiddick Island, a short ferry ride across a channel from Edgartown, for a cookout and party after the races.

On Regatta Day, the women arrived at their motel and then were driven to the cottage where they went swimming at a nearby beach before the races. They included Esther Newberg, twenty-six, Rosemary Keough, twenty-three; Susan Tannenbaum, twenty-four; Nance Lyons, twenty-six; her sister Maryellen, twenty-seven; and Mary Jo Kopechne, at almost twenty-nine (her birthday would be the following week), the oldest of the group.

Ted joined the women at the beach before boarding the *Victura*, which later placed ninth among the thirty-one competing vessels. He remained there for about an hour. *It is crucial to bear in mind that Kennedy knew where the beach was and how to reach it.*

Joe Gargan, Paul Markham, a former United States attorney from Massachusetts; Charles C. Tretter, an attorney; John B. Crimmins, Kennedy's part-time chauffeur, and the women were to watch the races from a chartered fishing boat.

At 8:30 that evening, the group met again at the plain, shingled Lawrence Cottage with its small, paneled rooms, and split-rail fence separating it from the road. The party was pleasant. Steaks and sausage hors d'oeuvres were grilled outdoors on the scrubby lawn, and there was some drinking. Campaign songs were sung, and a few couples danced. Neighbors reported talking and laughing. Ted said later, "As parties go, it was dull."

About 11:15 or 11:30 P.M., Ted, who had been talking with Mary Jo, glanced at his watch, said it was getting late, and he was tired. He was going to catch the ferry to Edgartown and go back to his motel. Mary Jo said she wanted to leave, too, and asked for a lift. Kennedy got the car keys from Crimmins, his part-time chauffeur, and the two climbed into the Oldsmobile and took off along the island's one paved road which ran past the cottage.

About a half mile ahead was a T-shaped intersection. A paved road to the left led to the ferry. To the right, a dirt-and-sand road led to the Dike Bridge, beyond which was the beach.

When the Oldsmobile reached the T, Kennedy turned right. Dike Bridge was only six-tenths of a mile away. The span is ten and one-half feet wide and did not have guardrails. (They were installed later.)* The bridge veers leftward from the road. To cross safely, a driver must proceed slowly and turn the wheel to the left. Kennedy did not, and his car shot straight ahead, toppling upside down to the bottom of Poucha Pond.

Kennedy's official account of what happened next is contained in his testimony at the inquest, held at Edgartown, January 5 to January 8, 1969:

"I remember the vehicle itself going off Dike Bridge, and the next thing I recall is the movement of Mary Jo next to me, struggling, perhaps hitting or kicking me, and I, at this time, opened my eyes and realized I was upside down, that water was crashing in on me, that it was pitch black. . . .

"There was complete blackness. Water seemed to rush in from every point, from the windshield, from underneath me, above me. It almost seemed like you couldn't hold the water back even with your hands. What I was conscious of was the rushing of the water, the blackness, the fact that it was impossible even to hold it back. . . . I was sure that I was going to drown."

Ted said the strong current swept him to the bank, where he called Mary Jo's name several times. Then, still gasping for breath, he says he swam back to the submerged car and tried "seven or eight" times to reach her.

"I would come back again and again. . . until at the very end when I couldn't hold my breath any longer. I was breathing so heavily it was down to just a matter of seconds. I would hold my breath and I could barely get underneath the water. I was just able to hold on to the metal undercarriage here, and the water itself came right out to where I was breathing and I could hold on, I knew that I could not get under water anymore.

---

*The bridge has fallen into disrepair and is no longer used.

"I was fully aware that I was trying to get the girl out of that car, and I was fully aware that I was doing everything that I possibly could to get her out of that car, and I was fully aware at that time that my head was throbbing and my neck was aching and I was breathless, and at that time, the last, hopelessly exhausted."

Carried to the bank again, he made his way back to the cottage, one and two-tenths miles away. It took him fifteen to twenty minutes, he recalled; along the way, he said, he saw no people, houses, or lights.

Outside the cottage he met Ray LaRosa, who had crewed for him in the race, and asked him to get Gargan and Markham. "There's been a terrible accident," he told the two men," We've got to go...."

Gargan drove to Dike Bridge, where he and Markham said they stripped off their clothes and dove repeatedly into the water in an unsuccessful attempt to reach Mary Jo. Exhausted, they drove toward the ferry slip. Markaham and Gargan told Kennedy that it was necessary to report what had happened to the authorities.

Kennedy testified: "A lot of different thoughts came into my mind at that time, about how I was going to really be able to call Mrs. Kopechne at some time in the middle of the night and tell her that her daughter was drowned, to be able to call my own mother and father and relate it to them, my wife. And I even—even though I knew that Mary Jo Kopechne was dead and believed firmly that she was in the back of that car—I willed that she remained alive."

At the ferry slip, the two men again told Kennedy to report the accident. He later recalled saying, "You take care of the other girls and I will take care of the accident." Then he jumped into the 500-foot-wide Martha's Vineyard Channel and began to swim across. The tide was strong, but Kennedy managed to reach the mainland. He said he made his way through the dark streets to the Shiretown Inn about 2:00 A.M., where he removed his wet clothing and fell asleep on the bed but was awakened by noises from the motel next door.

A half-hour later, Ted arose and went out and spoke to Russell G. Peachey, a co-owner of the inn. He asked the time. Peachey told him it was 2:30 A.M. Ted complained about the noises where a party was being held. Peachey said he would take care of it, called the motel and the noise subsided. Peachey said he noticed nothing unusual about Ted's behavior.

Meanwhile Gargan and Markham had returned to the cottage, where the party guests, having missed the last ferry, had made makeshift sleeping arrangements. The men said nothing about the accident. The next day, the women went back to their hotel, still unaware of what had happened. "We were fully expecting to find Miss Kopechne there," said Nancy Lyons, one of the boiler-room girls, "but she wasn't, and we waited."

When they got to the Shiretown Inn the morning after the accident, Gargan and Markham learned that the police had not yet been told what happened on the Dike Bridge. They again advised Kennedy to call the authorities, but he wanted to contact Burke Marshall, an attorney who had formerly headed the civil-rights division of the Justice Department. Ted tried unsuccessfully to reach Marshall.

Meanwhile, the Oldsmobile had been found in the pond by two fisherman, who notified Police Chief Dominic J. Arena. At the scene, Arena radioed the Edgartown Fire Department to send a diver down into the pond. Soon John Farrar, captain of the department's Scuba Search and Rescue Division, arrived and found Mary Jo in the rear seat. Tying a rope around her waist, he and Arena hauled her body to the surface.

While Farrar was in the water, Arena, who had borrowed a pair of swim trunks and dived into the pond, had obtained the license number, L78207, Massachusetts. He had the ownership checked and found it was registered in Ted Kennedy's name. Chief Arena asked that a radio call be dispatched to find him.

Arena returned to the police station. At that moment, Kennedy walked into the station house and told him what had happened. The police chief typed up a statement of the accident, dictated by Ted, which presented his version, and Kennedy signed it.

The order in which Kennedy made telephone calls after the tragedy is revealing.

He gave top priority to extricating himself from the mess. After the first call to Marshall, he made the others from the police station. The second was to Helga Wagner, the former German stewardess—not to inform her of what happened, but to ask where he could reach Steve Smith, the family damage-control expert, who was vacationing in Spain.

Next were Mary Jo's parents in Berkeley Heights, New Jersey. "I was alone," Gwen Kopechne said later. "I think he said something about her being in an accident. 'Is she dead?' I screamed. He hesitated but he had to say yes. From then on I don't remember anything." Neighbors rushed to the house after hearing Gwen Kopechne's anguished cries.

Then Teddy called his mother, who was about to leave for a fund-raising party at the St. Francis Xavier Church where she was to autograph books about her sons. Rose canceled the appearance.

He called Joan last.

Now Ted had to tell his father. He left Chappaquiddick that day and went to Hyannis Port. Rita Dallas, Joe Kennedy's nurse after his stroke, recalled that day the senator came to his father's bedside. He appeared "drawn, downcast," she said.

Placing a hand on Joe's shoulder, he said, "Dad, I'm in some trouble. There's been an accident, and you're going to hear all sorts of things about me from now on. Terrible things. But, Dad, I want you to know that they're not true. It was an accident. I'm telling you the truth, Dad. It was an accident.

"Dad, a girl was drowned. I stopped by at a party Joe was having for some of our girls from the office. One of them wanted to catch the ferry and get back to the motel on South Beach. I said I'd take her but I turned off the road, and my car went off the bridge into the tidal pond. I got out, Dad, and I tried to save her, but I couldn't. I guess, after that, I went to pieces. I walked back to Joe's, and then we drove back to the bridge. He tried to get her out, too, but he couldn't. I must have gone a little crazy, Dad, because I swam across to Edgartown. I left the scene of the accident, and things aren't good because of that.

"But I want you to know that I'm telling you the truth."

Joe Kennedy closed his eyes. Six months later he was dead.

Ten hours after he told his father Ted Kennedy appeared on national television from his father's home in the Kennedy compound to describe the events of July 18 and 19. He spoke for seventeen minutes, explaining that he could not discuss the events of that fateful night until after the matter had been settled in court.

He denied the "widely circulated suspicions of immoral conduct that have been leveled at my behavior and hers regarding that evening." He also denied that he had been drinking heavily that night and admitted that his failure to report the accident immediately was "indefensible."

He concluded by asking Massachusetts voters whether they thought he should resign from the Senate. The next morning, 7,500 telegrams arrived at his home; another 7,500 were still in the Western Union office. "They're calling by the millions," said the editor of the *Boston Globe*. Sacks of mail came to the Compound and, within a week, there were more than 100,000 letters, cards, and calls, most of them telling Kennedy to keep his Senate seat.

The following January, the inquest was held in Edgartown. A total of twenty-eight witnesses were heard in the four-day proceedings, which were closed at the request of the Kennedy lawyers.

Four months later, the 763-page transcript was released. It included a 12-page summation by District Court Justice James A. Boyle which concluded that "negligent driving" "appears to have contributed to the death of Mary Jo Kopechne." Pointing out that Mary Jo had told no one she was going and had left her pocketbook at the cottage, and that Kennedy, who was usually driven by a chauffeur, had requested the car keys, the judge wrote; "I infer a reasonable explanation...is that Kennedy and Kopechne did not intend to return to Edgartown at that time; that Kennedy did not intend to drive to the ferry slip, and his turn onto Dike Road was intentional."

Despite his conclusions, Judge Boyle did not order Senator Kennedy's arrest, which he could have done under Massachusetts inquest law. Without explanation, Boyle retired from the bench the next day.

There was speculation that he feared Kennedy reprisal for his ruling contradicting Ted's story, but the answer was a lot simpler. Judge Boyle, an avid golfer, was anxious to leave the bench and retire to the golf course. "He had already planned to leave, and his departure just after he made his ruling was a coincidence," said Leo Damore, author of *Senatorial Privilege*.

On Sunday morning, July 20, two days after the accident, a cadre of long-time Kennedy advisers had gathered at the Compound. They included former secretary of defense Robert S. McNamara, Ted Sorensen, Jack Kennedy's chief speechwriter, Burke Marshall, Steve Smith, Dave Burke, Paul Markham, Joe Gargan, Milton Gwirtzman, Richard Goodwin, and Arthur M. Schlesinger, Jr. John Kenneth Galbraith, JFK's ambassador to India, gave advice by phone.

Their job; to develop a plan for damage control which would minimize any adverse effects the tragedy could have on Ted's political career.

For a week, as the conferences went on and newspapers and magazines went wild with speculation about what had happened that night, Ted Kennedy walked along the beach, going over the events in his mind. On Friday, accompanied by Joan and Ethel Kennedy, his neck in a soft brace, Ted flew to Plymouth, Pennsylvania to attend Mary Jo's funeral. On Friday he returned to Edgartown to plead guilty to leaving the scene of an accident. Judge Boyle gave him a two-month suspended sentence.

Those are the facts placed upon the record. As many investigative journalists and historians have noted correctly, they have given rise to a host of questions. Rumors, too, have proliferated; rumors that have changed into possibilities, then hardened into convictions.

Here are the questions most people ask and, perhaps, the best answers that can be given:

Was Senator Kennedy drunk when he drove away from the party with Mary Jo beside him?

Whether or not Kennedy was drunk cannot be proved. What *has* been proved legally is that Mary Jo was close to being intoxicated.

After the race, which he lost, Ted went aboard the winning vessel, *Bettawin*, which had been skippered by Ross Richards. Here, at a victory celebration, Teddy drank three rum-and-Cokes, according to Stanley Moore, another contestant. The time was about 6:00 P.M. Following the party, Ted went to his room at the Shiretown Inn, where he changed clothes and was driven by Jack Crimmins, his part-time chauffeur, to the Lawrence cottage, where the party would be held.

Ted arrived at 7:30 P.M., undressed, and soaked in a hot tub for twenty minutes. (He took hot baths as often as he could to ease his back pains.)

During the party, Kennedy, by his account, drank two more rum-and-Cokes in the course of the evening as he ate and socialized with the guests.

Kennedy did not have a test of his blood-alcohol level, which is the concentration of alcohol in the blood and brain tissue expressed as a percentage, nor did he undergo a breathalizer test. Since he did not show up at the police station until ten hours after the accident, neither test would have proved much, because alcohol leaves the body at the rate of 1.5 ounces every two hours.

Alcohol metabolism studies have shown that, after six hours, the blood-alcohol level of a 190-pound male would be .027; this level would cause feelings of warmth and relaxation in the individual. At .04, most people would feel relaxed, talkative, and happy.

The effects of alcohol depend on such variables as body weight, tolerance, and whether food has been ingested before drinking. Since Ted weighed 220 pounds and was able to tolerate liquor well, he would probably have been less affected than the average 190-pound male.

Assuming that Ted's drinks were stronger and contained two ounces of alcohol each, he would have consumed a total of ten ounces, 4.5 ounces of which would have left his body after six hours, leaving 5.5 ounces still to be metabolized.

At that level, an individual's judgment is somewhat impaired, and normal ability to make a rational decision about personal capabilities, such as driving, is affected.

But this can only be speculation because the amount of alcohol Kennedy drank cannot be proven.

The only person whose blood-alcohol level was tested chemically was Mary Jo. According to Dr. John J. McHugh, the Massachusetts State Police chemist, the alcohol content of her blood measured .09 percent. Testifying at the inquest, Dr. McHugh said that this reading in a person of Mary Jo's body weight (110 pounds) "would be consistent with about 3.75 to 5 ounces of 80 to 90 proof liquor within one hour of death."

At the time, Massachusetts law considered a reading of .15 percent evidence of driving while intoxicated. The level has since been reduced to .1 percent. Robert Sherrill, in his hard look at the incident in the *New York Times Magazine*, wrote: "At that rate, Ms. Kopechne would appear to be perhaps the heaviest drinker at the party—assuming that the others were telling the truth about their own alcohol consumption."

Everyone who knew her said Mary Jo rarely, if ever, drank. However, the question must be asked: "Did she, on this party occasion, decide to drink a good deal more heavily than ever before?"

At the inquest, Esther Newberg said that the amount of liquor "would have been completely out of order with the way she lived."

Judge Boyle replied, "I am only telling you what a chemical analysis shows. And the chemical analysis is practically irrefutable."

According to studies by the California Department of Alcohol and Drug Programs, a blood-alcohol concentration of .05 percent—almost half the amount in Mary Jo's blood—produces "lightheartedness, giddiness, lowered inhibitions and less control of thoughts...both restraint and judgment are lowered." This will become significant a few pages further on.

Since Mary Jo was not driving, whether or not she had drunk heavily had nothing to do with the accident. The level of her sobriety is significant only when we seek to understand why she did not realize that Ted had taken the wrong turn, as we will see shortly. Kennedy himself took the blame for the tragedy.

It is difficult to square the testimony about drinking at the inquest with some hard facts.

Two days before the party, Jack Crimmins had come to the cottage with food, cookout supplies, and liquor. He put the steaks and other groceries in the freezer and stocked the cabinets with the following: three half-gallons of vodka, four fifths of scotch, and two bottles of rum. He also brought two cases of canned beer and put as many as he could fit into the refrigerator. After the party, Crimmins said he removed two bottles of vodka, three of scotch and the beer. Thus a half-gallon of vodka, a fifth of scotch, and two bottles of rum (the size was not specified) were consumed. Assuming that the bottles of rum were fifths, this adds up to 140.8 ounces of liquor. With an average drink containing 1.5 ounces alcohol, 93.8 drinks—or an average of 7.8 per person—were consumed during the evening.

The women testified that they had a total of nine or ten drinks, and the men, including Kennedy, said they had only six, for a total of sixteen. *That leaves 77.8 drinks not accounted for.*

Why wasn't an autopsy performed on the body of Mary Jo Kopechne? Were Kennedy's people afraid that an autopsy would show she was pregnant, thus opening up a whole new line of investigation?

Clamor for an autopsy grew in the months following the accident. Kennedy people wanted to prove that no sexual act had been performed and wanted to end the pregnancy rumors. Edmund Dinis, district attorney for the Southern District of Massachusetts, wanted to eliminate any doubts of foul play. On December 1, 1979, following a hearing, Judge Barnard Brominski denied a petition by Dinis to exhume the body for an autopsy on the ground that no evidence had been presented to show that Mary Jo had died from any cause other than drowning.

Mary Jo's parents, Gwen and Joseph Kopechne, were adamantly opposed to an autopsy, according to their attorney Joseph Flanagan. Gwen Kopechne repeated her objection in several interviews she gave later, saying that she saw no reason for exhumation.

Shocked at the ugly rumors that Mary Jo was pregnant, she revealed that her daughter had had her menstrual period only three days prior to the cookout.

"We would have agreed to an autopsy only if it could have been shown that foul play had been the cause of Mary Jo's death," Gwen Kopechne said. "We said this to Edmund Dinis before the hearing [on exhumation] began. We didn't feel that an autopsy would yield new evidence, and the thought of it was grossly offensive to us. It would have been like a second funeral."

Was there a sex orgy at the Lawrence Cottage? After all, there were six unmarried young women there and six men. Wasn't the party planned that way?

There was no sex orgy.

Joe Gargan's wife, Betty, was asked to attend and had agreed, but had to cancel because, at the last minute, her mother fell ill in South Bend, Indiana. Joan Kennedy, too, was invited and was hoping to attend but, pregnant with her third child, wasn't feeling well.

The fact that six men and six women were present has fueled the speculation that an orgy had been planned. That was just happenstance because a number of other men had been invited but didn't show up. They included Dun Gifford, who worked in Ted's office and later became a campaign aide for him; David Hackett, Bobby's lifelong friend, who had been in charge of the work of the boiler-room women; Ed Martin, of Ted's Boston office, and several others.

Nor was this the first party ever given to show appreciation to the women. It was the fourth. The previous spring, Hackett had had a party for them at his Maryland home. The *Washington Post*, whose reporter was present, said that it was "merry but a completely decorous affair." In January there had been another get-together organized by Hackett and Gifford. At this one, Hackett said, the girls were outnumbered two-to-one by men and, he told biographer Burton Hersh, "It was one of those great times, really memorable. There wasn't any hanky-panky at all."

Ted has insisted repeatedly that he took a wrong turn at the T-intersection. Is this creditable?

No, for three reasons:

One, the road to the ferry is twenty feet wide and paved. The road to the bridge is narrower and unpaved. It is extremely unlikely that a motorist would not realize at once that he was driving over a dirt road, not a paved one.

Two, Ted had crossed Dike Bridge early that afternoon and swam at the beach just beyond it.

Three, at the T, there is a road sign which clearly reflects an arrow pointing to the ferry when headlights shine upon it.

What then, would be a plausible scenario of what happened?

Ted Kennedy's low threshold for sexual excitation is well known. He may have fully intended to drive to the ferry, drop Mary Jo, then go to his motel, but was probably turned on by the young woman at his side despite his weariness. Aware that the beach would be deserted at that hour, he apparently decided to take Mary Jo there.

Why didn't Mary Jo, who had also been at the beach that morning, realize he was not driving toward the ferry? Why didn't she object?

By all accounts, she was a devout Catholic with an excellent reputation for hard work, morality, and personal integrity. Willing participation in a one-night affair would have been entirely out of character for her. One cannot rule out the possibility that, having consumed more alcohol than she ever had before, her normal inhibitions were lowered. "It is easy for uninformed and inexperienced drinkers to misjudge the drinks they can safely handle," declared Margaret Bacon, Ph.D., a clinical psychologist specializing in alcohol research. (Kennedy had denied any "immoral conduct" with Mary Jo or that there had ever been a "private relationship between us of any kind.")

Why did Ted Kennedy wait about ten hours to report the accident to the police? Why didn't he go into one of several homes in the vicinity and ask to use their phones to make a report?

Because, he has continued to insist, he was in shock and was suffering from head injuries. However, he was capable of discussing the tragedy with Gargan and Markham; when he showed up at 2:30 A.M. outside his motel, Russell Peachey, one of the owners, did not observe anything unusual about him.

At 7:30 A.M., Kennedy, fully dressed, borrowed a dime from the motel desk clerk to make a call from the outside pay phone. Mrs. Frances Steward, the clerk, said he was "quite calm and collected." After the long-distance call, Kennedy got back his dime and returned it to Mrs. Stewart with a polite "thank you" and a smile.

Kennedy was apparently attempting what is known inelegantly inside the Beltway as a "CYA" tactic—cover your ass.

Kennedy was sharply criticized for his inability to think clearly and act positively in the face of a crisis. The opposite—that he thought *very* clearly—was probably true. While he was doubtless extremely concerned about the death of a girl—its full impact would hit later—he acted at the time as Drs. Burner and West point out, "with a calculation we normally expect and want from public figures in a crisis." His political career, important to him, was on the line and, following Kennedy behavior, he weighed the problem, considered alternatives, and consulted members of his family and their close associates.

In fact, William F. Buckley said that Ted disqualified himself from the presidency, not because he was "drunk and horny"—doubtful on the first count, probable on the second—but because he was unable to extricate himself from the situation more artfully!

Kennedy's failure to report the accident at once lies at the core of the tragedy.

Still, assuming that Kennedy was in shock and unable to reason clearly, why didn't Gargan and Markham report the accident to the police?

They asked him to, insisted he should, but he told them he would handle the situation. As loyal Kennedyites, they could not—or would not—go against his wishes.

Did Ted ask Joe Gargan to take the blame?

Columnist Jack Anderson said he did at first, but abandoned the idea. True or not, Garry Wills said, "The theory naturally arose, since those who know Gargan have little doubt that he would have taken the fall if he was asked."

But when I put the question to Gargan in the late 1992, this was his impassioned reply: "It's an absolute lie. Ted never asked me to take the blame, never asked me to take the fall. If he had asked me to say that I had driven the car, I would have refused and we would not be friends anymore, and we are good friends today."

If Ted Kennedy had called the police or a fire-department rescue squad immediately, could Mary Jo's life have been saved?

John N. Farrar, captain of the Edgartown Fire Department Scuba Search and Rescue Division, who brought her body to the surface, believes that prompt action could have averted her death.

Farrar said he found Mary Jo's head "cocked back, face pressed into the foot well, holding onto the front edge of the back seat. By holding herself in a position such as this, she could avail herself of the last remaining air in the car."

In the past, he said, persons trapped underwater had survived as much as five hours by breathing in a pocket of air. At the inquest he testified that he could have had her out of the car alive in twenty-five minutes if he had been called immediately.

Why have the "boiler-room girls" kept silent all these years? Weren't they paid off by the Kennedy family to say nothing?

They have not been silent. They testified at the inquest, telling all they knew, which added little of substance. They have refused interviews simply because they had nothing to say. Why would the Kennedys "pay them off" when all they could "reveal" was that there was a party, that they ate, danced, sang some songs, and drank?

Why didn't the Kopechnes sue Kennedy over the death of Mary Jo?

"We figured people would think we were looking for blood money," Joseph Kopechne told Jane Farrell of the *Ladies' Home Journal*. The Kopeches received $90,904 from Kennedy as a settlement and another $50,000 from the insurance company. They built a house with part of the total of $140,904. Kennedy offered to pay the funeral costs, but the Kopechnes refused.

Does Ted's behavior demonstrate a callousness on his part about the drowning?

No. Coldness toward the death of a young woman, especially one who had been so devoted to his brother Bobby, cannot be reconciled with Ted's compassionate nature. While he was trying desperately to salvage his political career and keep his presidential hopes from being derailed, he was devastated by the tragedy, which has haunted him ever since. He has never been able to put the death of Mary Jo behind him.

On September 1, 1971, two years later, a Sunday morning, I visited Kennedy at Squaw Island, arriving in time for breakfast. An unwashed white Pontiac GTO stood before the white door where Kennedy had parked it the night before when he returned from a five-day sailing and camping trip with a few young Kennedys.

We had breakfast on a railed-in terrace at the rear of the house. Beyond was a small patch of lawn, with a lazily turning sprinkler, and then the slope to the beach. Originally there had been a wall here, but Joan had replaced it with sliding-glass doors for a view of Nantucket Sound.

After breakfast, Kennedy stood at the rail and pointed. The sun had burned his nose and forehead, which were bright red and peeling. He was wearing deep purple knit slacks and a black open-necked shirt, exposing a mat of white chest hair. "Over there," he said, "at the foot of the breakwater, is Dad's house." Kennedy turned his eyes ahead and pointed. "Just at the horizon is Martha's Vineyard. You can just barely make out the outlines of the shore. It's about twenty miles, a nice sail."

To the left, unseen, was Chappaquiddick Island. Kennedy stared in that direction. Suddenly his eyes brimmed with tears. "It's with me," he said, "and always will be with me." His voice dropped and he spoke almost to himself. Moving closer, I caught his words. "I'll never forget that," he was whispering. "I'll never forget that." Quickly he turned, sat on a metal chair, and changed the subject. As he spoke of other matters, his eyes were still wet.

A few years later, Teddy was vacationing with Joan at a Caribbean resort. At dinner in the hotel restaurant, Joan was overheard saying, "But Ted, you've got to forget about it. You just have to put it out of your mind." Ted was sitting silently, pecking at his food. They had been talking about Chappaquiddick.

Twenty years later, Senator Alan K. Simpson, Washington Republican, told me the following story: "I was on a train just recently with Ted. A woman came over to him and said, 'What do you think of what you did to that woman on Chappaquiddick?' Ted turned pale, then replied, 'Ma'am, that's with me every day of my life.'"

Kennedy did not join in the discussions with the counselors who rushed to Squaw Island. I was told by those who saw him that he was clearly in anguish. One said, "He had this look of utter sadness on his face and, as the days went on, his face became haggard from the lack of sleep. He seemed to be perpetually on the verge of tears."

Another recalled, "There was sheer horror in his face. His eyes would mist over, and you could almost feel his pain."

When Teddy returned to the Senate three weeks after the accident, colleagues agreed that he seemed an emotional wreck. Sylvia Wright wrote this stark description in *Life* magazine:

"He seemed devastated. The massive body had grown thin, the jowls which always made him look like a caricature of himself, were barely noticeable. The ashen face was melted down.... The tortured eyes looked out tentatively, seeking signs of loyalty or defection, then were cast down again. He walked and moved more slowly."

"Even his enemies felt sorry for Ted," said Fishbait, the congressional doorkeeper. "It was too terrible for words. There was almost the same sadness and hushed shock as when his two brothers were assassinated. Congressman and senators went around saying, 'Why? But why?' And they still don't know."

If his name had been Edward Moore, would he have been dealt with more harshly?

More than twenty years later, many believe strongly that his name and position protected Ted Kennedy from the more rigorous treatment an ordinary citizen would have received.

Lester Leland, foreman of the grand jury which investigated the affair, has declared that its members were pressured by the judge and the prosecutor to drop the case.

"I think that we were manipulated," he said. "And I think that we were blocked from doing our job, and if you want to use the word 'cover-up,' then okay, that's what it was."

Other critics have questioned the handling of the affair. Why did Police Chief Arena allow Ted Kennedy and others to leave the island without questioning them? Why was the Kennedy statement withheld from the press, at his request, for three hours? Why was there no autopsy, and why was the inquest delayed for six months at Ted's request and then closed to the public and the press?

The prevailing opinion seems to have been that Edward Moore would have had a much harder time.

Is Ted Kennedy the arch villain in the tragedy?

He will always bear the blame for the death of Mary Jo Kopechne, and he knows it. But the Kennedy loyalists who gathered at the Compound the day after and, coolly and dispationately, schemed to find a way to preserve the Kennedy dynasty were reprehensible, too. The sorry spectacle of New Frontiersmen of high status planning strategy to minimize Ted's involvement was a low point in the Kennedy political saga. It underscored old Joe Kennedy's credo that Kennedys must win, whatever the cost.

Thirteen

Teddy and Jackie and Ari

The Kennedys were appalled when, in the spring of 1968, Jackie told them of her intention to marry the elderly Aristotle Onassis, the billionaire Greek shipping tycoon.

He had been courting her since the previous year. Without receiving much media attention, they had dined quietly in such elegant restaurants as El Morocco, "21" and the Colony in New York, in his penthouse apartment on Avenue Foch in Paris, and at hideaway spots in Greece. In May 1968 Jackie went on a five-day Caribbean cruise with Onassis aboard his palatial yacht *Christina*, during which he was at her side almost constantly.

During the cruise, Onassis proposed marriage. On her return, Jackie told Bobby, her closest adviser and confidant in the family, that she was seriously inclined to accept. Bobby was stunned. He was then in the midst of his primary campaign for the Democratic nomination. Only half-jokingly, he told her, "For God's sake, Jackie, a thing like that could cost me five states!"

Word spread quickly. The family was horrified.

Jackie, a national icon since the murder of her husband five years before, had become one of the world's most famous women. Books were written about her. Magazines that featured her on their covers sold out.

There was an almost-mythic majesty about her, a living reminder of the glory that was Camelot, which the nation refused to give up.

The family knew that a worshipful nation would be confused and angered if Jackie married Onassis. "The American public," she had said when she was First Lady, "would forgive me anything except running away with Eddie Fisher." (Fisher had shocked America by leaving his wife, Debbie Reynolds, and marrying Elizabeth Taylor.) After a dazzling Prince Charming, she would be marrying a swarthy, homely Caliban; she was young, beautiful, and artistic; he seemed to care for little more than money and power; she was not a social climber because she had already arrived; people would believe that he wanted another jewel in his crown of acquisitions, which had already included the opera star Maria Callas; he was considerably older (sixty-two to sixty-eight, no one was sure); she was thirty-eight; and she was marrying out of the Catholic church, which Rose Kennedy could never forgive.

Moreover, in 1954 Onassis had been indicted by the federal government on criminal charges of falsifying the ownership of a number of Liberty ships. The U.S. claimed that Onassis had used American cohorts as "fronts" to buy up, at low prices, the surplus Liberties which, by law, could be purchased only by Americans. Onassis had been arrested, fingerprinted, and released on $10,000 bail. Subsequently, he paid a $7 million fine to escape jail.

Ethel Kennedy and several of the other women in the family pleaded with Jackie in her Fifth Avenue apartment. "If you hurt our men by marrying this man, you will hurt the America they have been raised to serve," Ethel said.

Jackie listened politely but would not yield.

The billionaire shipowner was not a newcomer in her life. She had known him casually since the late 1950s. When her second son, Patrick, died of hyaline membrane disease, a respiratory ailment, on August 3, 1962, after only forty hours of life, she had retired to Cape Cod, emotionally drained, speaking to nobody outside her family. To help her recuperate, Onassis offered to put the *Christina* at her disposal for as long as she wished.

Jackie accepted gratefully. With her sister, Lee Radziwill, Ari's sister Artemis, and Undersecretary of Commerce Franklin D. Roosevelt, Jr., she flew to Greece for a cruise. Later she told *Eleftheros Cosmos*, an Athens newspaper, "He rescued me at a moment when my life was engulfed in shadows....I will be eternally grateful to him."

Ted Kennedy was the only family member who did not merely wring his hands, but took active steps to stop the marriage.

He was still in mourning over Bobby's murder, but the perpetuation of the family name, honor, and future was important enough to him to jolt him into action.

After Bobby's death, Ted became Jackie's confidant. They talked often by telephone, and she was a frequent visitor to Squaw Island. (One morning, when I had spent several hours there with Ted, he suddenly looked at his watch and quickly ended our talk, ushering me out. It was 12:30 P.M. As I left, I saw a black limousine pull into the driveway. Caroline Kennedy was in the front seat, Jackie at the wheel.)

Late in August of 1968, Ted called Onassis on the *Christina*. Despite an erratic connection, he was able to get his message across. Jackie would be coming to Greece in a week. Could he and Ari meet for a private conversation of great importance?

"Of course, of course," Onassis replied. He invited them both to come to his private island of Skorpios in the Ionian Sea, two miles east of the fishing village of Nidri. They could chat uninterrupted as long as they wished. And afterward, Ari said, "we can have a little fun."

Jokingly, Ari told Willi Frischauer, his biographer, "As I did not expect a dowry, there was nothing to worry about." But, Frischauer said, he did realize that Ted might try to talk him out of the marriage.

Newspapers and newsmagazines published photographs of Jackie and Ted leaving for Greece, but were unaware of the real purpose of the trip. Jackie's intention to wed the shipping magnate was still a closely held family secret.

When Ted arrived on Skorpios, Jackie spent hours sunning herself as negotiations between the two started. Ted began by cautioning Ari that being a stepfather to Caroline and John, Jr., would not be easy. After all, Ari's business interests forced him to travel almost constantly, and he would rarely get to see them. Ari brushed the argument aside, telling Kennedy that he knew children, loved them, and had raised two of his own; his daughter Christina and son Alexander. They were now fine young people, he said.

Ari's assessment of his children omitted the fact that Christina and Alexander had been confused and upset ever since Onassis and their mother, Athena, were divorced in 1960, when the girl was eleven and the boy was thirteen. (The emotional damage lasted all their lives. Christina married four times and, grossly overweight, died of a pulmonary embolism in 1988 in a Buenos Aires suburb. Alexander, an angry young man throughout his young adulthood, died at twenty-four in a plane crash in 1973.)

Ted warned Ari that the marriage would be extremely unpopular in the United States, if not the entire world. Waving his hand dismissively, Ari stated that what others thought was irrelevant. Ted then turned to the subject of money. "You do know," he said, "that Jackie would no longer have an income from the Kennedy trust if she remarries." Ari wanted to know how much she received. About $150,000 annually, Ted replied. Onassis told him that he would arrange to have Jackie receive a significantly larger sum.*

At that point, Ted threw up his hands. He had lost. He and Jackie went to the *Christina* for a bouzouki party. (Bouzoukis are similar to mandolins.)

The *Christina*, which Winston Churchill once described as the world's most magnificent yacht, is all white, with a canary yellow funnel. Some 367 feet long, the yacht carries six lifeboats, a glass-bottomed fish-watching boat, a sailboat, two kayaks, an automobile, and a seaplane. Its furnishings, including antiques, paintings, and artifacts from all over the world, were once estimated conservatively at $25 million.

The *Christina* has a sick bay with modern surgical and medical equipment superior to that of many small hospitals, a swimming pool, game room, and an all-white dining room. Drinks are served in a large circular room at a bar with stools covered with tanned skin from whales' testicles.

That night, Jackie, radiant in a fiery red blouse and long checked skirt and scarf, stood next to Ari as he greeted his guests. Later, nibbling on white grapes, she listened to the music of the bouzoukis as Ari whispered a translation of the romantic songs in her ear.

By October 1968, rumors of the marriage had spread around the world. The *Boston Herald Traveler* broke the story on Thursday, October 17, 1968. That afternoon, Nancy Tuckerman, Jackie's social secretary, released a short statement:

---

*Actually, Jackie had inherited about $70,000 in cash from President Kennedy, plus his personal effects and the Cape Cod house, and the income from a trust fund, which amounted to $200,000 a year. When she married Onassis, she asked for—and received—what amounted to a bride price: a cash payment of $3 million and $1 million for each of her children. In return she gave up all claims to his estate.

In 1955, nineteen-year-old Joan Bennett was selected College Queen at a beauty contest in Bermuda during spring break from Manhattanville College of the Sacred Heart. The following year, she was named queen of Bermuda's annual flower pageant. (Bermuda News Bureau photo)

In her lily-covered coach, she was presented with the "key to the city" of Hamilton by its mayor, E.R. Williams. (Bermuda News Bureau photo)

During her senior year at Manhattanville and for a brief time after, Joan worked as a model. This is a series of three pictures submitted to Candy Jones, a cover girl and wife of Harry Conover, who headed a major model agency. Joan's measurements were 36-35-37.

Ted and Joan were married on November 19, 1958, a year after they met. He proposed on the beach at Hyannis Port near his father's house. John Kennedy, then a senator from Massachusetts (center), was Teddy's best man. The marriage was performed by Francis Cardinal Spellman, at Joe's insistence, even though Joan and Ted would have preferred to have John Cavanaugh, president of Notre Dame University, officiate. (Boston Herald photo)

Ted Kennedy campaigned actively for his brother Jack in the 1960 presidential race against Richard Nixon, the GOP nominee. (John F. Kennedy Library)

He was named Rocky Mountain coordinator and campaigned vigorously, but, unhappily, Jack lost in the heavily Republican western states. (John F. Kennedy Library)

Bobby, Ted, and Jack in the White House after Kennedy defeated
Nixon in 1960. Bobby had been named attorney general and Ted would
run for the Senate seat Jack had vacated, as soon as he passed his
thirtieth birthday in 1962. (John F. Kennedy Library)

Ted easily defeated Edward J.
McCormack, Massachusetts
attorney general, for the
Democratic nomination in June
1962, and on to win the election on
November 6 by more than 300,000
votes. He is pictured here in his
Senate office. (John F. Kennedy
Library)

Dignitaries from all over the world, including dozens of heads of state, gathered at the White House to follow the body of the assassinated President Kennedy to St. Matthew's Cathedral for the funeral mass. Jackie, a black veil shielding her face, walks between Ted (right) and Bobby. (John F Kennedy Library)

While flying to Springfield, Massachusetts, on June 20, 1964, where his nomination for a full Senate term was virtually assured, Ted's back was broken in the crash of a twin-engine plane. Two persons were killed in the accident, and Ted spent months immobilized in a special frame while his back healed. (Boston Herald photo)

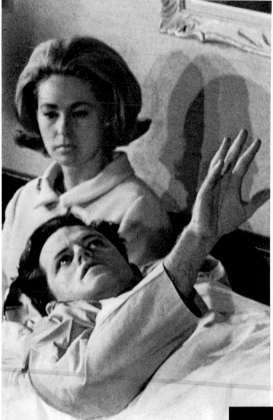

While Ted was in hospital, Joan wa
a daily visitor. (Boston Herald
photo)

With Ted lying prone in hospital,
Joan took over the entire campaign,
installing herself in an office next to
his room and traveling all over the
state for almost five months. The
work exhausted yet exhilarated her,
especially after Ted won by 76.5
percent of the votes cast. (Boston
Herald photo)

Lawrence Cottage on Chappaquiddick Island, which was rented by Joseph. F. Gargan, Ted's cousin, for a party following the annual regatta of the Edgartown Yacht Club. The celebrated cookout, with six "boiler room" girls and six men, including the senator, was held there on the evening of July 18, 1969. (Boston Herald photo)

The dirt road to hump-backed, unrailed Dike Bridge. Note that the span veers sharply to the left at the end of the road. Had Ted followed the dotted line, he would have crossed safely, but he went straight ahead and plunged into the icy waters of Poucha Pond. Ted managed to escape from the black Oldsmobile, but his passenger, Mary Jo Kopechne, drowned. (Boston Herald photo)

Ted Kennedy appeared at the funeral mass for Mary Jo, held in Plymouth, Massachusetts, wearing a soft brace. A cartoonist pictured the collar as a vise, choking off his hopes for the presidency in 1972. (Courtesy of Boston Herald)

In January 1970, Bill Barry, Bobby's security chief during the 1968 campaign and Ted's close friend, accompanies the senator and Joan to the inquest into the death of Mary Jo at the Edgartown District Court. In May of that year, Judge James A. Boyle released the 763-page transcript and his report in which he concluded that Ted's turn toward the bridge was "intentional."

"Mrs. Hugh D. Auchincloss has asked me to tell you that her daughter, Mrs. John F. Kennedy, is planning to marry Mr. Aristotle Onassis sometime next week."

Rose and Ethel said nothing. Only Ted said, "I talked to Jackie several days ago, and she told me of her plans. I gave her my best wishes for their happiness."

On October 18, Jackie, accompanied by Caroline and John and several Secret Service agents, came out of her apartment building on Fifth Avenue in New York City enroute to Kennedy Airport. About three hundred people waited outside. Amidst the murmurs of recognition one woman's voice could be heard. "I just can't believe it," she cried out. "Say it ain't so, Jackie."

Jackie and her children entered the limousine and were driven to Kennedy Airport, where other members of the wedding party, including her mother, stepfather, and sisters-in-law Patricia Kennedy Lawford and Jean Kennedy Smith, were waiting.

Newspaper headlines were not kind. "Jackie how could you?" asked the *Stockholm Express*. "Why did Jackie choose Onassis? There are over a billion reasons," wrote the *Long Island Press*.

A more reasoned appeared in *Time* magazine. "Her choice of Onassis may well represent a distillation of many reasons," it wrote. "Onassis is a man of considerable magnetism. Some of his friends profess to see him as part Alexander the Great, part a Hellenic Great Gatsby. He is iron-willed, infinitely considerate of his women, vain of his limitless ability to charm, entertain, and protect those whom he likes or loves."

Jackie and Ari were married in the tiny chapel of the Little Mother of God on Skorpios on October 20. There were only twenty-one guests at the simple Greek Orthodox ceremony, including Caroline and John and Alexander and Christina.

Jackie, in a two-piece beige chiffon and lace dress, and Ari, in a dark blue suit, exchanged gold rings and drank red wine from a single silver chalice to symbolize the "harmony of spirit and body." Archimandrite Ploykarpos Anthanassion placed wreaths of white flowers on the heads of the bride and groom and led them around the altar three times in a dance of Isaiah.

The wedding dinner that night was far more elaborate, with flowers, music, champagne, and gold bracelets for the women and gold watches for the men. Ari gave Jackie a huge ruby-and-diamond ring with matching earrings. She also wore two new 24-karat gold bracelets, one inlaid with diamonds and rubies. The cost; $1,200,000.

The marriage was a misalliance almost from the start. They quarreled constantly. Ted Kennedy had been right: Jackie felt that Ari did not spend enough time with his stepchildren. "You're away so often, they don't know you exist," she complained. He, in turn, could not reconcile himself to the way American children dressed, he told Jackie, who came to breakfast one morning in the hated blue jeans.

Jackie, who insisted on separate sleeping arrangements, would not allow Ari into her bedroom without permission. Once, he slipped in and put an expensive jeweled bracelet on her breakfast tray. Instead of thanking him for the gift, Jackie was furious. Why, she demanded coldly, had he entered her bedroom without asking her if he could? Ari was dumbfounded.

They battled in private and public. In the Pan American VIP Lounge at London's Heathrow Airport in January 1972, they had a shouting fight. Said one Pan Am employee, "It sure was a flaming row. She was shouting at him to be quiet and to listen for once. It got so loud, I don't think they could even hear each other." Jackie boarded the plane, but Ari stalked out of the airport.

Not unlike the marriages of far less affluent couples, most of the quarrels centered around money. Jack Kennedy had been angered by Jackie's extravagance, once asking wistfully if there was such a thing as Shoppers Anonymous. Ari, too, was angered at the amount of money Jackie was spending. He had given her an allowance of $30,000 a month, in addition to charge accounts, but she always exceeded the limits.

The quarrels persisted, the rumors of an impending breakup of the marriage grew and even appeared in the *New York Times*. They were always denied.

On a hot morning in late May, 1975, I went to see Roy M. Cohn, the lawyer-financier, at his New York town house on West 68th Street, which did double duty as his home and office. I had heard that Cohn had been engaged by Onassis to seek a divorce.

The mail had just arrived and Cohn, in blue bathrobe and slippers, sifted through it as he sat in an armchair. I had known Roy Cohn for years. He told me candidly the harsh facts of the crumbling marriage.

The event that broke the union, he said, was the cost of the lawsuit Jackie brought in 1972 against free-lance celebrity photographer Ron Galella in New York Supreme Court to restrain him from taking pictures of her and the children.

Cohn said, "Mr. Onassis was not in favor of bringing the suit on the ground that it would create a lot of publicity for the photographer and not accomplish anything for her. But she insisted. Then a lawyer's bill came in from the law firm which represented her, something over $400,000, which was presented to Mr. Onassis. He blew his top when that bill came in.*

"I have been a friend for about twenty-five years of Johnny Meyer, who was Mr. Onassis' principal assistant and his constant companion when he was in the U.S. and his adviser on things related to the U.S. I reviewed this legal bill situation with Johnny Meyer and concluded that it was grossly excessive under the circumstances. As a result of some of the thoughts I gave, the bill was negotiated down substantially and was finally paid in the still very large amount of $235,000.

"However, Mr. Onassis was still extremely annoyed since he had not wanted the suit brought in the first place and didn't regard it as his business. Some time after that, probably around the fall of 1974, Mr. Meyer spoke to me about the matrimonial situation. The substance of that and several subsequent conversations was to the effect that Mr. Onassis wanted out of the marriage.

"There were financial problems. He felt the amount she was spending was enormous and that the sincerity was not there, with heavy emphasis on the fact that his daughter Christina was just horrified at the whole thing and so deeply upset she was threatening to commit suicide unless Jackie was out of the picture. He [Onassis] was doing some consulting with Greek lawyers and advisers concerning the implications there and wanted to know if I would be available in the event some proceedings were appropriate or helpful in the United States.

"I think there was an overall suspicion on his part concerning every phase of her activities. It [the marriage] had degenerated to the point of almost total distrust on his part. The discussions went back and forth a

---

*Jackie won a court order restricting Galella from coming closer than fifty yards to her and one hundred yards to her apartment. Later, the Court of Appeals cut the distance to twenty-five feet.

number of times in late 1974 and early 1975. After the last conversation with him, Onassis became ill and later died. And that was it." No divorce papers were ever filed.

After Alexander's death in 1973, Ari's zest for business seemed to disappear and he became deeply depressed. He was also ill, suffering from myasthenia gravis, a progressive neuromuscular disease of unknown origin. One of its earliest signs is weakness of the eye muscles. Ari's eyelids had to be taped to keep them from drooping.

He entered New York Hospital in the fall of 1974 but doctors said he could not be helped. On February 6, 1975, his gallbladder was removed at the American Hospital in the Paris suburb of Neuilly-sur-Seine. Both Jackie and Christina visited and sat on either side of the bed, not speaking to each other. Told by doctors that Onassis was in no immediate danger, Jackie flew to New York on Thursday, March 13, to view a television documentary on which Caroline had been working. Two days later, the hospital called, saying that Ari had died. Jackie returned to Paris that evening.

Ted Kennedy flew to France to be with Jackie. He accompanied her on the Boeing 727 which carried Ari's body, in a plain oak coffin, for burial on Skorpios. Caroline, John, and Jackie's stepfather, Hugh Auchincloss, had arrived at the airport earlier to join the funeral party.

After a short, simple Greek Orthodox ceremony, Ari was buried to the left of the Skorpios chapel where he and Jackie had been married. His son Alexander is buried to the right of the chapel. As the Greek prelate intoned a final prayer for Onassis, Jackie, Ted, and Caroline crossed themselves. Less than twenty-four hours later, they left Greece.

Years later, Costa Gratsos, a longtime friend and close aide of Ari, revealed a tasteless episode which took place at Ari's funeral.

Christina was riding in the back seat of a limousine with Jackie and Ted when he leaned across to her and said, "Now it's time to take care of Jackie."

"Stop the car!" Christina demanded. She got out and joined her aunts in another limousine.

One of Christina's oldest friends said, "Christina knew that Teddy wasn't there to share her grief, to hold Jackie's hand. He was there for a specific purpose; he was going to want to discuss business sooner or later. Ari always had money in his head; Christina understood that. The Kennedys had it in their hearts; she understood that, too. But Teddy's timing blew her mind. And that's why she stalked out of the limo that day."

Ari's death made Jackie a very wealthy woman. She contested the agreement she had made in 1968 to give up all claim to his estate and, after lengthy negotiations, received a $20 million settlement, plus an extra $6 million to pay the taxes on the inheritance. In return, she gave up her share of the island of Skorpios and the *Christina*, which Onassis had left her.

In Jackie's Fifth Avenue apartment, there are many photographs of JFK and the family, but only one of Onassis.

Fourteen

The Best Chance

If Ted Kennedy had a golden opportunity to win the presidential nomination in 1968, his chances were even greater in 1972. This was astonishing in view of the almost universally accepted belief that his chance for the presidency had died with Mary Jo on Chappaquiddick Island.

Despite the tragedy, Ted's popularity was high. In 1970, only a year later, Ted placed third in the national poll of most admired Americans conducted by the Gallup Organization; he ranked just below Billy Graham. In 1971 he took third place again. The year after, he slipped to fifth, but rose to fourth in 1973 and 1974.

Pundits wrote Kennedy's political obituary after Chappaquiddick. Three weeks after the accident *Newsweek* said "Teddy's nomination in 1972 was a *fait accompli*. But now he could only retire to home base, try to put together as impressive a re-election victory [for the Senate] as he could next year and bank everything on the notoriously short memory of the electorate and the extraordinary magic of the Kennedy name and style."

The announcement of Ted's political demise was premature. One evening in 1979, I was chatting with Theodore H. White, prior to

155

presenting him with the Author-of-the-Year Award of the American Society of Journalists and Authors.

White, the chronicler of four presidential campaigns, said, "The brass ring was Teddy's to grab in 1972. Everywhere you'd go before the convention—in hotel lobbies, restaurants, wherever—you'd hear the name Ted Kennedy. He was the party favorite by far."

According to Dan Rather, the TV anchorman then covering the White House for CBS, "Ted was coming on like a tidal wave. Public opinion polls showed him so far out in front for the 1972 nomination that it was embarrassing for other party luminaries, whose names were listed as also-rans."

By March 1971, the Gallup Poll showed Kennedy tied with Ed Muskie,* the front runner; by May, he had pulled far ahead. Hubert Humphrey ran a poor third. Other candidates included Senators Henry Jackson of Washington, Vance Hartke of Indiana, and George S. McGovern of South Dakota, former Senator Eugene McCarthy, Congresswoman Shirley A. Chisholm of New York, and New York Mayor John V. Lindsay. Gallup cited "the strong and persistent appeal of Senator Edward Kennedy," despite the drowning of Mary Jo. "Memories of Chappaquiddick are fading fast," wrote Washington commentator, Clayton Fritchey in the *New York Post*.

Why was a Teddy ground swell moving so far and so fast? Was much of the media, which condemned him severely after the drowning and was still hammering away at his behavior, reflecting its own views and not those of the people who elect presidents? Is it possible that Americans were more forgiving of his "indefensible" actions than the journalists, editorial writers, TV commentators, and op-ed experts?

Possibly. The more likely reason for Kennedy's attraction was his liberal politics. American liberalism still carried considerable weight among the electorate: labor unions were strong, though less powerful than they were after World War II; the Vietnam War had pushed moderates to the left; the champions of human rights in a world oppressing people from South Africa to Russia to the Far East were

---

*Senator Edmund S. Muskie of Maine self-destructed during the primary campaign when he wept openly at a campaign rally as he assailed published criticism of his wife, Jane, and his own alleged comments describing French-Canadians as "New Hampshire blacks." The comments were scurrilous, and the country applauded his defense of his wife and himself, but viewed his tears as a sign of weakness, unacceptable in a president. Muskie left the race in April.

finding their voice. Only a few years later, liberalism would become a heavy chain which, like Marley's ghost, would have to be dragged around by politicians seeking public office under its weight.

But not then. After ten years in the Senate, Ted Kennedy's legislative performance appealed to the Vietnam veterans and their supporters. They loved it when he left his office in Washington and marched along with protesters, carrying a stop-the war placard. He had introduced another, stronger National Health bill; he had taken the bold step of calling for a detente with Communist China two years before Richard Nixon's unprecedented visit; he was one of the first to seek a minimum income tax so the rich could not escape paying all taxes; he was also one of the first to seek an annual cost-of-living increase in Social Security benefits.

When hundreds of veterans and their supporters camped on the Mall in defiance of federal orders and declared their intentions of resisting arrest, Ted Kennedy visited them at 2:00 A.M. and met with their leaders in a closed session in one of the tents.

Later he told journalists, "I'm an admirer of these people. They represent the best of America. They've fought, and they've fought gallantly. If they could be bivouacked 10,000 miles away from here, they certainly ought to be able to bivouc here."

If political economy is the "dismal science," as Thomas Carlyle said, politics is more dismal still, and a great deal more bizarre. Just as Ted Kennedy emerged as the country's most important Democrat, his party members in the Senate ousted him as their majority whip.

The move at the opening of the 92d Congress on January 21, 1971, was not only a surprise coup, but involved a dramatic deathwatch over Senator Russell who was lying critically ill of a respiratory infection and emphysema at Walter Reed Hospital. At 10:00 A.M. on that mild midwinter morning, the Democratic senators closed the door of the caucus room to elect their assistant majority leader. Kennedy was certain that he controlled at least twenty-eight votes, barely a majority of the fifty-five needed to win, but enough. But he did not know that Senator Robert C. Byrd, the short, colorless but ambitious junior senator from West Virginia, had been campaigning secretly for the post, collecting on his IOUs from colleagues whose measures he had supported, and putting together a coalition of conservative-minded Southern and Western members, plus a few swing members.

Neither was Ted aware that Russell had given his proxy to Byrd. Thus the cliffhanger. If Russell was still alive when the vote was taken, his proxy could be counted under Senate rules, but would be voided on his death. If Russell had died, Byrd would not have challenged Kennedy, he said later, because he believed that he would have fallen short of a majority by a single vote.

When he arose early that morning, Byrd called Senator Herman Talmadge, Russell's fellow Georgian, and asked him to stay in close touch with Walter Reed. Russell was still alive at 9:00 A.M. and at 9:30 A.M. Just before the caucus began, Talmadge reported that Byrd was still breathing.

Byrd made his move.

As it turned out, the West Virginia Senator had more support than he thought: he won 31 to 24. Kennedy left the caucus room bewildered. How, he wondered, did he lose the vote of four senators who had pledged their support to him? Byrd was elated, of course, but was also puzzled at winning three backers he never thought he had.

Four hours after the vote was taken, Russell, the Senate's dean and the symbol and keeper of its traditions, died at the age of seventy three.

Ted's defeat was widely construed as a stunning and humiliating setback. Even Kennedy-friendly Dr. Burns called it "a second Chappaquiddick." Anthony Prisendorf wrote in the New York Post that Ted's loss "makes it clear that the Kennedy name has ceased to be a sure-fire symbol of success." Stanley J. Hinden of Newsday called the loss "a major blow to his political prestige, to his role as a Senate policy-maker and to his chances of becoming a Democratic Presidential candidate in 1972."

Kennedy lost the whip job because many senators felt he had not given enough time and attention to the post while Byrd, a plodding but meticulous man, worked diligently on the dull but essential housekeeping chores. Byrd was always in the capital, while Kennedy took long absences because of the Chappaquiddick accident and for his reelection campaign in Massachusetts in 1970.

There were many more analyses like these, all tolling the same death knell. All of them were wrong.

Richard Nixon saw the setback as anything but a fatal blow to Ted's career. Even though Kennedy kept insisting he did not plan to seek the nomination, Nixon did not rule out the possibility that Ted would be persuaded to run, and Nixon was frightened at the prospect of facing him in a presidential campaign. So frightened, said Dan Rather, that "there were days when the entire place seemed to be in the grip of a morbid obsession, not unlike the mood aboard the *Pequod* when Ahab was at the helm."

Right-wing journalist Victor Lasky was one of Nixon's few friends permitted to visit him in his self-imposed exile at San Clemente after he resigned the presidency. Lasky recalled, "The Old Man detested Ted Kennedy because he represented all the things that were repugnant to him morally. Richard Nixon, you must understand, was a prude. Hell, he wouldn't even hold his own wife's hand in public, even though he really loved her. To him, Ted Kennedy was a Class-A roue´ with no sense of marital fidelity."

The accident at Chappaquiddick was still being headlined in July 1972, when a covert plan was launched to rid Nixon of the Ted Kennedy threat once and for all. It was dirty tricks, pre-Watergate, with many of the same cast of characters; it was also one of the lost stories preceding the scandal that would unseat a president.

The plot was financed by a $100,000 fund from the Committee to Re-elect the President (CREEP), which paid for an undercover investigation of Kennedy's role at Chappaquiddick. The mission: to snoop in and around Martha's Vineyard for any evidence that would refute Kennedy's account of the tragedy.

Even Secretary of State Henry A. Kissinger found time to become involved in Chappaquiddick, busy as he was in pursuing the elusive prospect of peace in Vietnam, with the strategic arms limitation (SALT) talks and with the continuing guerrilla attacks from Lebanon and Jordan on Israel.

The plan began when John Ehrlichman, Nixon's assistant for domestic affairs, called in John Caulfield, a former detective, second grade, for the New York Police Department. Ehrlichman thought that Caulfield had done an excellent job as police liaison to Republican campaign headquarters in New York and was a good choice to head up an intelligence system for the president. Caulfield was installed in a small suite at the Executive Office Building adjacent to the White House.

When Ehrlichman told Caulfield that he had a special assignment for a seasoned investigator, Caulfield suggested Anthony Ulasewicz, a former colleague on the New York police force. In June Ulasewicz met with Herbert W. Kalmbach, a deputy finance chairman of CREEP and

Nixon's personal attorney, who told him he would receive $22,000 annually, plus expense of $1,000 monthly, and take orders directly from Caulfield on assignments. "Whether it is within the law for a president in the White House to command as his party's leader such a private intelligence capability is unclear; but the style is dirty," Teddy White said.

Caulfield instructed him that his first job was to go up to Martha's Vineyard to find out anything that would discredit Ted Kennedy's account of the Chappaquiddick incident. Ulasewicz spent four days there on his first trip—there would be others—posing as a newspaperman, sitting in on press conferences, talking to anyone he could find who could disprove Ted's story.

He came up with nothing every other journalist did not know.

Thereafter, John Dean, White House counsel, received a note weekly from H. R. Haldeman, Nixon's assistant and chief of staff: "Does Caulfield have anything new on Kennedy?"

On August 17 Caulfield flew to Hawaii to shadow Ted Kennedy, who was returning from a trip to India. The sleuth discovered that Kennedy had been a guest at the home of a wealthy Japanese industrialist. That he had played tennis doubles at the estate of a Honolulu contractor named Lloyd Martin. That the players included Martin and his wife, and a Mrs. Warnecke. That a survey of all hotels, cocktail lounges, and other hideaways turned up nothing. "No evidence was developed to indicate that his conduct was improper," Caulfield reported.

Early in August, Kissinger had a talk with J. Kenneth Galbraith, the ambassador to India during JFK's administration and a close Kennedy family friend. Galbraith said that Kissinger had a hot tip. The secretary of state rushed to the president, who sent Ehrlichman a note: "Talk to Kissinger on a very confidential basis with regard to a talk he had with J. K. Galbraith as to what really happened in the EMK matter. It is a fascinating story. I'm sure H.A.K. will tell you the story and then you, of course, will know how to check it out and get it properly exploited."

Ehrlichman did check out the story and found it was nothing but gossip that could not be verified.

The low point in the plot came in the winter of 1971, when a sumptuous apartment was rented in midtown Manhattan. To John Dean, who was opposed to the idea, the place "looked like a Chicago whorehouse," with its red velvet wallpaper, black lace curtains, and white furniture.

A number of studs had been engaged to date some of the "boiler-room girls", bring them to the apartment and, presumably during an amorous dalliance, attempt to extract from them the story of what happened at Chappaquiddick. According to one report, hidden cameras were placed in the bedroom to record the scene, if it took place, and the film would be used to blackmail the women into their "secrets."

The plan failed. No boiler-room women ever came, and the boudoir operation ended.

Before Chappaquiddick and after, Ted had played a cat-and-mouse game with the press and the voters, dropping hints all over the country that he would run, then confusing everyone with his quips.

On January 22, 1969, speaking at a fund-raising dinner to help pay off Bobby's campaign debts, he said, "The campaign of 1968 never really ended in California because it remains with all of us. He [Bobby] often said, 'We have promises to keep.' And these are the promises which will bring all of us together many times in the future."

That sounded like a broad—and serious—hint to his audience. But then he shifted gears:

"I've read numerous stories that there would be a Muskie-Kennedy ticket or maybe a Kennedy-Muskie ticket running for the Democrats in 1972. Let me just say that Ed Muskie hasn't picked a vice-president yet." He paused. "And neither have I."

Ted began to make more and more appearances in 1971 denouncing Richard Nixon's policies in Vietnam. In Washington on April 2, he assailed the president's conduct of the war as "misguided and inhumane." The following week, in Peabody, Massachusetts, he said, "This is the time to begin to get out of Southeast Asia, lock, stock, and barrel." In October, at the Harvard Law School Forum, he delivered a comprehensive attack on the Nixon presidency, the sharpest so far, for his "trickle-down economics and trickle-up unemployment and for his vetoes on housing, health, and unemployment legislation."

But again coyness. Asked whether he could support Hubert Humphrey for the 1972 nomination, he replied, "He would make a good vice-president." The *National Observer* reported on October 9 that "his

political juices are beginning to flow" and that his determination to have
Nixon ousted from the White House might force him into the race.

Excitement heightened as convention time—July 10 in Miami
Beach—neared. "A moment of electric tension seems to be in store for
this generation of Americans," wrote William A. Honan in the *New York
Times Magazine*. "No one can be sure when it might occur, yet it
appears to be written into the script of contemporary history as a
obligatory scene. . . . It is the moment when Ted Kennedy appears on the
television saying: 'Help me finish what my brothers began.'"

But Ted had no intention of running.

He wavered only once in April, when the legacy of his brothers Jack
and Bobby was threatened by Alabama governor George C. Wallace,
who sought the nomination. Wallace's primary campaign proved surprisingly strong. "I'm going to watch that very closely," Ted said. If the
nomination of Wallace, whose segregationist policies had been opposed
bitterly by his brothers, appeared even remotely likely, he would go to
the floor and battle against it. But he didn't have to. On May 15, Wallace
was paralyzed from the waist down in an assassination attempt during a
rally in a shopping center in Laurel, Maryland. Although Wallace
continued campaigning, the bullets effectively destroyed his hopes.

But Ted, now forty years old, still said no.

He needed more time, he said, to learn about foreign affairs, time to
build even stronger fences in the Senate, where firm alliances are
essential if a president expects to win cooperation for his programs, time
for more legislative experience.

While George McGovern moved steadily ahead, Ted, with his three
children, sailed Nantucket Sound in his sloop, the *Patrician*. A friend
said that Ted might go to Miami, but only to urge Democrats to unite
behind the nominee. "Until then," the friend said, "he's going to be Joe
Six-Pack and watch the convention on television."

Which is precisely what he did. After McGovern won the nomination,
Kennedy flew into Miami and, in the early hours of the morning,
delivered an endorsement which was the best speech of the convention,
by most reckonings. McGovern named Senator Thomas F. Eagleton of
Missouri as his vice-president, then dumped him in August, when it
was revealed that Eagleton had undergone electroshock treatments in
1960 and 1966 for nervous exhaustion and fatigue. Sargent Shriver, Ted's
brother-in-law, was named in his place.

Had Ted Kennedy said yes, the course of American history could have been changed. While the Vietnam War was finally coming to an end, a deep chasm still divided the antiwar insurgents and the party regulars. "Kennedy was uniquely situated to make peace between the warring factions," said William Schneider, political analyst for the American Enterprise Institute for Public Policy Issues. "A great historic opportunity to pull the Democratic party together was lost."

Had he healed the rift, the Democrats might have retained the White House for eight years, and possibly longer, preventing the swing of the country toward the political right.

Fifteen

Joan's Agony

After Chappaquiddick, Joan hit bottom. The following incident is heartbreaking evidence of how sick she had become:

At 1:00 P.M. on a Saturday afternoon in September 1971, the telephone rang in the home of the managing editor of a major national magazine who, months before, had overseen the preparation of a two-part article on Joan. He had gone to her Virginia home with a photographer to supervise the picture-taking for illustrations and to interview Joan for more specific material he felt the article needed.

"We had a sort of cordial relationship," the editor told me. "Earlier that summer, I wanted to take my family to the Cape for a vacation. Since it was a last-minute decision, there were no accommodations available. I called Dick Drayne [Ted Kennedy's press aide] and he arranged it for me—not on the cuff, but we got very nice accommodations.

"While there, Joan invited my wife, the children, and me to Squaw Island. We sat on the terrace overlooking the sound and drank soft drinks. Joan's was a diet drink, which she poured from a can over ice; she drank no hard liquor at all.

"Joan pointed out a whole convoy of small boats going round and round like Indians around covered wagons. She said to my wife, 'That's

Ethel out there with about twenty of the kids. She's out there all day! I wish I had the strength and patience to do it. They go out about nine in the morning and don't come back until late afternoon.'

"It was four or five weeks later that the phone call came. It was Joan Kennedy, calling from Squaw Island. It became rapidly apparent that she was under the influence. She was slurring her words. She was quite drunk, and she was sexually aggressive with me, very specific.

"I was stunned, horrified, and saddened. I gestured to my wife to get on the extension phone because I didn't believe what she was saying.

"She was talking about wanting to fuck me and that what she needs is to get laid and couldn't I come up and forget about the world and have a good fuck. It wasn't an awful lot more, but it was said repetitively. She would say it seven or eight times. I kept trying to deflect it, to sort of cool it, to push it away, and yet, what do you say when this famous senator's wife....My wife couldn't believe it. It went on for literally twenty minutes, incoherent, weepy, all the things someone on the sauce does.

"She'd say, 'I know you don't believe me, but I'm a good fuck, I really am. It's just a short flight up here. You know, you've been up here. Nobody would know. Your wife won't know. We could just fuck our brains out.' Words like that over and over again.

"'You don't know what it's like,' she said. 'There's no affection up here. I could be dying of thirst for affection, and there is no affection. I need someone who would really care about me.'

"I don't know why she picked on me, other than the fact that I had always been sympathetic and kind to her personally. I had never done anything to offend her. I had sent her advance copies of the magazine with the articles. It really came out of nowhere.

"I finally managed to get her off the phone and I said to my wife, 'What'll I do?' She said, 'You should tell someone. That woman needs help and obviously she's not getting it.'

"I called Ted Kennedy's office in Washington and spoke to a young woman. I said it was essential I talk to Dick Drayne, that it was of utmost importance concerning Mrs. Kennedy, and that I'd never call on a Saturday if it wasn't something he should know immediately. Drayne called back fifteen minutes later. I told him exactly what happened, and he said, 'My God! I appreciate your call. I owe you one.'"

Then came another family catastrophe.

In the fall of 1973, Teddy, Jr., then twelve years old, complained of a sore right leg. When his leg failed to improve, the boy was taken to Georgetown University Hospital not far from his home for tests on a lump that appeared below the knee. The diagnosis: the boy had been stricken with chondrosarcoma, a rare form of cancer that originates in the cartilage. Though dangerous, cartilage cancers spread less rapidly than osteogenic sarcomas, tumors that form in the bone.

Joan and Ted were vacationing separately. He had spent much time at Hyannis Port and in Colorado. She toured Europe. She was still there in November when Ted called with the news. Teddy was in Georgetown University Hospital. His right leg had to be amputated above the knee.

Joan rushed home. The surgery had been scheduled for the day after her arrival, but the boy hadn't been told he would lose his leg. To make sure that he would not hear or see any news of his illness, Kennedy ordered the radio and television to be removed form his room. That evening, he and Joan went to the hospital. Joan was in no condition to tell her son, so Ted went alone into the boy's room.

Sitting on the bed, Ted explained what the swelling he had for ten days meant and what had to be done. "It was," he said afterward, "the hardest thing I have ever had to do." The boy began to cry. Kennedy hugged his son, and they wept together. Joan and Luella, the Kennedy nurse, who had come from Boston to care for Teddy, were in the adjoining room.

At 8:30 the next morning, young Teddy's leg was removed. At 10:00 A.M., he was back in his room, where his parents were waiting. Less than a half hour later, Ted Kennedy went a block away to Holy Trinity Church for the wedding of his niece Kathleen to David Lee Townsend. Inwardly distraught, but smiling for the cameras, he escorted the bride up the steps of the red stone church at 11:00 A.M. "He had made a commitment to give Kathleen away, and he stuck to it," Luella marveled. "There aren't many who could do what he did that day."

While he was still on the operating table, Teddy had been fitted with a temporary artificial limb consisting of an aluminum pipe with a foot of molded rubber. Within two weeks, he took his first steps in one of the hospital's physical-therapy rooms. Rising from a wheelchair, he walked a dozen steps to the parallel bars at the other end of the room, grabbed them, and looked back, grinning at the doctors.

Dr. Donald A. Covalt, a rehabilitation specialist from the Rusk

Institute in New York, supervised the construction of his artificial leg.
Dr Covalt said, "He was shaky, but he never shed a tear. He was also
scared to death, as anybody would be, but he did as we asked."

After several weeks of physical therapy, Teddy was fitted with a
permanent artificial limb, consisting of metal and a wood knee, which
bends with the same resistance as a human one, a plastic leg section,
and molded rubber foot. It weighed 7½ pounds.

After the boy came home, he was taken to Palm Beach, Florida,
where Joan watched him pedal a tricycle, pulling his crutches in a wire
basket behind him. Each morning and evening, she helped him into his
artificial leg. then she went to her room to cry. The doctor's assurances
that he would eventually run, walk, play, go camping, sailing and skiing
did little to ease her suffering.

Joan, now thirty-six, wept and drank more.

That spring of 1974, Joan signed into the Silver Hill Foundation in
New Canaan, Connecticut, a small private hospital which treats all
emotional ills but is known for its clinical work with alcoholic patients.
She remained for three weeks then returned to her McLean, Virginia
home the third week in June. Two weeks later, she went back to Silver
Hill for a much longer stay. Afterward, she spent additional time at a
small hospital in Capistrano, California, which is also known for its
treatment of problem drinkers.

At year's end, *People* magazine named her one of the year's "losers,"
linking her with Representative Wilbur Mills, who was arrested for
drunken driving after his friend, stripper Fanne Fox, landed in the Tidal
Basin, and John W. Dean, the White House counsel jailed for his part in
the Watergate scandal.

Joan underwent psychiatric treatment, but could remain sober only
for a short time. On October 9, 1974, she was arrested for drunk driving
in McLean after a minor car accident, the first of several. She pleaded
not guilty, was fined $200, and lost her license for a year.

So it went. Periods of sobriety, periods of heavy drinking, signing in
and out of alcohol-rehabilitation hospitals, the butt of countless jokes
inside the Beltway.

Muffy Brandon, one of Joan's closest friends, said, "What happens to
the human spirit is like what happens to a high cliff when the waves are
too strong and too high and too constant. The cliff erodes and the
underpinnings get shaky. That's what happened to Joan.

"When you have two brothers-in-law assassinated, when your son has cancer, when your husband almost died in an airplane crash, when you've had several miscarraiges—how much can the human spirit endure?"

The gorgeous girl whom Jack Kennedy once called "The Dish" was pitied by many, scorned by others and, in a stunning act of cruelty, put on display by her husband.

A journalist friend visited Ted at Squaw Island one afternoon. On his way out, Kennedy suggested that the friend say hello to Joan, who he said was at the rear of the house. The friend was aghast when he saw her lying in a drunken stupor in the rear of a car. "I've seen drunks often enough," the journalist said, "but what I was looking at there was the result of a two- or three-day bender."

The marriage deteriorated through the 1970s. It was an open secret in Washington and Boston, but the public was fed a stream of disinformation by the Kennedy staff that nothing irreparable had occurred. Reports that the marriage had soured were answered with comments such as "That's so ridiculous it doesn't even deserve attention." Dick Drayne, Ted's loyal press secretary, called one report "nonsense."

But it wasn't nonsense, and Joan's father, Harry Bennett, knew it. Harry was too honest to deny the truth. Although Joan called him frequently from Virginia to assure him that she was happy and not to worry, Harry's paternal instincts told him she was not happy, and he worried. I talked to him often during the seventies. He told me he hoped Joan and Ted could resolve their differences, especially because of the children. But he was not certain they could.

In the fall of 1977, after nineteen years of marriage, Joan made a watershed decision. "She realized that she had to do something about herself and that the only way to do it was to make a physical break with Washington," said her friend Joan Braden. She packed her bags and took a cab to National Airport, where she boarded a flight to Boston and a new life.

At Logan Airport, a taxi driver took her to 250 Beacon Street in the exclusive Back Bay section, where Ted had bought a pied-à-terre to stay in when he was in town. The nine-story brick-and-limestone building with a green-and-white canopy was only a short walk from Louisburg Square, her first married home. On either side of the entrance, two small patches of grass were fenced in by old iron railings. There was no doorman, just iron doors opening into a small foyer. A visitor had to press a bell to be admitted. Once inside, there was a large foyer with a faded circular green rug covering a marble floor.

A month after she left McLean, Joan made her first public admission that she was an alcoholic. She said, "It's good to talk about it after you've been sober for a year, and I have. I've talked about it with my friends until they're bored silly, but I've never talked about it publicly before."

Joan decorated her new apartment with graceful furniture which reflected her own quiet taste: a deep-green carpet in the L-shaped living and dining room; a sectional couch upholstered in black and white, graceful end tables and some green and white wicker chairs. Plants hung from the ceiling in front of a large picture window that looked out on the Charles River. She placed a few family photographs on the walls and furniture, but wanted no political memorabilia to remind her of the Washington years; no banners, no campaign signs, not even pictures of crowds cheering the Kennedy brothers. Most important to her was the shiny black Steinway baby grand placed prominently in the living room.

In Boston, she was shielded from the unending gossip about Ted and his women. "That's another nice thing about being here," she told me soon after she moved. Then, with curiosity mingled with apprehension, she lowered her voice and asked, "Tell me, what are the latest rumors?" It was like someone with an aching tooth unable to keep a tongue away, making it ache a little more.

I answered truthfully, "There aren't any."

Joan echoed incredulously, "There aren't *any*?"

"There are not any," I repeated.

"Oh!"

I told her that her separation from Ted appeared to be having a salutary effect on the senator. Ymelda Dixon, widow of newsman George Dixon, who had known capital celebrities since FDR's day had said, "There's just no gossip about him anymore." Betty Beale, the society columnist who had entertained Washington's elite for years and knew everything that went on, agreed. In the Senate pressrooms and at the bar of the National Press Club, where talk of private lives of the legislators over Bloody Marys was as common as discussion of power politics, stories about Ted's girl chasing had all but disappeared.

Ted, approaching forty-five, attended very few social events, came by himself, and left early—and alone. Once he went to a small dinner party for twelve at a fellow senator's home, arriving after cocktails still in the dark blue suit he had worn all day. He had a quiet dinner, sipped a glass of wine, talked quietly with the other guests, and left at about 10:00 P.M. Reports Mrs. Dixon, who was present, "He was dignified, very serious, very much the senator."

He rose between 6:30 A.M. and 7:00 A.M., jogged for twenty minutes around his estate, breakfasted, usually with aides, and was off to his office, arriving before 9:00.

Was there really a "new" Ted Kennedy? Some observers maintained that his increasing prestige in the Senate capped, after sixteen years in the Upper House, by assumption of the chairmanship of the powerful Senate Judiciary Committee in January 1978, had imbued him with a new seriousness of purpose. Others, more cynical, said that he intended to seek the presidency the next year and could ill afford new scandals.

Still others, like Betty Beale, said, "I don't think a man of his type changes his instincts. Maybe he's trying to be more discreet now. He never was before. I presume he's still doing the things he's always enjoyed doing, but more quietly. And as you get older, the urge does get a little less, doesn't it?"

Or had Ted been jolted by Joan's departure into the realization that, to keep his home and marriage intact, he had to change? Kara was nineteen, Teddy, Jr. a year younger, and frail Patrick only twelve. While Ted had never considered marital fidelity essential to a stable home, the physical separation of parents from one another was a different matter.

Joan became a full-time student at the Lesley College Graduate School of Education, a small teachers college in Cambridge, where she enrolled in an independent studies program leading to a master's degree in music education. She planned to become a music consultant for children's television programs. Each morning she drove to the school, about fifteen minutes away, parked in a small lot or on the street, and hurried to Room 203 on the first floor of Wolford Hall. Classes were informal, with fifteen to twenty students ranging in age from twenty-five to fifty, seated randomly at small tables around the large blue-carpeted room. In jeans stuffed into boots and an old sweater, she was indistinguishable from the other students.

Her courses met three times a week, two hours each time. Her classmates knew who she was, of course, but after the first days of surprise and some awe, they treated her as just another student. They conferred with her over knotty problems, exchanging ideas. Often after class, Joan would drop into Charlie's Bookstore, actually a small·snack shop on the ground floor of Wolford Hall, for coffee and more talk with her classmates.

Then she would be off on her busy daily schedule. She went to the library for research, study, and preparation of reports and papers. She would go for the private piano lessons she was still taking at the highly regarded Long School of Music on Follen Street in Cambridge. She always found time to see close personal friends, "people who are not in the news but whom I've known for years and whose friendship means so much to me."

Joan told me that she thoroughly enjoyed her new freedom from the "Washington goldfish bowl," but denied that she had abdicated forever from the political world of her husband.

Why did she leave McLean and her family?

"I had to," she said. "I had to be doing something for myself. And it's easier to do it up here. I'm not far from my family at all. It's only an hour and ten minutes to Washington. But up here I have the time and the space to work on myself.

"Leaving was essential for me. I had some real worries, worries about my drinking. I received some very good advice and was told that I should solve that problem before I did anything else. I had to get sober first, and up here it's perfect for me because there are fewer distractions."

There had been much speculation that it was only a matter of time before the marriage dissolved, but Ted dismissed the talk as "the same old gossip about the Kennedys." However, Joan was much too honest to lie or even fudge facts.

She admitted to me the future course of the marriage was at best "uncertain." She was not ever sure, she said, that her husband was still in love with her. "I don't know," she admitted in response to my direct question. "I really don't know."

Joan was making a desperate effort to control her drinking. She attended AA meetings regularly and had thrice-weekly private sessions with a psychiatrist, which helped. Mieke Tunney, former wife of California Senator John Tunney, called her progress "incredible."

"Joan," Mieke said, "is no longer taking orders. She's doing what *she* wants to do, not what Ted or anyone else wants her to do."

Despite press releases from Ted's office, that he was pleased that Joan was making a tremendous effort to regain her strength, he was furious at her departure. He had been convinced that Joan would remain the pliant woman she had always been and that he could conduct his life as he wished. But he quickly learned that her declaration of independence was very real.

One late afternoon she looked out her window and saw Kennedy and several aides getting out of an automobile. When he came up, she told him he could no longer come without an invitation.

"This is my pad," she told me. "It's not open house here for any of them anytime they want to come. They must let me know in advance and get my permission to come. I may be having some friends and relatives of my own here and, if it's not convenient, I tell them so. Ted used to come whenever he pleased and usually bring a few aides, but no more. He calls ahead."

In 1980, when Ted challenged incumbent President Jimmy Carter for the nomination, Joan was no longer available for speeches whenever his staff wanted her. It was she who told *them* when she would appear, and when she would not. Ted was astounded. Said Mieke Tunney, "He began seeing her through new eyes, and what he saw was an entirely different Joan."

No more could Ted's strategist plan her campaign schedule with dates from early morning until late evening. When Ted made his formal announcement on November 6, 1979 and began his drive the next day, Joan told his aides she wasn't ready yet. Ted had to be content with having his sisters accompany him on his campaign swings. Finally, on December 11, Joan made her campaign debut, but "on her own turf," Myra McPherson reported, her grandmother's farm in Florida.

At a crucial point, Joan announced that she was cutting short a tour of Pennsylvania because she needed time to cram for final exams. Aides were dismayed. Pennsylvania had a large electoral vote. They protested but got nowhere. Ted himself did nothing to stop her. Joan went home to Boston.

In Boston, Joan's consciousness was raised about the women's movement. Only a few years back, she had confessed to me that she knew little about the issue and had "never even met a women's-lib member."

In Washington, when she was asked about a problem or a situation, she had replied hesitantly that she'd have to ask her husband. In Boston she began to speak her own mind. "I had never read the newspapers," she admitted, "never read magazines. Now there are not enough hours in the day to study, to learn, to grow."

According to Nancy Korman, head of a public-relations company which had worked for Ted Kennedy, "Joan discovered the women's movement." She talked to feminist leaders, read widely, and came to resent the exclusion of women from equal participation in every area of life. She became a strong advocate of women's rights. "She learned that women aren't just pretty adornments," Ms. Korman said. "They have clout."

On February 15, 1980, Joan was asked to address the Ted Kennedy for President Women's Advisory Committee. Joan leaped at the chance. "I'll talk to the committee," she said, "but I'll write my speech myself."

And she did. Here, in part, is what she said:

> My own life experiences in the last few years have brought me to an increased awareness of the central importance of the women's movement. Two years ago. . . . I returned to college. . . . and when I receive my graduate degree I will be a professional in my chosen field. . . . Yet the reality is that most women who might wish to return to school are unable to afford it and that few of them have the proper counseling to direct them back into the stream of education and work.
>
> In speaking of my *choice* to work, I fully recognize that the majority of women today are working out of *necessity* not choice. . . So great are the economic pressures today that six out of every ten women with children at home are working and these mothers are contributing twenty-five to forty percent of their family's incomes. This means that millions of women are struggling frantically each day, rising early enough to get their children ready for school, then driving off to a full day's work, then afterward rushing out to do the shopping, to pick up their kids, to make the family meal.

Joan called for more child-care facilities, experimentation with different forms of neighborhood centers, flexible work schedules, job sharing, decent part-time job opportunities for women, equal pay for equal work, and the best possible health care for children. She concluded with a ringing endorsement of the Equal Rights Amendment.

The ERA, she said, "is more than a symbol; it can become the mandate for the federal government and for every state to ensure equality in both the law and the life of the land."

In 1981 Joan had the strength to end a marriage that had become a mockery in the eyes of all Washington and, at long last, her own as well. By doing so, she cast off the shackles once and for all that had chained her to a life that held out no promise of fulfillment for herself.

"If it wasn't going to work, and clearly it was not, it was better to break than to go on," said Joan Braden. Washington society columnist Betty Beale declared, "The chapter in her life had to be closed and a new one begun. Joan no longer felt that she had to be married to Teddy. He hadn't been the best of husbands."

A joint announcement in early 1981 of the marital collapse said that they arrived at the decision together but Joan's friends scoff at this view. Several pointed out that it was Joan who no longer wanted to remain a partner in what they termed "a nonmarriage."

Said a close friend of Joan, "Although she loved her husband and probably always will, she finally decided that she wasn't going to take his shit anymore."

As a cold drizzle fell on the morning of December 6, 1982, Joan and Ted Kennedy arrived at Barnstable Probate Court, an unpretentious structure less than five miles from the Compound. Joan, trim in a black-and-white tweed jacket and gray slacks, seemed calm as she chatted quietly with Ted, who wore a dark blue suit. They had filed for divorce, citing an "irretrievable breakdown" in their marriage. They sought a no-fault separation agreement.

Probate Judge Shirley Lewis took the bench, and the small group in the courthouse rose. No movie cameras recorded the drab little scene that followed as they had twenty-three years before in Bronxville, when Ted and Joan were married. No glittering guests were present; only several clerks, two uniformed court attendants, and four lawyers. Alexander Folger, Joan's attorney, who occasionally represented Jackie, and Paul Kirk, Jr., one of Ted's three lawyers, approached the bench and whispered a few words. Ted and Joan were called, sworn, and asked several questions by Judge Lewis. She granted the decree, which would become final in one year.

Joan looked around, somewhat dazed. She whispered to Folger, "It's over, so quickly," and he nodded. Ted came over, said something to her, and brushed his cheek against hers. They left separately, no longer husband and wife.

Under the divorce agreement, Joan received a lump sum of $5 million, plus child-support payments and annual alimony of $175,000. She and Ted were to share joint custody of Patrick, then fourteen, who was living in McLean with his father. Ted, Jr. and Kara were away at college. Joan retained ownership of the Beacon Street apartment, and title to the Squaw Island home was transferred to her. Ted wanted the house, too, but Joan insisted.

"That house means more to me than any other place in the world," she said. "It is where my children, their friends, and I go from late May until September, and we are there often in the winter months, too. I use the house as a retreat. I go there to be alone to think, read, walk on the beach, play my piano. Just a few days there and I'm renewed."

Ted capitulated.

There were reports that Rose, then ninety-one, was so frail, and would be so hurt and angry, that Ted would try to keep the news from her. The stories were absurd. Rose always had enormous emotional strength, greater perhaps than any of the other Kennedys.

In Palm Beach, her housekeeper, who has been with her since the mid-1970s, said that Rose was "not upset" by the announcement. In a rich brogue, she asserted, "Mrs. Kennedy just asked him if there was anything she could do." Ted did not confer with his mother about his divorce, nor ask her permission. "Mrs. Kennedy does not interfere in her children's lives and what they are doing," the housekeeper said.

Was Rose surprised at the news? "With Mrs. Kennedy you can never tell," the housekeeper replied. "She's so smooth, and she accepts everything as the will of God. She doesn't think about whether divorce will hurt Ted in his political career. She's been in politics too long. She knows the ups and downs, and she expects anything."

When Ted and Joan made their joint announcement on January 21, 1981 that they would end their marriage, Harry Bennett took the news badly.

"Are you surprised?" I asked him.

"No," he replied, "but I was hoping they would resolve their differences. The whole thing was just plain wrong. Politics and the Washington scene just wasn't for her."

Harry, ever the nice guy, said he didn't blame anyone—not Ted, not the Kennedys. "It's just over," he said. "She will be happier not being married to him." It was obvious to me that he was close to tears.

He added after a pause, "It [the marriage] never should have happened."

A few months later, in August 1981, Harry Bennett suffered a heart attack in Metairie and was flown to a Boston hospital, where he died. Harry may have died of a broken heart over the failure of his beloved daughter's marriage.

Joan's life as a divorced woman followed a zigzag pattern of ups followed by a few downs, but its overall trend has been upward. Her life was filled with cultural activities, family affairs, travel, a fitness program, and many friends. With each passing year, she grew stronger emotionally and physically.

Her sister Candace McMurrey, who Joan says is her "best friend," encouraged Joan every step of the way. Candy lives in Houston, with her lawyer-husband, Robert. She talks to Joan several times a week and visits her often.

"Joan is no longer devastated by the down periods in her life as she was during the Washington years," Candy told me in June 1991. "It has taken a long, long time, but now she has the strength and resilience to bounce back."

In 1984 Joan decided to redecorate her Beacon Street apartment. The result was so smashing that *Architectural Digest* published a five-page feature on the apartment, calling it an "American Classic in Boston." The entire interior was gutted and rebuilt. Picture windows were installed, a narrow central corridor replaced a wastefully large one, and living and bedroom space were dramatically increased.

Joan's new living room is decorated in lavender, beige and brown. Colorful cushions are tossed upon an upholstered sofa. Joan's baby-grand piano is in one corner and a huge picture window offers a magnificent view of the Charles River. Off the living room is a library with bright green walls and a green sofa. Joan uses it as an informal gathering place for her children, their friends, and her own guests. To one side is a George II mahogany table used when Joan hosts small luncheons.

The entire apartment is filled with antiques, mostly eighteenth-century pieces, which she and Ted collected during their marriage. Several mornings a week, Joan dons sweats, wraps a scarf around her head, and heads for the riverbank a couple of blocks away to join the other joggers. She runs a couple of miles, returning to keep a round of appointments made by her secretary: a visit to a doctor, a dentist, her hair stylist; a meeting of a charity committee; a luncheon with several friends or a large affair; an afternoon of more meetings.

Joan goes around town in a low-key manner, a kerchief around her head to avoid being recognized, though often she hears a cheery "Hi, Mrs. Kennedy," from passersby and cabdrivers.

Dinner is usually a quiet event with close friends, in homes or restaurants. A favorite is the main dining room of the Ritz-Carlton hotel overlooking Boston's Public Gardens. She has a small circle of intimates whom she sees often. "They are women I've known for ages and ages," Joan has said. "They're not well known, not anybody you'd read about, but they mean a lot to me. Some were friends since I was seventeen or eighteen." After dinner, she may go the theater, a concert, or a museum showing. She will frequently fly to New York for a concert or a play. And she sees and talks almost daily with her three children.

Joan makes frequent trips abroad. In Italy, not long ago, she narrated Aaron Copland's *A Lincoln Portrait* in Turin. One year, she and Patrick went to Israel by themselves; another time she went to Egypt with Kara. In 1984 Joan traveled to China with a group of experts to study Chinese music. She has been to Salzburg, Austria, the birthplace of Mozart, a number of times for the annual festival of music and drama. In winter she skis in Aspen.

Joan watches her diet carefully, eating almost every kind of food in small portions. There is plenty of cottage cheese and diet soda in her refrigerator at home. But when tension strikes, she will go on food binges. Once she devoured a dozen slices of toast. Another time, just before her decision to seek a divorce, she ate three hot-fudge sundaes and brought home a container of ice cream. Later that day, she stuffed herself with a huge submarine sandwich at a drive-in.

In the spring of 1988, doctors discovered a tumor on the top of young

Patrick's spine. Fifteen years ago she was near collapse when the right leg of her older son, Ted, Jr., had to be amputated. Even though she was aware of the dread consequences if the tumor was malignant, she was with Patrick constantly, diverting him with lighthearted talk. Nurses reported hearing bursts of laughter from his room at Massachusetts General Hospital.

By coincidence, at 10:00 A.M. on the morning of April 21, the day the biopsy was to be performed, I called Joan from New York. She chatted amiably about her latest projects, the progress of her children, the newest charity in which she was involved. At the time Kara, her oldest daughter, and young Ted lived only a few doors away on Beacon Street. "That says a lot," Joan told me, "because if we didn't love each other, we wouldn't want to be so close. I'm lucky. I love and am loved. My family, my friends, my children—I love them and am loved in return."

Not once did she mention the surgery Patrick was to undergo that afternoon to determine whether his tumor was cancerous. Fortunately, the growth was benign.

Recovery from alcoholism rarely takes a steady course. That same year, Joan's need for liquor reasserted itself, and she rammed her car through a fence in Centerville, a few miles from her summer home on Cape Cod. "It was a terrible, terrible experience," she said. She expressed disgust with herself for giving in to the urge and could think of no compelling reason for seeking solace in alcohol, but she had to pay the penalty.

After the Palm Beach rape scandal in 1991, she drank heavily, foolishly got behind a wheel, and was arrested for drunk driving in Quincy. It was her second arrest in Massachusetts in three years. Even though Patrick, a Rhode Island state legislator at twenty five, had not been involved, Joan was terrified that his reputation might be stained and his future blighted.

Publicly shamed again, Joan wept when news of her arrest was published in newspapers and flashed on television screens in millions of homes. On orders from the judge, she spent the last two weeks of May 1992 in an alcohol-treatment center.

This time, however, there was a significant difference from earlier years. The old Joan would have drunk herself into oblivion in private to blot out her shame and hurt, but the new Joan recovered swiftly.

Her sister Candy said, "The very day after her arrest, she was back at her desk in her apartment hard at work on the book she was writing about classical music for families.* When I talked to her that day, she regretted the incident deeply but was otherwise fine."

Dr. Michael A. Greenwald, a friend for fifteen years, who is also her dermatologist, said, "Sure she was upset over the Palm Beach episode. What mother wouldn't be? But she coped with it, and her other pressures, extremely well."

How does Joan feel about marrying again? She has firm opinions. "There is no remarriage in my future," she told me. "I love my life the way it is. Right now, there are no men in my life," adding with a laugh, "at least none that I want to talk about."

Joan has had four romances during the past decade. Soon after arriving in Boston, Dr. Greenwald introduced her to Dr. Gerald Aronoff, a handsome young neurologist, then thirty nine, six feet tall, with a strong jaw and full head of salt-and-pepper hair. They were together constantly for more than two years and friends began to think that marriage wasn't far off. But the romance cooled.

Were there any other men? Joan was coy about replying, but Candy wasn't. "Since Gerry, Joan has had three others, all of them pretty serious," she said. However, Candy wouldn't say who the men were. "That wouldn't be fair," she said. "They are all good friends now. She does have dates and I'm not going to say she won't fall head over heels in love with someone and marry him. But right now there's nobody in sight."

In 1984 Joan received the honorary degree of Doctor of Humane Letters from her alma mater, Manhattanville College. The citation accompanying the award read:

"Today we recognize the quiet courage of one who confronted serious illness and personal tragedy, of one who has prevailed against circumstances to emerge victor rather than victim."

---

*Joan's book, *The Joy of Classical Music*, published in November 1992 by Nan Talese Books, received excellent reviews.

While they were no longer husband and wife, Joan continued to be friendly with Ted. She would call regularly, often twice weekly, to discuss their children and her financial matters. Occasionally, they would dine together when he came to Boston. Aides in Kennedy's offices had standing orders to put her through to him whenever she called. And they would both attend the Thanksgiving and Christmas dinners at the Big House, sometimes sitting next to each other and appearing to have a good time.

The divorce did not shock Ted into curtailing his free-and-easy ways. He drank as much as ever, and he continued to pursue women as much as he ever did.

Sixteen

The Reluctant Candidate

Ted Kennedy never wanted to be president.

Judging by his actions from 1968 on, the conclusion is inescapable. After Bobby was assassinated, when Ted could have had the nomination, he said he had "no stomach" for the race. His decision was understandable at the time. Ted ultimately decided against running in 1972 and in 1976.

Again and again, Ted was asked if he wanted to sit in the Oval Office. He would dance around the question, hinting, teasing, but turning away at the moment of truth.

"Sure I'd like to be president," he said in 1975. "It [the office] affords the greatest opportunity to bring about the kind of changes that are needed." But—dancing away—"I don't foresee any circumstances for seeking it in the foreseeable future."

"Do you want to be president?" I asked him in the early 1970s. Ted waffled. "I can make the best contribution in the Senate," he said. "Who knows what the future will bring? Who can plan? I won't say that perhaps sometime in the future I won't have a turn of interest or heart, but I cannot say whether that will be so or won't be so sometime in the future."

While many associates believe that Ted would happily round out his political years in the Senate, others disagree. David Burke, his former administrative assistant, recalled the time that a health-care bill, which Ted had maneuvered through the Congress, was vetoed by President Nixon. "That reminded him how much an executive could do, and that a senator is just a special pleader."

But former California Senator John Tunney said that Kennedy told him he planned to make the Senate his "career."

Asked in the mid-1970s by conservative journalist and commentator George Will if his goal was the Oval Office, Kennedy replied that he had no trouble seeing himself in the Upper House for two more decades. But when he was asked bluntly by Paul Duke of the Public Broadcasting System if he wanted to be president, Ted answered yes.

As John N. Mitchell, Nixon's attorney general, said in 1969, "Watch what we do, not what we say." Watching Ted Kennedy's actions belie that yes.

In three presidential election years, Teddy offered excuses for refusing to run. It was too soon. His family pleaded with him not to enter the race. The political climate was not favorable. He felt "in my guts" it was wrong.

"One must ask if Ted wanted the presidency mainly because it was expected of him," said journalist and teacher Max Lerner. "He was happy in his Senate harbor. Why should he venture into the dangerous presidential sea?"

Former Senator Smathers, a personal pal of JFK and a family intimate, put it bluntly: "Never, never, did Teddy want the job, no matter what he said publicly. Some politicians need recognition, some thrive on being in a more important and powerful position. It's food for them. Ted Kennedy grew up with power all around him; the power his father possessed, power of his brothers, and surely his mother, who was important in the Catholic church. Teddy knew all the big guys. He even knew the Pope. He didn't need more power. He didn't need to be a bigger shot than what he already was.

"Jack wanted the presidency because, as he used to tell me, he was bored with being a congressman and a senator. 'I don't want to stay here doing this for the rest of my life,' he told me. 'I might as well go for the big ring.'

"But Teddy did not have the burning zeal to scale the heights because there were no heights to conquer. He had seen enough of presidents, been close to power and had seen what a difficult job it was. There was no privacy in the job, and Ted likes to live his life the way he wants to live it—not under a spotlight that bright."

Both Dr. Thomas Reeves of the University of Wisconsin and Prof. Herbert Parmet, author of *Jack: The Struggles of John F. Kennedy,* who has also studied the family and its influence on Ted, agree that seeking the presidency was bred into the youngest Kennedy from his earliest years. Reeves, the harsher critic, said, "Ted may have had enough sense to know that he was just not in any way qualified or up to it, which is why he refused each time until he was finally pushed."

Parmet declared that Ted never needed or wanted the office, nor hungered for it as did Nixon and LBJ. "The legend drove him on," he said.

Milton Gwirtzman, his former aide, said, too, that Ted "never wanted it terribly."

Finally, in 1980, when he was pushed by Democratic leaders into trying to wrest the nomination from the incumbent Jimmy Carter, and by the internal pressure to live up to the Kennedy "legend," Ted was a candidate who began his race with little enthusiasm. "It looks to me that he plain doesn't want to run," said syndicated columnist Ellen Goodman.

"His campaign was painful to watch, even for reporters who had gloated at earlier setbacks," said Garry Wills.

According to TV journalist Roger Mudd, "By 1980, Ted thought he could ascend to the presidency without going through the interviews, the long hours of travel, and all the other trials and tribulations that a candidate must endure. He thought all he had to do was say he wanted the nomination and he could have it. He just didn't go through the process of thinking through why he was running and what it was he wanted to do when he got there. He didn't go to the mountain and examine himself, to have a purpose in mind."

So certain were Kennedy courtiers that his declaration to run was all that was needed that Steve Smith rehearsed for weeks how to ask Jimmy Carter to quit the race without total humiliation.

One of John Kennedy's many women said, "The old man would push Jack, Jack would push Bobby, Bobby would push Teddy, and Teddy would fall on his ass."

He did, with a thump, in 1980.

Four years earlier, he was considered the man to beat, but chose not to run.

By mid-1975, it was hard to find a Democrat who didn't believe that Kennedy would be the Democratic candidate, opposing the incumbent Gerald R. Ford, or that he could not win. Clearly, Chappaquiddick was not the stake in his heart that everyone believed. A Gallup poll suggested that the tragedy had done substantial damage but was not fatal. More than half of those polled said they felt little or no concern about the accident as it reflected on Ted's candidacy. Moreover, the poll cast serious doubt on the conventional wisdom that Chappaquiddick had destroyed Ted with women voters. On the key question—did his behavior there disqualify him from the presidency?—51 percent said not at all, or a little, and another 7 percent had no opinion.

Despite the accident, despite mounting numbers of stories about his excessive drinking and womanizing, despite the shakiness of his marriage, by then widely known, Ted was the only candidate who excited voters. All of the polls reflected his popularity.

The other hopefuls were being greeted with modified rapture. Senator Henry Jackson of Washington was considered the front-runner, but he had a serious recognition problem: a Gallup poll found that 40 percent of Americans did not know who he was. Old reliables such as Ed Muskie and Hubert Humphrey did not set voters ablaze. Neither did Senators Lloyd M. Bentsen of Texas, Fred R. Harris of Oklahoma, or former governor Terry Sanford of North Carolina. A little-known governor, Jimmy Carter of Georgia, was mentioned, but party leaders greeted his name with indifference. Every now and then, someone brought up George Wallace.

Edward Moore Kennedy, the only outstanding name, denied almost daily that he was a candidate but appeared to be acting as though he wanted the nomination. He was highly visible. In *New York Magazine*, Kandy Stroud noted:

> Suddenly in 1975 he blazed onto the Senate and social scene like some political transfiguration. Just count the *New York Times* stories. He masterminded the entire realignment of committee positions in the Senate, knocking out the old conservative order and flooding the important committees with his favored liberal colleagues.

Kennedy was on the popular side on many issues, such as lowering tariffs on imported oil, seeking a reduction of oil-depletion allowances, offering a plan to boost homebuilding and, of course, hammering away at the need for national health insurance.

Throughout 1974 and the early months of 1975, Teddy did not make many speeches, but when he did appear, audiences went wild. He acquired a new dignity: his full head of hair was beginning to show gray, the lines had deepened in his face. He could pull spectators out of their chairs when he talked.

In May 1975, Speaker of the House Tip O'Neill issued a lengthy statement saying that Kennedy would definitely run, and followed it with an appearance on a Public Television broadcast. Asked by Paul Duke whether Ted would win the nomination, O'Neill replied:

I think that indeed. As a matter of fact, I'll be surprised if Ted Kennedy is not the nominee. I think he'll be nominated on the first ballot and I think that he'll be elected president of the United States. I think that he had some problems, home problems, concerning the boy which naturally would affect anybody, but I think young Ted is out of the woods, and everybody is happy and pleased about that. He knows the issues better than anybody, he's better received than anybody. No matter where you go, if any of the candidates are in the same city together, the Pied Piper will be Mr. Kennedy—they just flock to him.

Observed Rep. James A. Delaney of New York, who knew O'Neill and Ted Kennedy well, "Tip isn't a guy who shoots from the hip, and therefore, I have to believe he knows what he's talking about." Scoop Jackson conceded Ted could have the nomination.

"Kennedy is available," wrote journalist Carl Rowan. "No primary contests for him, probably, but he'll be sitting there between the window and the door, waiting for a draft to blow him into the White House."

But Ted didn't want the nomination.

He stunned every leading Democrat by ruling himself out of the race. On September 23, a few months after O'Neill's confident statement, Ted stood before a noisy crowd of journalists in Boston's Parker House hotel, with Joan at his side, and said, "This decision is firm, final, and unconditional. There is absolutely no circumstance or event that will alter the decision. I will not accept a draft. I will oppose any effort to place my name in nomination in any state or at the national convention." It sounded Shermanesque.

Ted explained that his decision could be summed up in two words: "Family responsibilities. I simply could not do that to my wife and children and other members of my family."

Still, Democrats were not totally convinced. Ted's friend Senator Tunney was "certain" Ted could be persuaded to run if the Democrats really wanted him. Pundits were busily analyzing his words. No, they said, they were not *really* Shermanesque. Ted had not rejected a bid as completely, as firmly, as unambiguously as Gen. William Tecumseh Sherman, the Civil War hero, did in his famous telegram to the Republican convention in 1884: "If nominated, I will not accept; if elected, I will not serve." Asked whether he were willing to echo Sherman's statement, Ted had replied with a smile, "I think he's gotten too much publicity anyway."

Even Ted's brother-in-law Sargent Shriver, who had shared the ticket with Senator McGovern in 1972, thought there was a chance that Ted would run. He spoke from inside knowledge. There had been many talks within the Kennedy family on the forthcoming campaign, he said, and there was a possibility that Ted's personal situation could change, particularly if the Democrats could not agree on another candidate.

Despite his loud refusal, Teddy still titillated the media about his intentions. In February 1976 he took Joan, his children and a large assortment of nieces and nephews on a skiing holiday in the Berkshires in Massachusetts. He made sure that the family vacation would be publicized heavily by inviting a press-association reporter and several photographers, who snapped Ted and his sons on the ski lift at Mt. Tom, Ted and Joan on the slopes, Ted and Joan waiting in line at Brodie Mountain, and the whole family at meals.

Plainly, Ted was keeping the prospects of his candidacy alive, a fact that did not escape President Jerry Ford.

On the same day that the account of the skiing holiday appeared in the *Holyoke Transcript*, an article by Godfrey Sperling, Jr, of the *Christian Science Monitor* News Service, was printed on another page. It began:

> President Ford is not ruling out the possibility that Sen. Edward
> M. Kennedy will be his opponent in 1976. Mr. Ford . . . is known to
> feel that the Massachusetts Senator may be drafted by the

Democratic Party, despite the Sherman-like Kennedy assertion that he will under no circumstances be a candidate in 1976. Further, the President views Senator Kennedy as a most formidable candidate—despite Chappaquiddick. The President sees a prospect of a deadlocked Democratic National Convention out of which would come a call which Senator Kennedy could not resist.

But Ted was playing the teasing game again. At the wire, he said no, and the Democrats nominated Georgia's Jimmy Carter, who defeated President Ford to win the White House.

Finally, four years later, on November 7, 1979, Ted said yes.

He was at his oratorical best as he stood before microphones in the Pennsylvania Room of the Sheraton Hotel on John F. Kennedy Boulevard in Philadelphia and once more evoked the memories of his slain brothers and the grand goals they had sought.

"We can light those beacon fires again," he thundered. "From the hilltops of America, we can send another call to arms, a call for more effective action on all the challenges we face." The six hundred Democrats hearing him roared as Kennedy smiled, waved, and strode off the podium as an orchestra played the title song from Lerner and Loewe's *Camelot*.

It was a speech designed to summon up the blood of the troops to charge once more unto the breach. Unhappily, however, unlike Shakespeare's King Henry V, Ted could not summon up his own blood for the assault. His candidacy was a joke. Jimmy Carter said he would "whip his ass" and did. Ted made the worst showing of any member of the Kennedy family in any political race.

Ted plunged in but was woefully unready. In all his previous campaigns, he and his staff had made exhaustive preparations, down to the most obscure facts and figures with which he dazzled and impressed the media and voters. But in this race, in what was probably the dumbest mistake he had made in his political life, he didn't bother to rehearse the most basic issue of all: why he wanted to be the nation's chief executive.

Lyndon Johnson, with his ambition and drive, would surely have known. Richard Nixon, Jimmy Carter, and Ted's brothers Jack and Bobby, equally as bold and aggressive, could have explained why. Teddy did not. Perhaps columnist Max Lerner was right when he wrote that

Ted "was happy in his Senate harbor. Why should he venture into the Presidential sea?"

Just three days before Ted's ringing announcement, CBS aired an interview with Roger Mudd, in which Ted made a complete fool of himself before millions of people. He was unable to articulate, clearly and forcefully, why he wanted to lead the nation. The interview had been taped on September 29 at Hyannis Port by Mudd, who was a neighbor in McLean and a personal friend. Kennedy expected a pleasant, relaxed chat about Jimmy Carter and politics, certainly with no questions about Chappaquiddick and his failing marriage. But Mudd zeroed in aggressively on all of his vulnerable points. Then, halfway through the interview, he asked Ted why he wanted to lead the country. The question was legitimate, considering that for months stories of a Ted Kennedy candidacy opposing the incumbent Jimmy Carter were a subject of major speculation.

Ted didn't know why he wanted to be president. He stuttered and stumbled in his response, which was painful to watch and listen to:

> Well, I'm—were I to make the announcement and to run—the reasons that I would run is because I have a great belief in this country that it is... there's more.... more natural resources than any nation of the world; there's the greatest educated population in the world; greatest technology of any country in the world; and the greatest political system in the world... the energies and resourcefulness of this nation, I think, should be focused on these problems in a way that brings a sense of restoration—in this country, by its people to.... in dealing with the problems that we face. Primarily, the issues.... on the economy, the problems of — energy. And—I would basically feel that—that it's imperative for this country to either move forward; that it can't stand still or otherwise it moves backward.

When Mudd asked him how his administration would differ from Carter's, Ted asked, "Well, in what particular area?"

Mudd replied, "Well, just take the—question of—of leadership." Kennedy's answer:

> Well, it's a—on—on what—on—you know, you have to come to grips with the—the different issues that we're—we're facing. I mean, we can—we have to deal with each of the various questions

that we're—we're talking about, whether it's in the questions of the economy, whether it's in—in the areas of energy.

Remorselessly, Mudd questioned Kennedy about Chappaquiddick, asking him if he expected people to believe his explanation of what happened. Supporters winced as he stuttered his way through his answer:

> On that, there's—the problem is—from that night—I . . . I found the conduct, the behavior, almost sort of beyond belief myself. I mean, that's why it's been—but I think that's, that's—that's the way it was. That—that happens to be the way it was. Now, I find it—as I have stated—I have found that the conduct. . . . in. . . in that evening and in . . . in the—as a result of the impact of the accident and of the . . . sense of loss, the sense of hope, and . . . the . . . and . . .

And so on. Author Gary Adler said that "Kennedy's reply reads almost as intelligibly backwards as forwards."

Following the interview, Teddy was skewered by opponents and supporters alike. Patrick Buchanan, the ultraconservative columnist and presidential candidate in 1992, suggested that Jimmy Carter could profitably use a tape of the interview, just as it was, as a television commercial for his reelection. Liberal journalists threw up their hands. Coleman McCarthy of the *Washington Post* wrote that "Kennedy did a job on himself." The interview, he said, "could only startle the Kennedy loyalists who have spent the past months pushing his candidacy."

Tip O'Neill, the fervent Kennedyite who had wanted Teddy to run in the three previous elections, changed finally in 1980. "I told him not to run," O'Neill said to me in the summer of 1992. "You can't beat an incumbent president," Tip told Ted. "Remember, he's got a hundred billion dollars at his disposal to distribute back to local governments, and he can send that money anywhere he wants. . . . Besides, you've got the morality issue."

Ted wouldn't buy Tip's argument, saying it was a factor in only a small percentage of the voters. O'Neill's own family was divided. His sons Tommy and Kip were in Ted's camp, while his daughter Susan and Kip's wife, Stephanie, supported Carter, prompting a Chicago newspaper to comment wryly that "the only time the O'Neills stand together is during the Gospel."

Why, then, did Ted decide to run? "The Kennedy crowd, the extended clan and their friends and allies, were yearning for a new Camelot," said former Florida Senator Smathers. "They pushed him, tugged at him and finally convinced him he could make it." They showed him polls taken in the summer of 1978 which had him leading Jimmy Carter by a margin of two-to-one nationwide. In a Massachusetts statewide poll, taken by the *Boston Globe*, Kennedy was favored by 69 percent of those interviewed and Carter by 20 percent.

After Chappaquiddick, Max Lerner commented, Ted "had been unable to say no to the circle of his advisers who had gathered around him."

"This was the year to trick him [Ted] out like Don Quixote and send him out on a nag as worn out as Rosinante, the now tarnished breastplate taken from the wall and clapped to his back," British journalist Henry Fairlie wrote. Unhappily, Kennedy was soon revealed as the Man from La Mancha, "a mere caricature of the noble Quixote."

In the country's first test of a candidate's strength in any state, the Iowa caucus on January 21, Carter trounced Kennedy by a two-to-one margin. Disheartened Kennedy aides noted that their man had taken only one of the ninety-nine counties. They wondered whether Ted had made a disastrous mistake. Ted, too, was shocked but slogged up to New Hampshire, where on February 26 Carter again won a clear victory, polling 49 percent of the vote to Kennedy's 38 percent.

The two outings were crushing blows; no longer could Ted defeat an opponent anytime he wished. Half of his staff, seeing thunderclouds lowering, advised him to cut his losses and get out of the race before his reputation as a vote getter would be destroyed.

Teddy could see the same black clouds, but he "saw" also the specter of Old Joe Kennedy, like the ghost of Hamlet's father, bidding him on. The patriarch's influence stretched from beyond the grave in directing Teddy's life and career. We have seen how Joe ordered him to stay in the East, and he did; how Joe ordered him to seek the Senate seat, and he did; how much he worshiped Joe, even to the point of cheating on an exam to stay on the football team to earn approval for athletic achievement. Teddy had not kept faith with the Old Man in the three preceding elections; now he could try.

But, lacking the zest for the job that his brothers had, Teddy didn't try very hard. He was now forty-eight, five years older than Jack and Bobby were when they sought the office. Seventeen years had passed since

Jack was murdered; twelve since Bobby was killed. Ted's campaign was lackluster, with none of the excitement that had characterized his other drives. He toured the country, shaking hands, asking for "your help," making speeches. But he had no passion in his voice, and he aroused none in his audiences, who applauded politely but did not cheer. They were also puzzled by his disjointed replies to questions. He talked like a man who was disoriented, who barely knew where he was.

Wrote Ellen Goodman: "His voice is strained, his timing is off, his eyes are glazed. Everything is wrong."

Said Smathers, "Jack and Bobby went into their campaigns with all guns blazing. Teddy walked in with his guns in their holsters, halfheartedly, and it showed."

"Halfhearted" was the term political observers used most often in describing his campaign. An aide told me, "Ted was going through the motions, nothing more."

Roger Mudd said in 1992, "Teddy wanted to be president but didn't know why." Is it conceivable that a politician who wants that high position would *not* know why? The suspicion darkens that Ted was in the race only because the specter of his father was crying out, "Remember me!"

By late February 1980, Ted was in a free fall in the polls; Carter was running ahead of him by twenty-five percentage points. The talk among Ted's aides was that their man actually wanted to lose.

The campaign was in total confusion. He had no war chest to conduct a presidential race and no national organization to run it. Everything had to be done from scratch. The money crunch became so embarrassing that in the critical New Hampshire primary campaign, twenty-five salaried workers at his Manchester headquarters had to be dismissed. Ironically, for a Kennedy race which had supplied endless gallons of coffee and tens of thousands of doughnuts to voters, all that was available in Manchester were stale doughnuts and coffee rebrewed from used grounds. Campaign literature was piled up in a corner, unmailed because no money existed for postage. Volunteers could not submit expense accounts for gasoline to go out to woo voters. It was budget campaigning, a far cry from the limitless sums spent in earlier races.

But by late April, Kennedy revived suddenly.

After his crushing ten-to-one defeat in the Iowa caucus, Teddy realized that the Kennedy name was no longer enough to ensure election, nor would his vaguely worded liberal convictions sway voters as they once did. It dawned upon him that a Kennedy could lose, and that was an unacceptable thought. So, just as President George Bush reinvigorated in October 1992, when he found he was lagging far behind Governor Bill Clinton, Kennedy made an abrupt about-face. He would not, could not, be the first Kennedy to lose an election.

Ted threw away the speeches written for him and barked out his program in a strong voice. He was funny, crisp, sarcastic, pungent. Again he called for national health insurance, arguing that "if free health care is good enough for members of Congress, it's good enough for the people."

He ridiculed President Ford's assertion that domestic exploration for oil would be given a big boost by decontrol of prices. Declaring that Mobil had bought Montgomery Ward with profits it made from increased fuel costs, he asked, "How much oil do you think they'll discover drilling in the aisles of their department stores?" His audiences guffawed

But Ted's revved-up drive came too late.

Teddy Kennedy, the "Rocky Mountain Coordinator" in Jack Kennedy's campaign, who couldn't win the Western states for his brother, was unable to win them for himself in the primaries either. He lost the Idaho primary by almost three to one—60 percent to 18—and Nevada 39 to 29. He won California 45 to 38 but lost Illinois 65 to 30, Wisconsin 56 to 30, Ohio 51 to 44, Texas 56 to 22, and Oklahoma 60 to 18.

Ted's campaign was a full-scale disaster. Of thirty-four state primaries, he lost twenty-four; of twenty-five caucuses, he lost twenty.

The evening before the convention in New York's Madison Square Garden, Kennedy withdrew from the race. He was a vanquished political figure, spurned by his own party. He lost his final and only real bid because the Mudd interview had shown the public that he was an inadequate candidate and because he proved it by conducting a weak campaign.

But the major reason, as Henry Fairlie put it, was that "he was a man out of his time."

Kennedy-style liberalism was going out of style, giving way to the moderates and centrists. Jimmy Carter had slashed the budget, reducing programs for the old, the poor, and the sick, while Kennedy asked for more spending for public housing, rent supports, unemployment compensation, and youth job programs. In the last days of the campaign, he called for a $12 billion jobs program, which Carter declared totally unacceptable. Carter had allowed the Consumer Protection Agency to die through benign neglect while Kennedy called for strong laws on product safety, truth in lending, and the right of consumers to bring lawsuits against companies that hike prices in violation of antitrust laws. Carter was a champion of nuclear power plants; Kennedy urged that they be phased out and a moratorium declared on licensing new ones. Kennedy's ideals were no longer fashionable and were being stifled by oncoming conservatism.

The glory days of Camelot were like the signs advertising household products on barns along little-traveled roads, fading, evoking nostalgic memories, but no longer used.

Fond recollections remained, of course. JFK and the wonder of those brief shining moments were hard to forget. But the American people, once caught up with the romantic notion of a dynasty, had recovered their balance. Most had been cured of what the psychohistorian Nancy Gager Clinch called "the Kennedy Neurosis." Realization was dawning that the family had taken unto itself too much that was undeserved: Robert Kennedy had been named attorney general with few qualifications, Ted had been picked up and deposited in the Senate with even fewer. Bobby had run for the Senate—and won—as an outright carpetbagger, and a kind of royal family was settling into place.

Ted never again would seek the presidency, though he continued his act of flirting with it and teasing the media, even into 1988, a dozen years later. Over and over he said he was "keeping his options open" but the only option he had after the 1980 debacle was to remain a leader of the loyal opposition, forever battling for his causes.

Meanwhile, as one friend observed Teddy was free to enjoy the lifestyle he desired—girls when he wanted them, drinking binges when he was so inclined, as any member of Congress could but a president could not: the kind of life "any bachelor with a $400 million trust fund might enjoy."

Seventeen

Close Call

John W. Hinckley, Jr., sat quietly in a wooden armchair in the tiny reception room of Suite 431 of the Old Senate Office Building in Washington. The slightly pudgy, blond, blue-eyed young man, barely looked his twenty-five years. He had told the receptionist he wanted "a moment" with Senator Kennedy.

Ted's staff never turns away citizens who ask to see the Senator, but emphasizes that they must take their chances on his availability. Hinckley was informed Kennedy had a busy schedule that day. Perhaps he might return to the office, perhaps not. Hinckley said he was in no special hurry and would wait.

Suite 431 was a warren of four small rooms and a larger one, twenty by thirty feet, for the senator. The space set aside for the staff—he had twenty-seven aides at the time—was strewn with books, papers, and reports. Typewriters clattered, phones rang continually, people bustled from one office to another, bumping into each other in the confined spaces. Behind the receptionist's desk hung an impressionist's painting of the French Riviera which Ted had created from memory while recuperating from his broken back in 1964. Below it was a letter from Norman Rockwell in which he had written that Ted had a "real future" as a landscape painter if ever he decided to leave politics. It is quite safe

197

to say that neither believed it, but Ted loved the letter and had it framed.

According to Gregory Craig, who served as an attorney for him and later joined Kennedy as a staff assistant, a loaded pistol rested in John Hinckley's pocket that December day. He planned to whip it out and shoot the senator the moment he entered the office.

But Ted never showed up. Senate business kept him away. After some three hours, Hinckley gave up and left. Craig believes if Ted Kennedy had returned to the office while Hinckley was there, Ted would almost surely have become the third Kennedy brother to be slain by an assassin.

Three months later, on March 31, 1981, Hinckley, of Evergreen, Colorado, the son of an oil executive, shot and almost killed President Ronald Reagan outside the Washington Hilton Hotel in an insane attempt to impress the actress Jodie Foster with whom he had become obsessed. He used a .22-caliber Saturday-night special, firing six Devastator bullets designed to explode on impact. This could have been the same weapon he had with him as he waited for Ted Kennedy.

The fear that Ted would be the next target haunts his family, friends, and associates—and not without reason. Of the five thousand letters he receives each week, ten are classed as hate mail by his staff. Two letters are usually considered ominous enough to send to the Federal Bureau of Investigation.

The ever-present possibility of being shot has caused Ted to react viscerally at times. Political columnist Jack Newfield remembers the time a tray was dropped when the two lunched in a Washington cafeteria. The loud noise caused Kennedy to flinch and shield his head protectively with his hands. Another time, marching in a St. Patrick's Day parade in the town of Lawrence, north of Boston, Ted paled and ducked when a cannon boomed nearby to signal the start of the march. Joan quickly grasped his arm.

Ted is sensitive to incidents that trigger memories. Less than a year after Bobby was killed, he attended the annual black-tie dinner of the Association of Radio and Television Correspondents at the Shoreham Hotel in Washington. Broadcast journalist and capital personality Barbara Howar was greeting guests on the receiving line. She slipped away to the ladies' room with Myra McPherson. To avoid having to elbow their way through the hundred of guests, they took a shortcut through a kitchen door. There they met Ted Kennedy, who had taken the same route to the men's room.

The three were frozen with horror. Howar recalled a "strange sense of giddiness" at the recollection that Bobby had been shot in a long, narrow serving pantry of a hotel kitchen. She said, "We fell suddenly silent. Teddy reached out and pulled Myra and me closer. We walked quickly down the rest of the long hall. The rest of the evening was not the same."

A longtime Kennedy friend says that Ted is always aware of his surroundings and swerves from one side to the other when he walks on the street.

"Invariably he turns as though watching for something. It's pretty clear that he constantly remembers that his name is Kennedy and he's the third brother. At crossings, he's anxious to move to the other side as quickly as he can. I've discussed this with others and they all feel the same way."

I, too, recall Kennedy's caution when we crossed a Washington avenue during an interview.

Once Joan burst into tears during an interview in her McLean, Virginia home. "I'm scared," she confided. "Scared something will happen to him. There may be a person out there trying to make a clean sweep of the Kennedy brothers. Look at us. We're naked here. Naked! My God! Someone can come down that road out there and come here.

"There's no name on the mailbox, but that doesn't hide us. The cabdrivers know where we are, and every newspaper has printed where we live."

Ted's children were severely affected by Bobby's death. Teddy had nightmares and often asked his mother, "If Uncle John was shot and Uncle Bobby was shot, will Daddy be shot?"

That is why, whenever Ted Kennedy was away from home, he telephoned every evening to chat with his children, asked about their day, and talked about his, all to reassure them that he was all right.

Kennedy's reaction to sudden loud sounds is autonomic, not fear of dying. He is a fatalist who believes "What will be, will be. What God will ordain will happen." While he has said that "the idea of death doesn't bother me," he doesn't want to "get it" from behind. "All I want," he said, "if someone's going to blow my head off, I just want one swing at him first."

There is no truth to published accounts that Rose wanted to see Ted in the White House before she died, and that she had once asked him, as a birthday present to her to make a supreme effort to be elected president. I was not the only journalist to whom Rose confided her terror that her sole surviving son would be killed. When stories surfaced that she had asked Ted to run, I put the question to her: "Would you want to see Teddy run for president in 1984"

She snapped testily, "Must you ask that stupid question? You ought to know by now."

Ted, too, told me that his mother had never made such a request.

In 1972, when Governor Wallace was shot in Maryland, Rose became agitated. She called President Nixon at the White House and asked him to provide Secret Service protection for Ted even though he was not a candidate.

President Nixon complied with her request. "I felt I should," he told Theodore White.

Feeling the pressure, Kennedy's staff sometimes relieved the tension by joking. "We plan the best funerals," one top aide remarked after Bobby's assassination.

"Often the tension is so great, only humor can get us through," added Dick Drayne.

Eighteen

Parenting

"Children evoked in all the Kennedy sons the strongest emotions they would ever know," remarked Doris Kearns Goodwin. Lem Billings said that they were all oriented toward their kids far more than to their wives. "There was nothing, flat nothing, the sons would not do for their kids."

Ted Kennedy's concern for his three children has always been deep and genuine, which makes it all the harder to understand why he took his youngest son and his nephew to the Au Bar that Easter 1991 weekend.

Once again the Good Ted/Bad Ted paradox appears.

Fifteen years earlier, in 1976, Ted was named National Father of the Year. He received a statuette at a luncheon in New York while Rose looked on beaming. Some may suspect the accolade is given to a celebrated person to obtain publicity for the awarding organization and that recipients may not truly deserve the honor. Perhaps. But a close look at Ted Kennedy's parenting provides abundant evidence that he was indeed a superb father during his children's youth.

His father's influence was a powerful factor. For all the vilification heaped on Joe Kennedy as a parent, the lack of moral guidance in sexual behavior, the drive to win whatever the price, the patriarch had many excellent qualities as a parent which his sons absorbed and followed.

Old Joe never gave his children extravagant allowances. He made them work for extra cash, and he didn't pay well for chores. Teddy would mow neighbors' lawns instead of his father's because "the pay is better there." Joe insisted on the ritual of family dinners. When he was home he made himself available for one-on-one talks about any problem a child might have. If he went on a business trip, a son or daughter could call a special number at his New York office, where operators were instructed to reach him at once. He would interrupt meetings involving multimillions to take the calls. Neither a smoker nor a drinker, he demanded the same of his children.

JFK was an adoring father who spent much time with Caroline and John, taking them sailing, teaching his daughter to swim, driving them and their cousins for ice cream in neighboring Centerville at Hyannis Port. He would even interrupt state business when they marched into the Oval Office.

Robert Kennedy paid close attention to his children's progress in school and sports. He was camp supervisor of activities at Hickory Hill, refereeing games and soothing the overly reckless who wound up on the disabled list. In her small, cluttered law office in Towson, Maryland, Kathleen, Bobby's eldest child, told me, "When my father came home from work, all of us would rush to the door and wrestle him down to the ground. We'd drag mother over, too, and we'd tickle-tumble each other, rolling on the floor, until he cried 'enough.'"

With Bobby, too, dinner was a family affair, except for the very youngest, and like Joe, Bobby would question them on historical events: "When was the Constitution ratified? Name the thirteen original colonies." The children would shout out the answers. Before bedtime, Bobby would read them stories from a children's version of the Bible. When he was attorney general, Bobby would take a child to work with him to observe at first hand what daddy did at the office.

In Ted and Joan's Georgetown house, there was no Hickory Hill-style pandemonium, no sense of domestic anarchy, and no animals except inanimate chickens, pigs and cows inhabiting a toy farm. The children were quiet and well behaved, playing by themselves or with friends in the garden at the back. As often as he could, Ted came home for dinner and, from the beginning, established "family time," at which, like with Joe, and Bobby, there would be discussions of history and current events at the children's level. If they did not understand what monetary policy meant, or how the electoral college worked, Ted explained in simple terms. Whenever a child would seem to lose attention, Ted would re-establish alertness by saying it was still "family time," a time that continued into the children's late teens and was adhered to even on vacation trips.

Gerald Doherty, who ran several of Ted's Senate campaigns, said, "He was absolutely fantastic with children, always compassionate and understanding. Not only of his own youngsters, but everyone elses'."

For example, one day on Cape Cod, Ted and several family members were attending a performance at the Melody Tent Theater. A young boy in the audience wanted Ted's autograph, but his father told him he must respect the senator's privacy. At intermission time, the boy, who had a weight problem, felt two muscular arms enfolding him and a voice booming, "How's my boy?"

Said Eddie White, the boy's father, "Is this the ogre the media is trying to portray? I thanked the senator, knowing he picked a child who probably stood out from the others." The boy got Ted's autograph and a memory he won't forget.

As reported elsewhere, Ted had a famous dispute with eight-year-old Teddy, Jr. in 1969, over homework. With student dissension at its peak around the country, the boy, then a second grader at Beauvoir School of the National Cathedral in Washington, opposed his father's insistence on supervising his assignment. The next morning, Teddy, Jr., pinned the following note on his father bedroom door; "You are not ascing me qestungs about the 5 pages. You are not crecting my home work. It is a free world."

Said the senator jokingly of his son's rebellion, "I called the campus police."

Ted's children always came first. Like his father, when they were young, he would interrupt anything—political strategy meetings, press conferences, committee sessions, interviews—to take a phone call from a child with a problem. He attended school plays and pageants, he was present at every graduation, even of his nephews. Once, he flew across the country for the commencement exercises of a Shriver boy, embraced and congratulated him, then flew back. He worried if any of his or his brothers' children were doing poorly in school and arranged for tutorial help if they were.

Ted's gift of mimicry could land him a television program for children which would be a worthy rival of "Sesame Street." He can imitate almost any animal or fish. He does a great frog, chipmunk, rabbit, and bear; he's a splendid shark, crocodile, dolphin, fox, and elephant, and he creates imaginative stories to go with the sounds. Ted performed nightly for the children when he was home, and over the telephone when he was not. When a child would call him with a problem wherever he was, politicians stared at each other as all business halted while the senator became a zoo, barnyard, or sea creature.

After the amputation of young Teddy's leg, the senator and his son became especially close. For two years, once each month on Friday afternoons, the boy checked into a Boston hospital to receive massive doses of methotrexate, a powerful drug that can prevent cancer cells from multiplying and ultimately destroys them. The treatments often caused violent nausea and vomiting. Ted sat with him, encouraging him, trying to divert him, holding him. By Sunday, Teddy would feel well and would leave with his father, sometimes returning to Virginia, sometimes going to a sports event.

Between the treatments, Ted took the boy camping in summer and skiing in winter. Teddy managed well on one ski with the help of poles specially fitted with shorter skis to enable him to maintain his balance. When Ted visited Russia in the spring of 1974, he took Teddy along. Later that summer, Teddy and five young friends flew to Ireland for a minibus tour. Only a few days after he arrived, his father showed up at the picturesque village of Loughrea, where they were staying, and took the boy on a holiday in Galway Bay. Father and son were together for five days. Later, young Teddy, with two schoolmates, went to work in his father's office for the remainder of the summer, sorting mail, filing, and doing odd jobs.

What effect will Teddy's behavior and Joan's alcoholism have upon their children? There have been a few rough times for each.

In June 1992, Ted, Jr., then thirty-one, checked himself into the Institute for Living for a three-week stay for alcohol dependency. "At times," he said on leaving, "life has presented me with some difficult challenges. My decision to seek help was based on the belief that continued use of alcohol is impairing my ability to achieve the goals I care about."

Patrick, who suffers from asthma, admitted late in 1991 that five years earlier, when he was nineteen, he had a drug habit but conquered it after treatment at a rehabilitation center. Said Patrick, "As a teenager, I started down the wrong path in dealing with the pressures of growing up. I mistakenly believed that experimenting with drugs and alcohol would alleviate them."

He added that rehabilitation treatment at Spofford Hall in Spofford, New Hampshire, "was the best step for me. It worked."

As a young girl, Kara experimented with marijuana and hashish, and reportedly ran away from home several times.

But all three are now on a steady course. Kara, a Tufts graduate, was married in September 1990 to Michael Allen, a Washington architect. Skilled in audiovisual techniques, she became a producer for Very Special Arts, a nonprofit organization which helps physically and emotionally handicapped people get into fine-arts institutes around the country.

Teddy, Jr., holder of a master's degree from the Yale University School of Forestry, where he majored in ecology, founded and is still active in Facing the Challenge, which promotes self-help programs which enable disabled persons to achieve their full potentials in life. He will be married in the fall of 1993.

Patrick, a frail youth, more contemplative than his ebullient father, is a graduate of Providence College in Rhode Island, and surprised the family by developing an interest in politics early. While still a student, he became a page in the Rhode Island State House and ran later for the state assembly. He defeated the five-term incumbent in the Democratic primary in 1988, won a second term two years later and a third in 1992. Reports have swirled around Boston for years that young Ted, raised in politics, affable and charming, will run for something, sooner rather than later, but neither he nor any one else confirmed this.

If he does go into the "family business," he will be facing stiff competition from his cousin, Representative Joseph Kennedy III, already in Congress, and others who have their eyes on a political career. Frank Mankiewicz, RFK's press secretary, who has remained a family friend, foresees an avalanche of young Kennedys descending on Washington. "In ten years," he joked, "there could be a Kennedy caucus in Congress."

Nineteen

Senator at Work

"The bottom line is getting things done," Ted Kennedy believes. He has mastered the art better than anyone else in the Senate.

Lawmaking and problem solving are complex and delicate. They require the application of just the right amount of pressure at just the right time, cultivating friendships and keeping them fresh, possessing an antenna finely tuned to receive signals from opponents and, perhaps most important, knowing when to use quiet backstage diplomacy and when to come out like a gunslinger.

Let us see how he uses both techniques.

One: Here is Kennedy using behind-the-scenes diplomacy to avoid a strike that threatened to paralyze the nation:

On the morning of April 17, 1991, Ted Kennedy was working the phones from his home. He had been awakened at 7:01. At that hour, some 235,000 railroad workers throughout the country had walked off the job, staging the first rail strike in a decade.

With the nation already mired in a deepening recession, disruption for only a few days of the flow of coal, steel, grain, automobile parts, and other raw materials to industrial plants could cause economic catastrophe. Moreover, a large volume of military hardware—tanks, armored

vehicles, jeeps and trucks—just brought back from the Persian Gulf War
was backing up daily in all the major ports.

Kennedy reached out to the contacts he had made over the years with
labor and management, calling in his markers. He telephoned Fred
Hardin, president of the United Transportation Union; James J. Kennedy, Jr., executive director of the Railway Labor Executives Association; William Mahoney, the association's counsel, and leaders of allied
unions.

Ted had been a friend of labor for decades and they all knew it.
"Come to my office," he told each of them. "Half-past six. Let's talk
about this." With a full-scale strike underway, the union officials
protested. They could not leave their posts. But Kennedy proved
persuasive, and they agreed reluctantly.

Railway executives were pleading with the government to halt the
walkout, and the government heeded, as it usually did when it came to
rail negotiations. A congressional resolution was drafted calling on the
unions to end the strike, a move unpalatable to labor. Said Richard I.
Kilroy, president of the Transportation Communications Union, "We
prefer that Congress not get into the picture and let us fight it out."

Fred Hardin growled, "We don't want Congress to cram [an agree-
ment] down our throats just because a few railroad presidents want to
make some more money."

Still, the union leaders heeded Kennedy's call and by 6:30 P.M. were
in his office. Kennedy told them frankly that he was hardly happy at the
prospect of congressional action to stop a strike. "But the country's
welfare has to come first," he said.

The strike had been called because negotiations between the unions
and railroads had reached a deadlock. Eleven months earlier, an
emergency board named by President Bush had submitted a list of
recommendations for a settlement, most concerning wages and work
rules. The unions had rejected the terms but had agreed to a cooling-off
period which expired that morning. An hour before sunrise, the workers
left their terminals, yards, ticket windows, and maintenance bases.

Seven hours of high drama followed.

Standing in the middle of his office, Ted read the brief text of the stop-
the-strike resolution which had been drafted that day by the Transportation Subcommittee of the House Energy and Commerce Committee.

Loud protests rose from the union officials, but Kennedy answered them softly, pleading, then urging more forcefully, assuring them they could make any changes they wanted.

Words and phrases were altered and, one or several at a time, were sent by fax to the Democrat-controlled House subcommittee at the Rayburn Building. They were returned with more alterations. The union leaders suggested other changes, which were faxed again and returned again, until a measure that finally satisfied everyone was finally cobbled together.

By 7:30 P.M. it was completed and sent to the House where at 9:00 P.M. the resolution passed, 400 to 5. After a quick dinner, Ted hurried to the Senate. At 10:30 P.M., he rose on the floor and asked for unanimous consent. Minutes later, the measure passed without a roll call. At 1:00 A.M., the president was roused at the White House, where he signed the legislation. The potentially devastating strike was over.

Wrote the *Boston Globe*: "It was a classic example of Kennedy at his best."

Said a union official, "He didn't miss a beat. He made a phenomenal effort on our behalf, not only that evening, but in the many months that preceded the April 17 deadline."

Kennedy's role in the April rail strike went almost completely unnoticed by all except those closely involved because the attention of the media and the public was riveted on the Palm Beach scandal, then less than three weeks old. (See chapter 20.)

"If you're interested in being effective," Kennedy said, "It's important to be able to build coalitions. You have to compromise to make progress." After all, he believes, "the bottom line is getting things done."

Two: This is Ted Kennedy in a blazing political fight.

In 1987, he lashed out hard and fast when Judge Robert H. Bork was nominated to the U.S. Supreme Court. He did so because he was convinced that the conservative opposition and the undecided members on the Judiciary Committee could be swayed only by a public battle which would reveal that Bork, a former judge of the United States Court of Appeals and Solicitor General, was unacceptable for confirmation. Kennedy counted on arousing strong public pressure to convince the members.

If Senator Kennedy had not acted swiftly and decisively, Judge Robert Bork would have sat on the United States Supreme Court, and *Roe* v. *Wade*, the landmark ruling which legalized abortion in 1973, would have been repealed in 1992.

Kennedy knew Bork's record and beliefs. He was a strict constructionist who saw no room for flexibility in the Constitution. The right to privacy, Bork maintained, could not be found in its seven Articles and twenty-seven Amendments. The sole legitimate basis for constitutional rulings is "original intent": that the courts could enforce only rights which appear in the text of the law of the land. By that rigid standard, he believed, *Roe* v. *Wade* was unconstitutional.

Kennedy knew that putting Bork on the Supreme Court could create a new majority that would almost surely overturn the abortion doctrine. Kennedy also objected to Bork's other views: he did not believe gays had a constitutional right to engage in homosexual activity, which strongly suggested opposition to gay rights; nor did he believe courts should make social policy, which again suggested opposition to affirmative-action programs.

The struggle to defeat Bork was one of Kennedy's most outstanding liberal crusades.

Bork had been named to fill the seat vacated by Lewis M. Powell, a centrist who had often been a fifth vote with the liberals on the Court on matters of abortion, affirmative action, and religion. Barely two hours after Bork's nomination was announced, Kennedy raced to the Senate, asked for the floor and denounced the appointment. In his bullhorn voice, he then declared: "Robert Bork's America is a land in which women would be forced into back-alley abortions, blacks would sit at segregated lunch counters, rogue police could break down citizens' doors in midnight raids, schoolchildren could not be taught about evolution, writers and artists would be censored at the whim of government."

The speech was a call to action, setting off an intensive drive to block Bork. While in the past the question of a nominee's fitness for the Court had been based on his legal ability and ethics, now Bork's opponents focused on his ideology.

"Nobody thought Ted Kennedy could prevail," wrote liberal commentator Jack Newfield. Ted planned a campaign as thoroughly as any race for office. He spent four months rounding up opposition to Bork, calling every black mayor in the South, all thirty vice-presidents of the

AFL-CIO, and, with the aid of a computer file, placed endless calls to black elected officials. Ted marshaled his arguments carefully, calling upon all the arts of persuasion he had learned in his decades as a senator, pleading with them to "join me in actively opposing this nomination."

On September 15, Joseph M. Biden, Jr., chairman of the fourteen-member Senate Judiciary Committee, banged his gavel to open the hearings. As commander-in-chief of the stop-Bork movement, Kennedy was front and center most of the time; not as the soft-voiced mediator he would be during the railroad strike, but on the attack, in a voice that needed no microphone to be heard.

Kennedy was sharp, sarcastic, and scornful. He said in his summation:

Mr. Bork has shown his bias against women and minorities and in favor of big business and presidential power....Mr. Bork has claimed that he is only applying the neutral principles, but there's something wrong with neutral principles if the result is that Congress and the courts must be neutral in the face of discrimination against women and in the face of gross invasions by the government of individual citizens' rights to privacy.

Mr. Bork has shown little respect for past decisions of the Supreme Court. Again and again, he's suggested that we roll back the clock, return to more troubled times, uproot decades of settled law in order to write his own ideology into law.

Mr. Bork is out of step with the Congress, out of step with the country, out of step with the Constitution on many of the most fundamental issues facing America.

Bork didn't have a chance. Responding, he denied that he had asked Congress or the courts to be "neutral" on racial discrimination, that he had upheld the laws that outlaw racial discrimination, and had "never, never written a word hostile to women or privacy."

Bork knew he was defeated well before the vote. On October 6, the Judiciary Committee recommended 9-to-5 to reject the nomination; later the Senate concurred by a wide majority.

Orrin Hatch, a Republican member of the committee, admitted that were it not for Kennedy's aggressive lobbying and slashing attack, Bork would be sitting on the Supreme Court. Instead, Justice Anthony Kennedy, named by President Reagan after Bork was rejected, lined up with the five-to-four majority backing a Pennsylvania statute *regulating* but *not overturning Roe* v. *Wade.*

Although born into wealth and privilege, Ted Kennedy has totally rejected his father's ultraconservative ideology. He has dedicated his political life to the legacy left not by Joe, but by Jack and Bobby.

Jack broke from his father's foreign and domestic views after graduating from Harvard, arguing with him about his isolationism during World War II and voicing his hatred of dictators and dictatorships.

Nurse Luella Hennessey told a revealing story about young Jack who had come to Europe to spend several days with the family in the summer of 1938. Joe Kennedy had rented a villa in Cannes, on the French Riviera. One stormy afternoon, with a fire blazing in the large sitting room, Jack told a story to his brothers and sisters who were housebound by the rain. Eunice, Pat, Jean, Bobby, and Ted sat spellbound as he talked about Hannibal, the Carthaginian general, Julius Caesar, who became dictator of the Roman Empire, and of Napoleon:

> All three were dictatorial rulers whose people received nothing despite the great renown they won for their countries. Eventually, the people revolted against their dictators and threw them out of power, but soon other strongmen arose. They too were ousted. This continued until these once-glorious nations were glorious no longer. They shriveled and died.
>
> But look at the United States. Why are we the most powerful country in the world? Because power lies in the people who make their laws through elected representatives, enforce them, and govern themselves. The great question for Americans is how to avoid the great mistakes that led to the downfall of other nations.

As he read and studied more about history and political science, as his intellectual development expanded, Jack Kennedy opposed his father in virtually every political area. So, too, did Bobby, after he left his sheltered life and saw for himself the injustices suffered by millions in the United States.

Jack was troubled by the conflict. He wondered whether a man could love his father and still disagree with him so completely. He put the

Joan, terrified that her husband would become the third Kennedy brother to die by an assassin's bullet, smiles with relief as Ted announces that, despite considerable pressure, he will not seek the presidential nomination in 1976. (Boston Herald photo)

After their divorce, Ted and Joan saw one another on Thanksgiving, Christmas, and other family occasions, particularly at events involving their children. On June 2, 1983, Ted and Joan attended the graduation of their youngest son, Patrick, from the ninth grade at Fessenden School in West Newton, Massachusetts. Left to right: Ted Jr., Joan, Patrick, Ted, and Kara. (Boston Herald photo)

Away from politics, which she admitted was "not my bag," Joan Kennedy has devoted much of her new life in Boston to musical pursuits. She earned a master's degree in music education at Lesley College in Boston. In addition to performing as a piano soloist, she narrated "Peter and the Wolf." Here she recites with the Boston Pops on June 26, 1983. (Boston Herald photo)

Members of the Kennedy family are active in the affairs of the John F. Kennedy Library and Museum, south of Boston, where a special suite is set aside for their use. Here Ted speaks at a press conference in 1989. Caroline and and J.F.K. Jr., are in the center, Jackie at right. (Boston Herald photo)

The road back from alcoholism was not smooth for Joan Kennedy. In May 1991, Joan, who had fought hard to remain sober, drank too much and rammed her car through a fence in Centreville, not far from her Cape Cod summer home. She had to pay the penalty, suffer humiliation before the country, and abide by the ruling by a judge that she spend two weeks in an alcohol rehabilitation center. She is shown here in Quincy District Court with her attorney, William Sullivan. (Boston Herald photo)

Massachusetts' official memorial to J.F.K. was unveiled in May 1989, on the lawn of the State House on Beacon Street. A competition to select the winning statue was supervised by Caroline Kennedy Schlossberg, who felt the entry by Isobel McIlvain best captured the essence of her father. Ted is shown at the dedication of the statue, which shows J.F.K. in a walking pose, elbows bent, left hand tucked characteristically in a jacket pocket. (Boston Herald photo)

Ted Kennedy is six feet two inches tall, and would like to get down to 210 pounds, his football weight, but ice cream and chocolate chip cookies defeat him. With strict dieting, he can lose thirty pounds in a short time, but his girth increases soon after. Here he is at Hyannis Port, earning the appellation of "Fat Boy" pinned on him by Howie Carr, a *Boston Herald* columnist. (Boston Herald photo)

On October 25, 1991, Senator Kennedy, seeking to mend his tattered reputation, admitted in an address at Harvard's School of Government in Cambridge that he recognized his "shortcomings," that he alone was responsible for them, and would "confront" his faults. (Boston Herald photo)

The Palm Beach scandal brought back memories of Chappaquiddick. In each, Ted ducked behind the family's legal barricades to avoid scrutiny by the law. At his trial on charges of sexual battery, the Florida equivalent of rape, William Kennedy Smith, Ted's nephew, arrives at the Palm Beach courthouse on December 8, 1991. (Boston Herald photo)

After his acquittal on December 11, Willie Smith talks to the press. To his right are his mother Jean and sister Kim. Roy Black, his attorney, is behind him. (Boston Herald photo)

On July 3, 1992, Ted Kennedy, sixty years old, married Victoria Reggie, thirty-nine, at his home in McLean. Vickie, daughter of Doris and Judge Edmund Reggie of Louisiana, is a strong-minded, self-assured young woman and is considered a brilliant lawyer. Joan was stunned when the engagement was announced, but later extended her best wishes to the couple. After a brief honeymoon, Ted, Vicki, and six-year-old Caroline, her daughter by a previous marriage, were seen strolling in Hyannis Port. Vicki also has a son, nine years old in 1992. (Boston Herald photo)

Ted bought a two-bedroom condominium on the second floor at 17 Marlborough Street at a cost of $350,000 as a Boston home for his new family. The building is only a few blocks from Joan's apartment. Curran and Caroline attend the Maret School in Washington, Vicki has resumed her law practice, and, with her help, Ted has begun a new life. (Boston Herald photo)

Ted, Vicki, and the children arrive at St. Francis Xavier Church parish hall in Hyannis, where he and Vicki cast their ballots on election day. (Boston Herald photo)

Vicki and Ted at the Big House in Hyannis Port in September 1992.
(Boston Herald photo)

question to Dr. Lawrence A. Fuchs, then chairman of the American Studies Department at Brandeis University in Waltham, ten miles from Boston.

"My father," he said, "is absolutely predictable on every political issue. We disagree on almost everything. Do you agree with everything your father believes?"

Dr. Fuchs replied that he did not.

Jack pressed on: "Do you love your father?"

Fuchs said that he did.

Kennedy's point, said Dr. Fuchs, was that even though he diverged almost totally from the views his father espoused, he would not allow his political differences to interfere with his loyalty and love for him.

Ted absorbed the ideology, not of his father, but his brothers, demonstrating what Ted Sorensen called "the quality of continuing growth." From his earliest years as senator, Joe's youngest son was drawn to the liberal programs.

Ted never stopped loving his father, whose personal behavior shaped his own. But he never stopped admiring his brothers for the changes they sought to make in government. And he has never ceased to believe in the legacy of Camelot and the role he must play in its fulfillment.

In Washington, Ted Kennedy is called "king of the Hill." And for good reason: he is the most prolific lawmaker of both Houses on Capitol Hill.

Now fourth in Senate seniority, Ted occupies much more spacious quarters in Room 315 of the Russell Building at 1st and C Streets, Northeast. His private office offers a stunning view of the Washington Monument and the Lincoln Memorial, and the two reflecting pools between them. As in all Kennedy homes and offices, photographs are all over the place: pictures of his mother, father, brothers, and sisters sailing, tossing footballs, racing at the Compound; pictures of Jack and Bobby campaigning and working; pictures of all the children.

In his office a visitor can read the framed letter written by Jack to Rose from the Choate School when Teddy was born in February 1932, asking to be the godfather to the new baby. Nearby is a note to Ted from Rose, admonishing him not to use the word "ass."

Ted also has a tiny office in the Capitol Building where he often goes to prepare for a debate in the Senate chamber, which is only a few yards away.

Unflaggingly industrious in pushing social-welfare measures he cares about, Ted scores dozens of times at every congressional session. Only two years after he became chairman of the Labor and Human Resources Committee in 1987, thirty-nine bills approved by it were enacted into law. In 1991 the list rose to fifty-one.

Ted's fellow senators couldn't care less about the personal scandals into which he catapults himself. Declared Tom Korologos, a Republican loyalist who has been around Washington for many years, "Not a soul will vote on anything based on what happened in Florida."

The list of major laws in which Good Ted has played key roles fills pages. The Comprehensive Child Care Act, expansion of the Head Start program, disaster relief for the communities overwhelmed by AIDS and drug epidemics, nutritional labeling, the Occupational Safety and Health Act, Bilingual Educational Act, Job Training Partnership Act, a law barring employers from routinely using polygraph tests on workers, the Fair Housing Act—all bear his imprint.

Kennedy is a superb legislator because he understands the inner workings of Congress the way a great football coach knows how and where to position his players and which plays are likely to succeed, which may fail.

Staff members explained his system: Before a single word of a contemplated measure is put on paper, Ted talks to legislators from both Houses, by phone or in person, and with other parties who have an interest in the issue, to obtain their views, pro and con. Then, after carefully noting where the thorny patches lie, Ted tailors the measures to sidestep them.

His goal is to win the backing of 70 percent of the members of both Houses. It is an important number since a two-thirds vote in the Senate and House can override a veto; the bill becomes immune to a presidential turndown. It also becomes filibuster-proof because two-thirds of the Senate and House can invoke the cloture rule which chokes off the endless speeches that can keep a measure from coming to a vote.

Discussing his legislative technique, Kennedy said, "If you're inter-ested in being effective, it's important to build coalitions. You have to compromise to make progress."

But it's not always softsell; sometimes Ted feels that some kind of persuasion is needed. In 1990, for example, he asked Elizabeth Taylor to appear at a press conference he called on an AIDS bill. As a measure meanders through Congress, Ted's aides follow its progress carefully and, when the bill encounters a roadblock, sharp letters signed by Ted are sent to newspapers in the wavering legislator's district or state. Few members hold out when editorials appear in their hometown papers urging passage of the bill.

While Kennedy remains a staunch liberal, in recent years he has moved to a more centrist position. In a watershed address at Hofstra University on Long Island in 1985, Kennedy proposed a new kind of liberalism, one which had "the daring to try innovations, and the courage to discard them when they fail." Speaking at a three-day conference examining the presidency of JFK, he redefined liberalism for a new era in the United States and recast the image and appeal of his party and his backers.

It was an astonishing speech for a Kennedy. In the university's field house, Ted spoke to several hundred people, among them some two dozen nieces and nephews, including Caroline and JFK, Jr., and many leading New Frontiersmen, now white-haired.

Breaking with his image of traditional liberalism, Ted asserted that it was time to take a step to the center by putting a lid on government spending programs:

> We cannot and should not depend on higher tax revenues to roll in and redeem every costly program. Rather, those of us who care about domestic programs must do more with less. And, in fact, some of the measures we should take will save money instead of spending it.
>
> The mere existence of a program is no excuse for its perpetuation, whether it's a welfare plan or a weapons system. Too much of our public-service jobs and public-assistance programs have done too little to break the cycle of poverty and dependence. And too often they have proven to be counterproductive.

Daniel Henniger, editorial-page editor of the *Wall Street Journal*, wrote that "it was a major repositioning speech." Kennedy, said Henniger, "held retirement parties for a certain collection of ideas, slogans and impulses with which he has long been associated."

The *Boston Globe* added: "There seems little doubt that Kennedy is in the midst of an effort to moderate his political standing; to become less identified with the far-left wing of the Democratic Party and viewed more of a centrist."

Again, in 1991, Kennedy reiterated the need for a change of strategy in dealing with social problems in a time of huge budget deficits. To the Committee on Economic Development, composed of corporate and university presidents, he described "a new kind of thinking about social programs in the country—what I call 'public enterprise.'

"We cannot afford to keep throwing money at problems," he declared. "We must apply the same vigorous standards that business uses in private enterprise... any good business looks at the bottom line and so must the government."

At another conference, Ted called for programs that are "cost effective, that save money in the long run."

Ted has stuck to this position, even with his top-priority program of universal health insurance. In 1991 his Senate committee proposed yet another plan called HealthAmerica that would not involve government spending. The plan would require all employers to finance health-insurance coverage for workers which would meet basic minimum standards or pay a 7.5 percent payroll tax into a fund, called Americare, which would cover both their employees and the unemployed.

The bill calls for guidelines for reimbursement for treatment. Kennedy says it will also put in place a comprehensive program to control health-care costs.

In a later address before the American Psychiatric Association, Kennedy said he would work to see that mental-health illness would also be covered by HealthAmerica. "A single psychiatric episode," he pointed out, "can easily lead to medical expenses that mean financial ruin for the average family."

Arguing for his program, Kennedy cited the "almost unbelievable fact" that 37 million people in this country have no medical coverage at all.

"More than most Americans, I know what it means to have serious illness in the family," he says. "My father was crippled by a stroke and required constant care for years. My son was stricken by cancer and is well today because of the miracle of modern medicine... I myself was hospitalized for several months, my back broken in many places."

His family could well afford to pay for good medical care, Kennedy declared, but for many "the tragedy of serious illness is compounded by the additional tragedy of a heavy financial burden.

"We can lift that financial burden from all the families of America. Through national health insurance, we can provide a decent health care system. . . . We can make health care a basic right for all, not just an expensive privilege of the few."

Ted has never swerved from his dedication to civil rights and bias issues. Hawklike, he has watched every legislative move, every bit of political gamesmanship attempting to water down laws.

In the late fall of 1991, a two-year effort to strengthen the laws barring job discrimination for any member of a minority group, women, disabled persons, and any other individuals was finally enacted. This law, the Civil Rights Act of 1991, was needed, proponents argued, because the Supreme Court had chipped away at antibias laws in five previous decisions, especially in an 1989 ruling that tilted sharply toward employers in disputes over the racial composition of their work force.

The law was scheduled to be signed at a ceremony in the Rose Garden on November 21.

But trouble erupted in the late afternoon of the previous day.

White House counsel C. Boyden Gray faxed an order to federal departments under Bush's name to begin abolishing affirmative-action regulations which had been American policy since LBJ began the programs in 1965. All government programs giving preference in hiring and promotions to women and racial minorities were to be terminated. Preference was no longer to be given to minorities in the awards of contracts to outside companies, in scholarships, and in college admissions.

Kennedy was incensed; he had worked hard for the bill. So, too, were civil-rights leaders, legislators in both Houses, and even some members of the president's cabinet. The Civil Rights Act had nothing to do with affirmative action or quotas, they pointed out. Its main thrust, as Kennedy said, was "to provide meaningful remedies, granting victims of intentional discrimination the right to recover compensatory damages and, in particularly flagrant cases, punitive damages of up to the greater of $150,000, or the amount of compensatory damages and back pay."

Kennedy was convinced that the Gray directive was a sneak attack to placate conservatives by undermining the spirit—if not the actual wording—of the law. "It was hyprocrisy at its worst," said Rep. John Conyers, Jr., of Michigan, a member of the Congressional Black Caucus.

There was turmoil in the Oval Office. Bush, who claimed that Gray's directive had been unauthorized, ordered Marlin Fitzwater, his press secretary, to announce that the president had been unaware of the order and that it would be rescinded at once. For his part, Gray admitted his order was a mistake. Supporters of the act were soothed but still cautious. "There is no question that the Bush administration will continue to do everything possible to undermine the act and the bipartisan enforcement policies of the past quarter century," declared Ralph Neas, executive director of the Leadership Conference on Civil Rights.

Kennedy, mollified but still wary, attended the signing ceremony at which Bush declared, "I say again today I support affirmative action. Nothing in this bill overturns the government's affirmative-action program."

Kennedy hailed Bush's remarks as a "statement of reconciliation, a statement bringing the country together on the issue of race."

Almost thirty years after he delivered his maiden speech in the Senate on civil rights, Ted Kennedy, with considerable support of course, from colleagues and private organizations, had won one of his great battles.

Consistent with his "new liberalism," Kennedy has an ambitious agenda. He will push for legislation to decrease high-school dropout rates, improve math and science education, attack the drug and violence plague infesting U.S. schools, raise literacy rates, increase minimum wages, boost teacher training and recruitment, and fight hard for summer-job programs for inner-city youth. He supports unpaid parental leave when emergencies strike, plans to push hard to lower illiteracy rates, and seeks to streamline the complex process that students must now undergo to obtain financial aid for higher education.

The consensus in Washington is that Ted Kennedy's staff is the best on Capitol Hill; brilliant, aggressive, and dedicated. There is a corollary to this belief. Cognizant of his personal wealth, some observers have commented it is "the best staff money can buy." Senator Edmund Muskie made such a statement in 1969.

"He said if he had Kennedy money he would have Kennedy staff," according to Theo Lippman.

This charge is denied by former Kennedy staffers. Gregory Craig, now a lawyer in private practice in Washington, was a senior adviser to Kennedy on national-security matters for five years. He does not believe that the senator "supplements salaries."

"Kennedy people get standard staff pay," he says.

"Why does he attract so many good people?" he asked rhetorically. "I think it is because excellence begets excellence. Deeply motivated and highly qualified people are able to attract excellent people.

"They come from some of the greatest universities in the country: Yale, Harvard, Stanford, the University of Chicago, Northwestern. They have enormously developed political and personal skills, powers of persuasion, powers of argumentation. And he gives them their head."

Former Kennedy staffer Dun Gifford says that the senator attracts the "best and the brightest because word has gotten around it is a great place to work. He does not pay more than anyone else."

Kennedy gets an allowance of $1,140,000 annually for staff salaries, a figure based on the population of Massachusetts, according to Tim Wineman of the Senate Disbursing Office. He can allot it as he wishes. Wineman says he knows of no instance in which a senator pays a staff member additional funds out of his own pocket.

Kennedy's chief legislative director, W. Carey Parker, who has been with the senator since 1969, earns $106,959, according to the 1992 payroll. Says Paul Donovan, Kennedy's press aide, "He's one of the most senior aides in the Senate, and his pay is commensurate with that level of experience and responsibility." The pay of other staff members ranges from $70,000 to $80,000 for more senior aides to the mid-$30,000 level for juniors.

Parker is not the only high-salaried Senate staffer. A payroll list released by the Senate reveals there are now 86 people on Senate staffs who earn salaries which top six figures annually, according to the Capitol Hill newspaper, *Roll Call.*

Kennedy's staff, one of the largest in the Senate, numbers about one hundred, including interns and visiting fellows. They are generally in their twenties and thirties, dedicated to pushing his agenda.

Craig says that Kennedy is on top of everything that his office is doing but he is "not restrictive."

"He delegates authority very well, in a way that produces efficient performance," he said. "His staff is given directions and instructions, he knows exactly what they are doing but, at the same time, he gives them a good deal of leeway to use their initiative."

For example, he said, "In 1985 I had full authority from Senator Kennedy to negotiate the terms and conditions of a trip to South Africa. I did not have to check back with Senator Kennedy every step of the way, on appointments, time, date, or place."

For Kennedy, no two working days are alike. Sometimes a day begins about 8:00 A.M. at breakfast in his home, where Kennedy opens his battered bag and hands back the memos his staff had jammed into it the day before. Each has been read and comments have been scrawled on it. Some are marked "OK," some get a huge "NO!" or an "Ugh!" Those items requiring more discussion are marked "See me."

Some aides wait until the end of the day before shoving a document into the bag. "That way," says one, "it stands a better chance of being pulled out by the boss first."

Said one staff member, "I was putting stuff in the bag cold, and then one day I noticed that the others were using all kinds of stunts to get his attention: big check marks, or items circled with brightly colored marking pens, especially red and yellow, or writing 'Must Do' or 'Must Read' on their memos."

On other days, Kennedy drives to his office where the memos are distributed. Full meetings are not scheduled and are held only occasionally. He tells aides what he expects them to do on walks to the Senate chamber, at drop-in visits to his office, and especially during trips, when he has more time.

Gregory Craig said that many times he asks several aides to come home for dinner, where issues are thrashed out and policies formed. "There's only a limited amount of time in the senator's day," Craig explained. "I recall when the senator's domestic initiatives were on the front burner it was impossible for me to get time for foreign-policy stuff and vice versa. When I got him out of the country, then he would focus on my agenda, and it was very hard for civil-rights people and the labor people to get access to him."

Said Eddie Martin, a former aide, "It's a whole life working for him. If you left the office before he left, you always felt guilty."

"You never really break away," confided Milton Gwirtzman.

One staff member has admitted that "Kennedy people get a reputation for being very pushy and obnoxious. You hear things coming out of your mouth that you can't believe you're saying. But the most respected trait on the staff is getting it done. No matter whose feathers you ruffle, get it done."

Early in October 1991 some two months before his nephew Willie's trial on rape charges, Ted underwent another painful experience during the confrontation between Anita F. Hill the soft-spoken, black, Yale-educated professor, and Judge Clarence Thomas, also black, of the U.S. District of Columbia Court of Appeals. In this amazing and ignoble episode, which sullied the reputation of the U.S. Senate, Kennedy was humiliated before more than 10 million people around the world.

Once again it was Good Ted, Bad Ted—good to those who believed in the causes he espoused; bad, unfortunately, for him and to many more who watched as he sat, hands on his chin, in silence, as the Senate Judiciary Committee heard charges of sexual harassment brought by Ms. Hill against Thomas.

Nothing like this hearing had ever been seen or heard before on Capitol Hill. Thomas had been nominated for the Supreme Court by President Bush and the Judiciary Committee, consisting of fourteen white male senators. Testimony on his confirmation was heard in Room 318 of the ornate, high-ceilinged Caucus Room.

Suddenly an explosive drama developed. Ms. Hill, a thirty-five-year-old law professor at the University of Oklahoma, appeared before the committee and charged that Thomas had made sexual advances to her when she was employed by him in two offices between 1981 and 1983.

In addition, she claimed he made outrageous comments to her on a number of occasions. She testified that he discussed with her a pornographic movie he had seen featuring an actor named "Long Dong Silver" because of the size of his penis; that he had described films depicting group sex, and sex women had with animals; that he had boasted of the size of his penis; that on one occasion "he told me graphically of his own sexual prowess"; that once he reached for a can of Coke and asked, "Who put pubic hair on my Coke?"

During the years Ms. Hill had worked for Thomas, he had been a supervisor in the Office of Civil Rights of the U.S. Department of Education and afterward headed the Equal Employment Opportunity Commission.

Following Ms. Hill at the green baize witness table, Judge Thomas, facing the glare of the klieg lights, the TV cameras, and the fourteen committee members, denied "each and ever single allegation against me today...unequivocally and uncategorically." He termed the hearings a "circus" and a "disgrace," an assessment with which most of America agreed.

Millions of viewers watched the spectacle of senators, sounding like a pack of Torquemadas, question the black woman sharply, showing little empathy—let alone fairness—to her. Ms. Hill underwent an ordeal at the hands of the panel of white men, some of whom were legislators of considerable importance, that she will never forget.

On Tuesday night, October 22, the Senate voted to confirm Thomas by 54 to 48, the narrowest majority any Supreme Court Justice had received since the turn of the century.

The Thomas-Hill hearings were a political tragedy for Ted Kennedy, the worst since Chappaquiddick. As the champion of women's rights, he had a golden opportunity to rise to greatness by lashing out at the senators who were assaulting the integrity and reputation of Anita Hill so bitterly.

But Ted was forced into impotence by his own personal misbehavior. He sat mute day after day, except to ask a few minor questions, though he ached to rise to Ms. Hill's defense. "Never in his political career did the boss experience such frustration," said a staff member.

Ted Kennedy knew only too well that speaking out would boomerang against Anita Hill. Flawed himself, he had no credentials to defend her against the senators who were attacking her testimony. Rising to her defense would not have been an act of courage, but of stupidity. The Republicans on the committee would have flung his own long record of misbehavior at him and ask witheringly: Who was this sinner to cast stones?

After the committee voted to approve the nomination and sent it to the full Senate for confirmation, Kennedy finally rose on the Senate floor to denounce the attacks on Ms. Hill at the hearings. Once more he was the voice of liberalism, the defender of the victimized.

"Are we an old-boys' club—insensitive at best, and perhaps something worse?" he said. "Will we strain to concoct any excuse? To impose any burden? To tolerate any unsubstantiated attack on a woman in order to rationalize a vote for this nomination? Here in the Senate and in the nation we need to establish a different, better, higher standard."

The predicted attacks began. Senator Arlen Spector, Pennsylvania Republican, shot back: "We do not need characterizations like 'shame' in this chamber from the senator from Massachusetts."

Orrin Hatch, defending Republicans from charges that the harsh questioning of Ms. Hill was orchestrated by the White House, declared, "The fact of the matter is, anybody who believes that, I know a bridge up in Massachusetts that I'll be happy to sell to them on behalf of the senator from Massachusetts." (Later, Hatch claimed he made an "unfortunate and insensitive mistake," apologized, and asked that his remarks be stricken from the record and that "a bridge in Brooklyn" be substituted.)

A mystery still remains unsolved about the hearings.

Anita Hill had made a statement to the Judiciary Committee, detailing her claims of sexual harassment, and later was interviewed by the FBI. A staff member of the committee had assured her that her confidentiality would be respected. Her name would not be mentioned at the hearings, and she would not be called upon to testify. The staff member told her that when Judge Thomas read the statement, he would withdraw his name from consideration rather than risk a public confrontation over the explosive charges.

But something went terribly wrong. The statement was leaked to Nina Totenberg of the Public Broadcasting System and to *New York Newsday*. Ms. Hill's name was mentioned prominently as the accuser. She had to testify.

Following the hearings, an independent counsel, Peter Fleming, Jr., of New York, was appointed as a special counsel to determine who had passed on the confidential information. After a four-month investigation, during which Fleming looked into reports that the leak may have come from Democratic senators, including Kennedy and Howard Metzenbaum of Ohio, Fleming wrote in a ninety-one page report that no source for the leak could be found, and the matter was dropped.

Twenty

Palm Beach: Chappaquiddick Redux

Whenever a Kennedy gets into serious trouble, the first rule of action is to confuse, hide, lie if necessary—and run for help from family loyalists and lawyers.

There was an eerie resemblance in the aftermath of the tragedy at Poucha Pond and the episode beside the swimming pool at the Kennedy mansion in Palm Beach. A pattern of evading scrutiny by law-enforcement officials and ducking behind the Kennedy legal barricades was repeated in both scandals.

In 1969 Ted had avoided police for nine hours after Mary Jo Kopechne was drowned, made a brief statement, then fled to the compound where leading Kennedy strategists planned ways to minimize his involvement. From Palm Beach, he flew to Washington without talking to police who sought to question him about charges of rape brought against his nephew, and conferred at once with the best lawyers and investigators on damage control.

Moira K. Lasch, the assistant district attorney who prosecuted Willie Smith, heard the echoes of Chappaquiddick when she attempted, unsuccessfully, to introduce Leo Damore's highly critical book, *Sen-*

atorial Privilege: the Chappaquiddick Cover-up, into evidence at a pretrial hearing.

"That book is relevant," Ms. Lasch argued, "because it shows the fact that public officials can come under the influence of Kennedy lawyers. They attempt to intimidate officials and try to control the dissemination of free information. . . . The Kennedys try to avoid the close scrutiny of their own conduct."

Dominick Arena, the Martha's Vineyard police chief, also sees parallels to the drowning at Chappaquiddick. The day after the accident, he said in 1991, he was not told that a party, at which liquor had been served, preceded Ted and Mary Jo's drive to the Dike Bridge. It was only later, he said, that he learned from a journalist about the cookout. Had he known earlier, he would have questioned all the guests present but, lacking this information, he did not.

"That gave everyone a chance to leave the island and meant we didn't have an opportunity to talk to everyone at the time."

The tawdry episode in Palm Beach began on the night of Good Friday, March 29, 1991, in the Kennedy winter home on North Ocean Boulevard. Once an elegant mansion when Joe Kennedy bought it in 1933, the seven-bedroom house had fallen into disrepair because Rose had refused over the years to pay for any refurbishing. Now it is dwarfed in size and magnificence by the surrounding homes, but it maintains its classic dignity as a creation of the 1920s. Fronting on the beach, the estate has a swimming pool, a tennis court, a wide lawn shaded by tall palms, and many memories of the winter vacations spent there by President Kennedy.

There had been a dinner party that evening, attended by Patrick, Willie, his mother Jean, William Barry and his wife and daughter and son-in-law. Barry, a tall, broad-shouldered former FBI agent, had been security chief for Robert Kennedy and has remained a close family friend.

Two pretty girls, Brigette and Cara Rooney, came over after dinner and, with Willie and Patrick, decided to go to a nearby discotheque. Ted and the older guests told them to have a good time and went out to the terrace where, unaccountably, the family tragedies entered the conversation. It was one of the rare times that the Kennedys talked about them. Luella, the family nurse, told me, "They have steeled themselves not to look back. It was the only way they could avoid being mired in sadness. So they never talk about the bad events, even among themselves."

But that night they did. Steve Smith had died only eight months before, and his widow, Jean, began reminiscing about him and campaigns past. Later, Ted described the ensuing conversation as "very emotional, very difficult."

Ted went to bed about 10:30 P.M. Usually, the wash of the surf outside his open window brought sleep quickly, but that night he remained awake, staring at the ceiling, haunted by memories.

About midnight, Ted saw Willie and Patrick, returning from the disco, walking past the glass windows adjacent to the patio. He called to them and asked if they wanted to go out for "a few beers." Ruefully, Ted admitted he should have gone for a long walk on the beach until sleepiness overtook him; instead, he took the men to a bar, and into yet another Kennedy scandal.*

The three, Ted seeking to exorcise the demons that had come unbidden into his mind, and Willie and Patrick, looking forward to a couple of hours of fun, drove to the latest "in" place, Au Bar on Royal Poinciana Way, opened only a few months before.†

Ted was recognized and seated at a choice table near the small dance floor. The older man and the two younger ones ordered drinks, sipped them, and chatted. After a while, Willie, 6'3", blue-eyed and a recent medical-school graduate, went to the marble-topped bar, where he felt someone brushing against him. He turned to look: it was a young woman, attractive but not beautiful. They began a conversation, not unusual between strangers there. Her name, she said, was Patricia Bowman. Willie asked her to dance.

While they were on the floor, Anne Mercer, Bowman's friend, walked by; Bowman introduced the thirty-three-year-old blonde to Ted and Patrick. Mercer, who disliked the Kennedy family, showed her feelings

---

*Late in December, John McLaughlin, moderator of a television talk show, asked his panelists: "What was the worst idea of 1991?" Syndicated columnist Fred Barnes responded, "Willie and Patrick, let's all go out and have a drink."

†Howard Stein, one of the club's owners, was the son of Charles (Ruby) Stein, a New York loan shark with Mafia ties, according to Murray Weiss and William Hoffman in their 1992 book, *Palm Beach Babylon*. The elder Stein disappeared suddenly in 1977; in May of that year, part of his body was found on the shores of Jamaica Bay, Queens, New York.

at once, at one point reportedly calling Patrick a "bore," adding, "With genes like this, there'll be no more Kennedy dynasty."

Ted bristled. "How dare you speak in this manner. This young man is a member of the legislature of Rhode Island."

Patrick reddened and, containing his anger, rose and went to the bar where he and Michelle Cassone, a twenty-six-year-old waitress, began a conversation and soon went to the dance floor. At about 2:30 A.M., Ted was ready to leave. Willie couldn't be found, so Ted and his son, knowing Willie could find his way to the mansion, left the bar. Patrick invited Cassone to the house; she accepted and followed them in her own car.

At 3:00—closing time—Willie discovered that his uncle and Patrick had gone and asked Ms. Bowman for a ride home. She agreed; on arriving, Willie showed her around the mansion, then walked with her on the beach where they talked and kissed.

Afterward, Smith said, he disrobed and dove into the surf for a brief swim. When he emerged from the water, Bowman said she wanted to leave. Followed by Smith, she went back into the grounds of the mansion. By the poolside, Bowman said, Willie tackled and raped her. Willie's account was that she permitted him to enter her, even guided him with her hand; at one point, he said, he called her "Kathy," who was not identified, which irritated her.

Bowman ran into the house where, in the kitchen, she called her friend Anne Mercer. Meanwhile, Smith cooled off by doing several laps in the pool. About 4:00 A.M., Mercer and a friend, Chuck Desiderio, reached the mansion and followed Patricia back to her home in Jupiter, about twenty miles north of Palm Beach. Bowman, twenty-nine years old, unmarried and mother of a two-year-old daughter, lives in a comfortable-looking three-bedroom house which was bought for her by her stepfather, Michael G. O'Neil, the retired head of the General Tire and Rubber Company, for $160,000.

Patricia, whose parents were divorced when she was thirteen, was born in Akron, Ohio, went to high school in Stow, a few miles northeast of the city. She attended college in Ohio for two years, then moved to Florida, where the climate helped ease the pain of arthritis which set in after she was seriously injured in an auto accident at the age of sixteen.

Meanwhile, her mother, Jean, became a top executive of General Tire and eventually married Mr. O'Neil. Patricia lived for a while in Orlando, then moved to Palm Beach, where her daughter was born out of wedlock in 1989. After Mr. O'Neil retired, he and her mother moved to an exclusive development in Jupiter which, like many others in the area, has security guards at the entrance checking on all visitors.

Bowman filed rape charges on Saturday, March 30, and the floodgates opened.

While Ted was not on trial, he was an integral part of the proceedings that unfolded in Palm Beach. Once again, the public's attitude toward him was polarized. He was ridiculed and re led by many and defended staunchly by loyalists. Anti-Kennedy columnists excoriated him for taking his son and nephew drinking, pro-Kennedy writers and several senators saw nothing essentially evil about it. Mike Barnacle of the *Boston Globe* fumed that Ted Kennedy believes he can do whatever he wants, and "get away with anything."

Pete Hamill in the *New York Post* said that many Irish fathers take their sons out drinking, and what was all the fuss?

Bob Shrum, a former Kennedy press aide, assailed the avalanche of media criticisms, and admitted that he, too, had taken a nephew out for a few beers and "I don't think it's an offense."

The editor of one major national magazine told me that Ted's action was beneath contempt. Another shrugged and said, "These weren't kids. One was twenty-four and a state legislator, and the other was thirty and a medical-school graduate."

What became clear from the start was that everything Ted Kennedy does that is even slightly unusual becomes an instant sensation. He has long since accepted this, saying, "It goes with the territory."

For example, after he returned from Au Bar, newspapers and TV broadcasts had a field day with the story of Ted Kennedy, minus his pants and wearing only a T-shirt, romping around the mansion. Actually, Michelle Cassone and Patrick were sitting on the seawall overlooking the ocean when Ted joined them. His appearance startled Michelle. She said he wore what appeared to be a long shirt, his bare knees showing.

The *New York Post* learned about the incident and published an article, stretching over two pages, under the headline: *TEDDY WORE*

ONLY A T-SHIRT. The story, reporting that he chased a girl around the mansion, soon escalated into another raunchy Teddy tale.

The simple explanation is that Ted, like many men, often sleeps in a nightshirt or equivalent garment. And all that happened was that he was still sleepless and wanted to talk some more about his family and his memories. Twenty minutes later, he yawned, said good night, and returned to his bedroom. No romp, no sex, nothing untoward occurred.

Two days later, however, Ted was involved in a problem that could have had serious repercussions. He and his friend Bill Barry came under police scrutiny for possible obstruction of justice.

After Bowman filed her charges of sexual battery, two detectives arrived at the mansion about 1:30 P.M. on Easter Sunday and asked to speak to the senator. Barry, answering the bell, told them Ted had already left town, "but it was possible he may still be around." Actually, Ted was inside the house, preparing to have Easter Sunday lunch with guests.

Ted did not leave for Washington until the next day. In her sworn deposition, Jean Smith declared that her son, Willie, ate quickly, then left for the West Palm Beach airport at 2:15 P.M. Mary Barry, Bill's wife, said in her statement that her husband told her that evening: "We have a problem. . . . It is potentially serious and I just don't want to talk about it until we are away from Palm Beach." After they left, Barry told Mary about the charges against Willie Smith. Others at the luncheon also said in sworn statements that the senator and Willie were indeed at the house that afternoon.

In Washington, Paul Donovan, Kennedy's press spokesman, said that the Senator had no knowledge of the rape charges until late Sunday afternoon. Ted himself said that Barry had not mentioned the word "rape" when he told him police were asking to see him, believing they were only checking out an instance of "sexual harassment." But young Patrick, in his May 7 deposition, contradicted his father, saying that Barry did indeed tell the Senator the police were inquiring into allegations of sexual battery. Responding to this, Ted said on May 15, "There was an honest semantic misunderstanding" over the phrase, which he did not know was the equivalent of rape under Florida law.

In December 1991, the trial of Willie Smith on two counts of sexual battery began, drawing unprecedented attention. Almost a thousand journalists and broadcasters from all over the globe converged on the West Palm Beach courthouse, across the inland waterway, from which the proceedings were telecast across the United States and, by satellite, around the world. Patricia Bowman, whose name had not been disclosed by most of the media, remained unidentified, her face covered in the television broadcasts by a large blue circle. Later, she emerged from behind the "blob" in an interview with Diane Sawyer, in which she reiterated her side of the story.

During the legal haggling of the preceding months, the "exclusive" stories and interviews in the newspapers, tabloids and lurid TV shows, the public became thoroughly confused. It was difficult to cut through the tangle of verbiage and legal technicalities and realize that the case of *the State of Florida* v. *William Kennedy Smith*, Docket Number 91–5482, concerned this single question:

Ms. Bowman claimed she had been raped. Smith, who admitted they had intercourse, said she had consented. The four women and six men of the jury were asked to decide who was telling the truth.

The stakes were high for Willie Smith—he faced five to fifteen years in prison if convicted and the end of his hopes for a medical career.

Once again, the public's attitude toward Ted Kennedy was polarized.

Outside the courthouse, vendors hawked tee-shirts illustrated with a caricature of Kennedy holding a foaming tankard of beer. Willie got even rougher treatment. After he testified that he assured Ms. Bowman he had been "careful", tee-shirts appeared bearing the inscription: "Don't worry. It's only a short prick." At the same time, Kennedy's office was flooded with sacks of mail expressing support.

Roy E. Black, a forty-six-year-old Miami criminal lawyer, chosen by Ted's legal advisers, headed Willie's defense team. Black, who commands huge fees, is considered one of the best criminal attorneys in South Florida. He is gentlemanly in his courtroom demeanor, yet subtle and crafty in his cross-examination. When he was still a public defender in Miami at the age of thirty, he was named one of the city's best defense lawyers, and since then his fame, and case load, have soared. He received a fee of $250,000 for his services.

Black's legal team recruited Cathy Bennett, an expert in jury selection to join the defense. Ms. Bennett, who was in a Houston, Texas, hospital where she was undergoing chemotherapy for cancer, checked out and flew to Miami despite her doctor's warning that if she halted the treatment she could have only a month to live. She had been stricken with breast cancer in 1985 which had spread to her lymph nodes, intestines, stomach, and bones.

The forty-year-old woman had helped lawyers select many dozens of juries for clients ranging from John Z. DeLorean to the Indians at Wounded Knee. Cat Bennett understood that jury choosing is the key factor in most, if not all, criminal cases. Using psychology (she had two degrees) and an uncanny intuition, she would frame artful questions, which she fed to the lawyers, that would reveal hidden prejudices as well as sympathies.

Bennett sat at the defense table throughout the sixteen arduous days of jury selection, looking paler and more tired each day. Six months after the trial ended, Cat Bennett died.

Ted had returned to Florida on December 6 and testified for forty minutes. Having crash-dieted, he had lost twenty-five pounds; his face had a healthy glow, and he looked fit in his blue suit, blue shirt, and muted striped tie. He spoke in a somber tone and would slip on reading glasses to examine documents showed him. He was, in short, the picture of a dignified United States senator.

Surprisingly, Ms. Lasch, who had been expected to attack furiously, asked only soft questions. Ted retold the story of that night, recounting his inability to sleep because of an "overwhelming wave in terms of emotion." Lasch allowed Kennedy to talk of his tragic memories. "I lost a brother in the war," Ted said in a somber voice. "When Jean married Steve [Smith], we had another brother. When Steve was gone— something left all of us when we buried him." No one moved as Ted spoke.

"I think he was terrific," Willie said later; everyone agreed.

Willie's mother Jean was at the trial every day. John Kennedy, Jr., attended one session, denying a published report in *Time* magazine that he bowed to family pressure to be there. Said young Kennedy: "No one in my family ever pressured me to attend. I went to Florida because I wanted to go, and it wasn't to get a tan." Neither Jackie, Ethel, Joan, nor any other family member was present at any of the sessions.

The bitterly fought trial lasted nine days, including a weekend session. On December 11, the Kennedys and their attorneys had barely arrived at the mansion after the jury received the case, when they were summoned back. Deliberating only one hour and seventeen minutes, the jury acquitted Willie of all charges. He bowed his head as though in prayer, then bounded up to embrace Roy Black.*

Willie soon dropped out of sight as the media lost interest; he is now a resident in internal medicine at the University of New Mexico Hospital in Albuquerque.

Patricia Bowman, still living in Jupiter, has resumed her life. From time to time she addresses women's groups around the country, on college campuses, and at victims' agencies on rape prevention and how to handle sexually aggressive situations when they arise.

She strongly opposes identification of rape victims by the media, asserting that publication of their names will make victims reluctant to file charges. Addressing a forum of the American Press Institute in September 1991, attended by editors from across the nation, Bowman assailed newspapers for disclosing her name, among them the *New York Times*. In a lengthy article about her on April 17, 1991, the *Times* dug into her background, citing intimate details about her life ("She likes to cook, listen to Bruce Springsteen music... her home has peach-colored walls.") At the forum, Bowman called the decision to reveal her name "unforgivable," said her daughter's walls were not peach at all, and irately denounced the article's intrusion into her privacy.

"The *Times* even told the titles of the children's books on the shelves in my daughter's room," she declares. "These book titles are visible only by trespassing on my property, going over shrubbery, and voyeuristically... peering into a baby girl's bedroom window." Each night, she asserted, she and the child "still walk to each and every window in our home and scare the monsters away so that she can go to sleep."

In a note accompanying the article, the *Times* stated that the customary policy of news organizations to withhold the names of rape accusers had been broken ten days before by the *Sunday Mirror* in London, followed a week later by the *Globe*, a nationally circulated

---

*Many persons insisted that the verdict was a miscarriage of justice because Judge Mary E. Lupo ruled that previous charges of sexual misbehavior made against Smith could not be introduced. However, it is a principle of American jurisprudence that a defendant's previous record cannot be brought up at his trial except under unusual circumstances. (Also, evidence obtained illegally by police and prosecutors, no matter how damning, is considered "tainted" and unusable in court.)

supermarket tabloid. The evening before, NBC News, anchored by Tom Brokaw, had disclosed her identity. "The *Times* had withheld Ms. Bowman's name until now, but editors said yesterday that NBC's nationwide broadcast took the matter of her privacy out of their hands," the *Times* stated.

Only too plainly, the case was a terrible event for the senator. It was "The End of the Line" for Ted, *Esquire* magazine wrote. Ted's handling of the rape case "echoes an old pattern of recklessness, evasion and irresponsibility," said *Time*. "It's Time for Teddy to Step Aside," said the *New York Post*.

The patriarch of the dynasty was beleaguered. His own future, and that of the dynasty itself, was facing extinction.

Twenty-One

Crossroads

Until 1992 the two divergent aspects of Ted Kennedy's personality have been able to coexist. But the time finally arrived when the Bad must reform if the Good is to remain in office.

Until then, his friends and political observers agreed that there has been no contradiction between the Senator who fights passionately for the rights of the underprivileged and the self-indulgent, pleasure-seeking private man.

Dun Gifford, his former aide, said bluntly, "Ted Kennedy's personal life has nothing whatsoever to do with his public life."

Senator Smathers, the convivial pal of John Kennedy, declared, "If you have a loose, relaxed social life, that does not mean you are going to be a bad Senator. Nobody wants to emulate his lifestyle. Nobody wants his or her children to be another Ted Kennedy socially. But once he gets on the floor, he knows what he's talking about, makes sound arguments, has good ideas as to what legislation ought to accomplish. And everyone knows that. There are two separate and distinct parts of the man's character and existence."

Television journalist Roger Mudd believes that the playboy image does not cancel out Ted's accomplishments. "In American politics," he said, "there is a tolerance of personal habits and lives....A lot of

235

Senators who have stubbed their toes and come under public scrutiny are generally judged by their legislative records, and his [Kennedy's] is an outstanding one."

Senator Simpson, the Wyoming Republican, declares that "whatever he does in his own life is his own business" and finds no conflict between the two sides of Ted Kennedy.

Even Senator John Warner of Virginia, a Republican—and a conservative one at that—had high praises for his liberal colleague, despite his irresponsible private deportment. "He works twelve to fourteen hours a day," Warner said, "and in the deepness of his heart he believes in what he's doing, which you can't say for everybody around here."

Some critics argue that Kennedy cannot be a true liberal, battling for his causes, without embracing and practicing in his own life, the values of middle-class America, such as being a faithful husband and a reasonably reliable individual who might go off on an occasional binge with the boys, but leads an essentially decent life.

"I like Kennedy's economic policies," a thoughtful Delaware voter commented during the 1980 primaries, "but I feel safer with Carter. He's more stable, a family man and all."

This voter is not alone. Many people believe that political leaders cannot be effective if they do not conform to the behavioral norms set by society.

The argument appears persuasive, but let us take a closer look at some historical examples of lifestyle versus political accomplishments.

Did Franklin D. Roosevelt have any less compassion for the poor and deprived because he was involved with Lucy Mercer Rutherford, Eleanor's social secretary? Did his affairs with a number of women make Martin Luther King, Jr. any less passionate in his lifelong battle for black equality? Dwight Eisenhower, who kept the nation on an even keel during his two terms from 1953 to 1960 is now considered by historians as one of the great presidents. Yet Ike had a wartime romance with Kay Summersby, one of his drivers.

Jack Kennedy's sexual exploits were monumental, yet even though his stature as an icon has been eroded by revisionist historians, few dispute his solid accomplishments in civil rights, aid to education, manpower training and, of course, the nuclear-war test treaty with the Soviet Union.

Did Lyndon Johnson's lusty lifestyle make him less capable of constructing a plan for a Great Society, his grand design for a prosperous and unified country, many of whose precepts were enacted into law?

Another question asked repeatedly about Ted is whether a man who privately shows so little respect for women can fight seriously for the rights of women in the workplace, in public life, and in the home.

Yes, he can, said Molly Yard, former president of the National Organization for Women, the country's largest group whose agenda is equality for women. "We can count on him," she said. NOW has high praise for his voting record on issues affecting women.

"Ironically," wrote James Carroll in *the New Republic*, "as a defender of a whole range of programs designed to help the poor, including especially prenatal care and child care, he is in public life one of the nation's greatest defenders of women."

Ted himself finds no contradictions between his private and public behavior toward women. The ones he bedded were individuals who offered themselves to him willingly; they were, as his father taught him, the "cake on his plate," his to take.

But the issue of women as victims of discrimination is another matter entirely. This is a wrong that needs to be corrected, Ted believes, and he goes about the task with verve and vigor. His support of increased opportunities for women in scientific careers, of efforts to narrow the wage gap between men and women, for the establishment of more day-care centers— these and other issues affecting women have, in the end, nothing to do with his private behavior, he feels.

His colleagues in the Senate understand this. "All of us have come to draw a line," said a Republican senator who has often opposed Kennedy on issues. "There's the Ted I see at 9:30 A.M. on the Senate floor with three staffers, and then there's the 9:30-at-night Ted. He separates his life, and so do we."

Nor has Ted seen any contradiction between hard drinking off hours and legislative effectiveness. He—and everyone else inside the Beltway—know that representatives and senators often drink to excess when work is finished.

What Ted Kennedy did not grasp until 1991 is that personal and private behavior have been merged in the voters' minds. The "character" issue has become increasingly significant in the acceptance or rejection of candidates for office. He got the message at last that voters would be likely to turn out of office a hard-drinking, womanizing official no matter how great his accomplishments.

Kennedy's friends and staffers plead for understanding of the negative side of his personality, the "Bad Ted." One staff aide, whom I have known for twenty-five years, became increasingly emotional in cataloguing the tragic events of his life.

"This is a man," the aide said, "whose three brothers and a sister suffered violent deaths, whose eldest son lost a leg to cancer, and whose youngest son was so asthmatic as a child that he had to sleep in an iron lung; whose father was a bed and chairbound invalid for eight years, unable to speak, whose first wife was an alcoholic, who lives every day of his life with the drowning of Mary Jo. What must it be like to be such a man, to try to handle those griefs, not in private as others can, but before the eyes of the world? For God's sake, can't we consider all these things as we judge this man?"

At the end, the aide was close to tears.

There is no doubt that Ted Kennedy is disliked by many people in the United States, although nobody, of course, can measure the extent of this critical view. Those hate letters every week, far more than any other senator gets, are significant. Opponents charge that his liberalism can wreck the country, that he is an arrogant rich man's son who acts as though he can do anything he wishes and emerge unscathed and, most of all, that he has irredeemable character flaws.

"The conservatives hate him because he's on the side of the poor, the workers and the middle-class," wrote Mike Dubson in *Curbstone* a monthly community newspaper published in Dorchester, south of Boston, where the JFK Library is located. "Too many of the poor, the workers, and the conservative middle class, duped by the propaganda of the rich, hate him for it too."

Ted's friends and staff argue that, while opposing him for his political views is surely everyone's right, hating him for his flaws misses a key point. Sympathy and understanding, they say, must be factored into the evaluation of the man and the senator. "Where is our sense of compassion for Ted Kennedy?" asked Dubson. "He has known great pain in his life, and it shows in every bulge and line of his face."

Dubson wrote in *Curbstone*: "It's no wonder he's turned to drink too many times. It's nowonder he's been horsing around a little too much.

We all have to get away from it, even the youngest son of a rich family who happens to be a senator."

While the argument can help explain Ted's conduct, it can no more excuse it than a person, born and raised in poverty, can be forgiven legal punishment for shooting a victim and stealing his wallet. We can *understand* his motives, blame the country's horrendous neglect of the poor and deprived, and try in every way to improve conditions, but the unassailable fact is that the law has been broken.

One would have to be inhuman not to feel compassion for a man who has had such losses as Ted Kennedy, but can we allow our sympathy, however profound, to forgive him his excesses?

Nor can the good in Kennedy ever cancel out the bad. Murray Kempton, a liberal journalist who "cherishes" Ted for his policies, said that even his supporters "cannot avoid conceding that indecency leaves a stain that never quite washes away." Kempton cited the assessment of Oliver Cromwell by British statesman George William Claredon that he was a man impossible to blame without praising or to praise without blaming. "There are worse things" Kempton observed, "than being both Edward Kennedy and worthy of so high a compliment."

The newest assault on Ted began in May 1992, when the bizarre story of "the book" roiled the publishing industry. For months until its publication the following September, the book became the subject of intense speculation.

In May G. P. Putnam's Sons announced that it would publish a "highly confidential" work which was "one of the most controversial and revealing biographies of a public figure to appear in many years." Putnam's refused to divulge the author, subject, or what it contained.

However, in late August, Putnam's dropped the book abruptly. The cancellation, so near the book's fall publication date was highly unusual. Phyllis E. Grann, president and chief executive officer, declared that "we simply cannot proceed for legal reasons." But about two weeks later, St. Martin's Press announced it had picked up the book, and that it would be published on September 28. By that time the news had leaked out that the subject was Ted Kennedy and the author was Richard E. Burke, thirty-nine, who had joined Ted's staff in 1971 and served as his senior aide from 1977 to 1981. Burke reportedly received an advance payment of $500,000.

The book, *The Senator: My Ten Years With Ted Kennedy*, charged Ted with many extra marital affairs and with using cocaine. Burke also claimed to have seen vials of amyl nitrate, a stimulant said to have aphrodisiacal powers, in Ted's desk drawer at his home.

Soon, however, Burke became enmeshed in credibility problems.

On February 4, 1981, Burke had told Washington police that he had received several death threats, that he had been fired upon while sitting in his car and chased up the stairs of his home in Glover Park by a knife-wielding intruder. But three weeks later, Burke confessed that he had lied. He claimed that the "accumulated pressure" of the 1980 presidential campaign had caused him to think irrationally. He admitted firing the bullet through his car window to validate his hoax.

After the fabrications were disclosed, Burke resigned. In a letter to Kennedy, he wrote that he was seeking "comprehensive medical advice" and was "currently receiving the recommended treatment." The *Boston Globe* said that Burke had quit after "having suffered a nervous breakdown."

Moreover, Burke was deeply in debt. After he left Kennedy, he had become involved in several enterprises, the latest of which was a company called Congress Video, which made self-help cassettes. But the company had failed. On September 1, 1991, the firm filed for bankruptcy, owing $3.3 million. It was claimed that Burke wrote the book to make enough money to get out of debt, a charge which he denied.

After ridding himself of his own drug problem, Burke said, he wrote the book because "the American people need to know what their leaders are like."

Burke could not—or did not—document most of his charges. He relied heavily on secondhand information from unidentified or "composite" individuals, prompting Paul Donovan, Kennedy's press aide, to charge: "It's not a work of biography. It's a work of fiction."

I asked Melody Miller, Ted's deputy press aide, how Kennedy reacted to the book. She replied, "He has not read it and will not promote the book by any statement other than the one he made when it was published."

That day he had said, "It is an outrageous example of say anything, sell anything, publish anything for a buck...this is the worst exploitation my family and I have had to endure in many years."

NBC's "*Today* Show," an important publicity exposure for new books, canceled a scheduled interview with Burke on September 28 because, executive producer Jeff Zucker said, "there were too many questions on my mind."

Tom Quinn, the head of the Secret Service team which guarded Kennedy around the clock for fourteen months during the campaign, declared that the book was "total b.s." Quinn, now retired from the agency, said he was "outraged" by the statements made by Burke. "There's no way that Senator Kennedy could have had any involvement with drugs," he asserted. "He did not exhibit any of the signs of illegal drug involvement whatsoever."

And Dr. Brian Billes, who served from 1975 to 1976 on the staff of the Senate Health Subcommittee, asserted that Kennedy showed "no signs of the type of erratic behavior we know to be associated with drug use."

As we have noted, the influence of Old Joe was central to the creation of Bad Ted and Good Ted. Joe was revered by his youngest son, whose desire to win his father's approval began his woes and whose insistence on the family destiny, which he never moderated compounded them. At the same time, it was Joe who instilled in Ted and the other children the importance of repaying in public service the wealth the Kennedys were able to accumulate in this country.

Pounding away at the power and continued glory of the family from Ted's earliest years, Joe developed in his youngest son an obsession with the responsibilities relating to the Kennedys. "He talks about the family and its meaning to him all the time," declared biographer and friend Burton Hersh. "It has put a burden on him that he didn't have to carry."

But Ted had no choice. He has been the bearer of the tradition for a quarter of a century and, year after year, the load became heavier until he buckled under the strain. Even though Ted never wanted to be president, he *felt* he had to be the dynastic heir and could not face the awful realization that he was failing to live up to the expectations of his father and brothers.

As the tragedies mounted inexorably, the despairing thought of the brevity and evanescence of life reinforced the hedonistic philosophy Ted had as a young man; that life should be enjoyed. So as Good Ted worked hard, Bad Ted sought to derive as much pleasure as possible from the life that still remained.

Alcohol helped, though nobody could tell for certain how much the tragedies contributed to his increased drinking. Jack and his father had stomach problems which were aggravated by liquor, and Bobby was strong-minded enough not to require any alcoholic boost.

Joe Kennedy's parenting was tragically wrong. By rearing his sons to be so interconnected emotionally, so dependent upon one another, he made each vulnerable to the fate of the others. Bobby was devastated when Jack died; Teddy was lost after Bobby was murdered.

After 1968, Ted had nobody in the family to whom he could confide his fears, nobody to whom he could go for suggestions and guidance. His sisters were supportive and loving, but none was trained in the art of politics. He leaned increasingly on Steve Smith, who was tough and shrewd, but Steve was not immediate family. And when Smith died, Ted's last lifeline was severed.

If his older brothers had survived, would Ted have led a more disciplined life? Judging by his own character flaws, John Kennedy would have been a poor role model; but Bobby, a moralist with a Calvinistic belief in absolute moral right and wrong, would almost surely have tried to exert a strong influence on Ted. Bobby, says John Seigenthaler, "was a devout Catholic, a mass-attending, confession-going, communion-receiving Catholic. He set himself standards and lived by them." Bobby disapproved of Jack's affairs, but accepted them as part of his brother's makeup. His relationship with Ted had always been big brother to little brother, and it is not difficult to imagine Bobby taking Ted for long walks at Hickory Hill to explain where little brother was heading and trying to persuade him to straighten out his own life.

Twenty-Two

Cleaning Up His Act?

As he entered his sixtieth year on February 22, 1991, just five weeks before the Palm Beach scandal broke, Ted Kennedy made a major lifetime decision: to make a radical course correction if he wanted to preserve his political life—or even if he wanted to live at all.

Troubled only by his back pains, Ted had been a vigorous and healthy man. He had suffered an easily excised skin cancer in 1982, but now he was on a frightening descent into life-threatening physical deterioration. While no medical evidence has ever been made public about the condition of Ted Kennedy's liver (or indeed of any of his vital signs), cirrhosis, the destruction of liver tissue that can cause death, was a clear possibility if his heavy and prolonged consumption of alcohol continued.

Up to the end of the 1980s, Ted's friends were wary of approaching him about his alcohol use. They recalled what happened in 1970 when John Culver, a former senator from Iowa and a Harvard classmate who had played football with him, cautioned Kennedy to ease off. Ted became furious and didn't speak to Culver for four years.

Ted's drinking progressed more heavily than ever. He started to suffer periodic blackouts, unable to remember in the morning what he did or where he was the night before. He gained an enormous amount of weight, looked glassy-eyed and sleep-deprived. He neglected his appearance and personal hygiene. He was observed by his worried staff, sitting at his desk, staring at nothing, barely responding to their questions. His capacity was amazing: it was not unusual for him to consume a bottle and a half of wine in about a quarter of an hour, followed by large glasses of scotch. Other times he would switch to rum-and-Cokes, drinking one after the other all evening long.

Ted's friends became deeply concerned and braved his wrath by telling him point-blank that his life was now in danger. Ted's early biographer Burton Hersh said, "Everyone around him was worried. We all told him that for the sake of his health and career, he had to make a drastic change." Some of his more intimate friends went to high-ranking Catholic clergymen for guidance on what could be done.

Senator Hatch cornered him a number of times in private and eventually went public with a plea to stop the toboggan slide. In May 1991, when Kennedy visited Hatch in his office two floors below, in Room 135 of the Russell Building, the Utah senator gave him a stern lecture.

"You're a great senator now," he told Ted, "but you could go down in history as one of the all-time great senators. To do that you have to grow up. And you really have to stop drinking."

Relating the story, Hatch reported, "He knew I was right. He acknowledged it would be better for him not to drink. He knows that sooner or later he must come to grips with it."*

This time Ted heeded the advice coming at him from all sides.

In October 1991, after a troubled summer, Kennedy met with his closest friends and advisers in Virginia and on the Cape on how to mend his tattered reputation, especially since he was facing a reelection campaign in 1994. Some favored a public apology and a promise to reform; others told Ted that if he made such a pledge and failed to keep it, he'd be in worse shape than ever.

Ted wrestled with the problem, finally deciding on making a public admission that change in his personal lifestyle was essential. Shrewdly selecting a Harvard audience, bound to be sympathetic because of its liberal leanings, and timing his *mea culpa* for the week before jury selection was to begin in Willie's trial, he addressed the Institute of

---

*Questioned on the *Today* show by Bryant Gumbel, Ted denied that he had an alcohol problem.

Politics at the John F. Kennedy School of Government in Cambridge on the twenty-fifth anniversary of its founding.

Some eight hundred persons jammed the lecture hall on October 24, including dozens of journalists. Television cameras and lights were set up in the rear. Departing from his speech, in which he once again pleaded for more and better civil-rights legislation and excoriated the "negative politics" of the Republicans, he issued a public apology to the people of Massachusetts for his private behavior. Without alluding to any specific actions, he said:

> I am painfully aware that the criticism directed at me in recent months involved far more than honest disagreement with my positions or the usual criticisms from the far right. It also involved the disappointment of friends and many others who rely on me to fight the good fight.
>
> To them I say: I recognize my own shortcomings—the faults in the conduct of my private life. I realize that I alone am responsible for them, and I am the one who must confront them. I believe that each of us as individuals must not only struggle to make a better world, but to make ourselves better, too.

However, while Ted said he would "confront" his faults, and that he alone was to blame for them, his speech was carefully crafted to avoid anything resembling a pledge to behave properly.

Helping Ted frame his speech was a tall, hazel-eyed, dark-haired and very brainy lawyer named Victoria Reggie. She entered—actually, reentered—Ted's life at the point where it had reached critical mass, when a destructive explosion had been virtually inevitable.

On June 17, 1991, Ted attended a party celebrating the fortieth wedding anniversary of Doris and Edmund Reggie at their summer home on Nantucket. He watched thirty-eight-year-old Vicki as she bustled around, introducing the guests and making sure they were served cocktails and canapés.

Finally they said hello. Ted had come alone. "What's the matter," Vickie teased him. "Couldn't you get a date?"

Ted wasn't dateless for long. He took Vicki to dinner the next week.

Victoria Reggie is the eldest daughter of Edmund and Doris Reggie's six children; four boys and two girls. Reggie, a wealthy attorney who lives in Crowley, Louisiana, had been a friend of the Kennedy family since the 1956 Democratic convention, when he steered his state's delegation to Jack Kennedy in his quest for the vice-presidency. He became a city judge in 1950 and served until 1975. Reggie ran three presidential campaigns for the Kennedy brothers in Louisiana: Jack's in 1960, Bobby's in 1968, and Ted's in 1980. A frequent visitor at the White House during JFK's administration, Reggie was offered a U.S. District Court judgeship, but turned it down because he preferred the slower pace of Southern life.

Ted met Vicki when she was ten years old and he had turned thirty-one at campaign headquarters in Louisiana while she was stuffing envelopes for JFK. He had waved to her casually when she was a teenager during her summers on Nantucket and had hired her as an intern in his office in 1975, when she was attending H. Sophie Newcomb Memorial College, but she had drifted out of his sight and mind when she went to Tulane Law School, where she edited the Law Review and graduated *summa cum laude*.

Years later when they met again at the Reggie party, Ted was smitten almost from the start, said Vicki's father. But Vicki was not. It took her several months after they began dating to realize that she was falling in love with the senator. Ted, however, was more vulnerable than Vicki. His two-year romance with Palm Beach socialite Dragana Lickle had cooled; the town buzzed with rumors that she had jilted him.

Vicki was more cautious about another commitment. Divorced in 1990 from Grier Raclin, a Washington lawyer specializing in telecommunications, she shared custody with him of their two children; Curran, nine, and Caroline, six.

That summer, Ted's newfound relationship with Vickie went unnoticed. This was surprising in view of the constant media surveillance of Ted's romantic life. They picnicked in secluded areas on Nantucket and went on long, private sails around the sound in his boat, which was kept moored at the Compound. They rarely, if ever, appeared in public. Flowers from Ted arrived at the Reggie summer home almost daily. The mailman delivered ardent love letters. Ted went trick-or-treating with her children on Halloween, read them to sleep, played tennis with her son, and filled out coloring books with her daughter.

By late October, the secret began to leak out. Vicki coached Ted on the testimony he would deliver at Willie's trial, and when he went on the witness stand, she sat in a front row. Occasionally he looked at her and smiled slightly as their eyes met.

By the time the trial ended, both realized they were in love. Late in

December, Vicki hinted to her friends that marriage might not be far off. Finally, in early spring, Ted asked her to marry him and she accepted.

Then followed an episode which recalled the past. In the spring of 1958, as detailed in a previous chapter, Ted, in the fashion of earlier generations, had asked Joan's father for her hand in marriage. Now, almost exactly thirty-four years later, he telephoned Vicki's father.

Judge Reggie relates the story: "We knew they were dating, so we weren't surprised when the Senator called [in March—ed.] and Vicki was with him, and he said, 'You know, I love Vicki very much and I've asked her to marry me, and I want to ask you and Doris' and, you know, Ted did it the proper way, and it was so nice." The four—Reggie and Doris and Ted and Vicki—talked together on the phone. Reggie gave them his consent. "It was just wonderful, just beautiful," Reggie said.

On March 16 Ted announced their engagement. "I love Vicki and her children very much," he said. "I've known her for a number of years. She has brought enormous happiness into my life. I look forward to our marriage and to our life together."

In Boston, Joan Kennedy was stunned. She knew little of the romance and nothing at all of Ted's plan to rewed. When a reporter from the *Boston Herald* called to tell the engagement was announced, Joan's only comment was, "Oh? Is that true?"

Assured that it was, Joan replied in a strained voice, "I can't talk now," and hung up.

My own efforts to reach her were futile. I learned from her friends that she remained closeted in her apartment for weeks, refusing to speak to anyone but her most intimate friends.

Joan never expected—certainly never wanted—to reconcile with her former husband. But in the years since their divorce, she had never completely severed the cord that bound her to him. She sought his advice often about her own life and the lives of their children. Aides in Kennedy's office had standing orders to put her through to him whenever she called. They would also dine together occasionally on his trips to Boston.

Joan had confided her own personal problems to him and believed that he would tell her about his. But he never said a word about the most important decision he would make since their divorce a decade ago.

On Friday afternoon, July 3, thirty family members and friends of the

Kennedy's and Reggies gathered at Ted's McLean home for the wedding. In the large living room, Ted and Vickie stood before Judge A. David Mazzone,* under a portrait of Joseph P. Kennedy—Ted, beaming, in a dark suit and small-figured blue tie, Vicki in a short-sleeved, knee-length dress of handmade white lace over white silk and carrying just three pink and white roses.

Doris Reggie, a slim, attractive woman whom Vicki closely resembles, said the couple "didn't even wait for Judge Mazzone to say, 'You may kiss the bride.'" Close to the end of the brief ceremony, they embraced and kissed.

"Hey," the judge remonstrated with a broad smile, "I'm not finished." He then pronounced them husband and wife, and told Ted to kiss the bride, which he did once again, fervently.

Ted's daughter Kara began to applaud, and the guests took the cue, clapping for a full minute. Young Ted and Kara rushed to the couple and embraced both, triggering more cheers and applause.

During the reception, well-known singer, Maura O'Connell, backed up by several musicians, sang the couple's favorite song, "You'll Never Know How Much I Love You." "They had heard it on a CD disk several months earlier in their courtship," Doris Reggie said, "and from then on it was 'our song'." Vicki and Ted held hands during the rendition, which was followed by several other favorites of theirs.

Ted's gift to his bride was a painting of a bunch of daffodils in a green vase. Daffodils, among the first flowers to appear in the spring, meant a new beginning. Every guest received a copy, and bouquets of daffodils filled the living room. The foot-high wedding cake was decorated with spun-sugar daffodils. Ted didn't want anyone to miss the point.

The wedding dinner was served on the enclosed rear terrace, overlooking the rushing Potomac. The couple had selected a menu which was a mix of Southern and Kennedy cuisine; crab salad, Louisiana style, and filet mignon. Ted's thirty-one year old son, Ted, Jr., rose to toast his father and new stepmother: "I can't remember the last time I saw my dad so happy," he said. "And it is all due to Vicki."

Early that evening, the couple left for a brief honeymoon in Stowe,

---

*Since the Catholic church does not recognize civil divorce and still considers Ted married to Joan, a church wedding was not possible without an annulment. So far as is known, Ted had not sought one. He can attend mass but is forbidden to receive the sacraments, including the remission of sin.

Vermont. On their return, Vicki moved into the McLean house. Shortly afterward, Ted purchased a $350,000, two-bedroom, air-conditioned condominium on the second floor of 17 Marlborough Street, in Boston, just a few blocks from Joan's apartment. Curran and Caroline were enrolled in the Maret School, an exclusive six-building day institution at 3000 Cathedral Avenue NW in Washington, where the tuition is $10,500 per pupil.

Vicki, her mother said, has resumed her law practice with Keck, Mahin & Cate.

Victoria Reggie is entirely unlike Joan. She is a self-assured young woman who would not shrink into Ted Kennedy's—or any Kennedy's—shadow. Said Barbara Smith, an old friend, "Vicki can handle the tremendous scrutiny and pressure this life brings." Joan buckled under the strain. Vicki can stand up to Ted, telling him frankly and directly what she thinks, and he listens. Joan rarely could; and on the infrequent occasions when she did speak, Ted listened disinterestedly and went his own way.

Vicki was no pushover as a date, either; at the start of their relationship, she would not return his calls for hours or even until the next day, taking care of her law business first. No Kennedy woman had ever done that. She can hold her own in discussions about politics, the economy and foreign and domestic affairs at dinner parties with leading experts. Joan could not.

Vicki told Ted bluntly that he had to curb his use of alcohol and set a limit of two drinks a day, plus a small quantity of wine. "Your life is going down the tubes and you have no one to blame but yourself," she told him in the spring of 1992. "If you don't straighten up, you'll end up in the gutter dead because of liver failure." And that, while she loved him, it was up to him to decide to turn his life around. Ted promised to stop heavy drinking.

In a courtroom, Vicki is tough and relentless. During her own divorce proceedings in 1990, she fought hard for what she felt was her due, at one point writing to Raclin, her husband: "I will not be bullied by you." Ultimately, she received annual child-support payments of $62,000, exclusive of school tuition, their $725,000 brick colonial house in Washington, their Nantucket vacation house, and three automobiles.

"Vicki has a lot more balls than Ted ever dreamed of having," a friend said.

By the late summer of 1992, Ted Kennedy was involved in image polishing.

His press staff often worked past midnight, grinding out releases under the heading in large letters, "From the Office of Edward M. Kennedy of Massachusetts," explaining, in minute detail, what he had done for the state. He traveled to college campuses, went on radio talk shows, and appeared at a fund raiser for gay rights. Usually he would pass up the state's Democratic party dinner, an annual event, but this time he was there, delivering an address and afterward wading into the audience to shake hands, slap backs, and tell party members how happy he was to see them.

Quite clearly, his senate seat was in jeopardy.

Back in 1990, Michael Kelly had written in *Esquire* magazine: "He'd have to hit the Pope and pee on the Irish flag to lose his Senate seat."

But the mood of the voters had changed drastically. By August 1991 a telephone poll conducted by the *Boston Herald* and TV station WCVB, showed an astonishing reversal of the near-reverence in which Ted Kennedy had been held in Massachusetts. In 1988 he had been swept back into office in a landslide, winning slightly more than two-thirds of the votes. This time, he plummeted. The survey reported that 62 percent of voters believed Ted should be replaced in the Senate. Only 34 percent said they favored his reelection.

Several candidates surfaced, including William Weld, a former Rhodes scholar serving his first term as governor of the state, Secretary of Transportation Andrew Card, and former U.S. attorney Wayne Budd. In the *Herald* poll, 59 percent said they favored Weld over Kennedy. Nationwide, a Gallup poll conducted in October showed that Ted's approval rating had dropped to 22 percent.

But Ted insisted that he would not retire. He declared, "The last Congress was the most successful one for me in all my years here. I will continue to run as long as the people of Massachusetts will reelect me."

He worked hard to make it happen, doing all he could to revive the Kennedy mystique by parading his family before a once-adoring, now skeptical electorate. Even before he and Vicki were married, Curran and Caroline were told to call him "daddy." In June, Ted, Vicki, and Caroline, accompanied by John Tunney and several other friends, went sailing in Nantucket Sound. Coming in, the boat dropped anchor, and the party boarded a launch to the dock.

Spotting a group of photographers onshore, Ted reached back, took the little girl's hand and said, "Come on, Caroline, help me get elected."

Caroline replied, "Yes, daddy," and was snapped hand-in-hand with him as they alighted from the launch.

Knowing that the appetite of the media for Kennedy "lifestyle" stories was insatiable, Ted revived a technique he had not used in years: offering personal interviews to newspapers and TV stations which would benefit him most. Ted does this only when he feels he needs the exposure; at other times the portcullis is lowered. In 1978, Joe McCarthy, who wrote the bestseller, *Johnny, We Hardly Knew Ye*, for Dave Powers and Kenny O'Donnell, was assigned by a major magazine to interview Ted. Ted refused to see him. Big, kindly Joe was stunned and aggrieved. "That book was probably the most favorable ever written about his brother, and yet he turns me down," he said sadly.

But in July 1992 Ted's press office called all the Boston newspapers, the *Cape Cod Times* and the NBC *"Today Show,"* announcing that Ted and Vickie would be pleased to sit for interviews. A day was specified for later that month, and the media visits were scheduled.

The scene outside the Big House bordered on the comical. Each newspaper was permitted to have one hour with the couple. Reporters and photographers gathered on the porch like patients waiting to see a doctor. Each journalist was ushered in by Melody Miller, greeted warmly, and offered tea and coffee. Ted and Vicki sat on a couch, holding hands. They exuded warmth, homeliness, and family as they answered the same questions in virtually the same words at each interview.

Vicki: "This is a change of direction for both of us."

Ted: "This is a new beginning for me as well. It's just wonderful having small children around the home again. They're such fun."

Vickie: "We both love to read, bicycle, and there's music."

Ted: "The children and I had an 'Olympic' competition, doing handstands in the water. They only gave me a 6.5."

Vicki: "I'm a sports fan, rooting for the Redskins and the New Orleans Saints and the Atlanta Braves."

Ted: "She's a good cook."

Vicki: "I love a kitchen. You know how people love to gather in a kitchen and eat and talk."

Ted: "I'm teaching her how to prepare Nantucket scallops and marinated bluefish with lemon sauce and mayonnaise on the charcoal grill."

Vicki: "His favorite casserole is eggplant with chopped meat, onion, pine nuts, and tomato sauce."

Each newspaper published long stories, with several pictures of the newlyweds. For the *New York Times*, which printed its article on page one of the home section, Vicki posed in the kitchen to demonstrate her cooking skills.

Ted needs a generous display of the family the nation took to its heart because he no longer can rely on the massive infusions of Kennedy cash which helped elect a president and kept him in office for six terms.

Once one of America's greatest fortunes, the Kennedy family wealth has declined sharply. In 1991 following an investigation of the Kennedy holdings, *Forbes* magazine stated that the family "barely qualifies for the *Forbes* Four Hundred," the list it compiles annually of the richest people in the country. In a separate list of ninety-eight "family fortunes", the Kennedys, whose wealth is now estimated at $350 million* is close to the bottom, about on a par with Frank Perdue, the chicken farmer, Gene Autry, the former cowboy star, and Aaron Spelling, the television producer.

Of all the assets Joe Kennedy amassed, the sole remaining money producer is the Merchandise Mart in Chicago, which earns about $20 million a year. It's big money, certainly, but significantly less than the superrich computer-software, merchandising, media, and other tycoons of today whose wealth is estimated in billions.

There are few buyers for the huge complex if the Kennedys ever decide to turn the Mart into cash; worse still, the recession had hit the Mart hard and, according to *Forbes*, it is a property "with no great future." Complaining that rents are too high, many are planning to move when their leases expire. Joe Kennedy, the ultimate insider, purchased the Mart in 1945 from Marshall Field because he had learned that the United States was planning to end the cap placed on

---

*In 1950 the Kennedy wealth was estimated by *Fortune* magazine at $400 million, an amount that Collier and Horowitz said "couldn't help but increase just by its own momentum." That sum, in 1950 dollars, would be many times higher in the 1990s. Joe Kennedy himself said then that while "some shopkeeping" remains, "no more acquiring is necessary." In 1957 he was listed as the ninth wealthiest person in the United States, richer than any of the Rockefeller brothers.

government leases during wartime. Assured that rents would soon zoom—as they did—he bought the Mart for $13 million and realized huge profits from the escalating rentals.

Nobody knows how much each Kennedy spends, but they all live handsomely. All that Kennedy cousins appear to know is that checks arrive in the mail regularly from the offices of Joseph P. Kennedy Enterprises at 100 East 42nd Street, New York. The office also pays their credit-card and other bills. The cousins do not seem to know how much money there is and how long it will last.

It won't last forever. The family's wealth is tied up in trust funds, the income from which is shared by Rose, her children, and grandchildren. According to Joe's will, the trusts will end upon the deaths of Rose and her five surviving children. What remains of the principal will be divided among the younger Kennedys.

The trouble is that nobody in the family is minding the store. With the death of Steve Smith, who kept a close watch on expenditures and investments, no member of the family is involved in the management of its financial affairs, and only one has exhibited any interest in helping to maximize the family fortune. Christopher George, RFK's son, born in 1963, is working as a vice-president of marketing at the Mart.

As far as the money is concerned, the bottom line is that if the Kennedy spending continues at its present rate and nothing is done to augment the principal, the family fortune will be tapped out in a few decades—certainly in the early part of the twenty-first century.

The overriding question is: Can Ted Kennedy straighten up? His family and friends hope and believe he can. His private behavior since the Palm Beach episode has been without incident, and that is a good sign.

Tip O'Neill, ever the apologist for Kennedy, but a man who always speaks his mind, told me, "There is no question in my mind that he will change. He is probably angry with himself. He loves the Senate and has been upset by the criticisms. Yes, he will surely mend his ways. His record will be exemplary."

The change shows. According to John Robinson of the *Boston Globe*, those who know him well, say, "He is happy, not merely companionable. He is focused, not merely well briefed. He is articulate, not merely enjoying momentary lucidity. He has a private life that befits a distinguished gentleman of senior rank, rather than of a rake in the flower of post-adolescent frenzy."

Ted is no longer seen in his favorite drinking places on Cape Cod and in Palm Beach. He dines out with Vicki and family members or friends, generally goes to bed early, and appears to be a man at peace with himself.

The good behavior is likely to last.

He has no more wild oats to sow. He has a new wife who loves him and whom he adores. A woman who won't allow him to drink too much, much less stray, which he is little inclined to do anymore. Former Senator Smathers, a cutup himself in earlier years, observed, "Ted has already straightened up. The combination of age and a new wife is doing the job. You don't see many debauchers who are over sixty years old. Mother Nature helps curb their excessive indulgence in sensual pleasures. You may, of course, see men with ambitions along these lines, but very few men of that age have been able to create much of a reputation as a debaucher."

The odds are good that Ted will make the transformation from world-class *roué* to righteous citizen, good husband, and responsible public official.

Appendix

The Kennedy Tragedies

1941 Rosemary, eldest of the Kennedy daughters, who was mentally retarded, underwent a prefrontal lobotomy to alleviate convulsions, but the surgery left her permanently incapacitated. She has resided ever since at St. Coletta's, a convent in Jefferson, Wisconsin, where she has her own apartment with an attendant, car, and chauffeur at her disposal.

August 1–2, 1944 John F. Kennedy, a naval lieutenant in World War II, suffered back injuries when a Japanese destroyer sliced his PT boat in two in the Pacific. Kennedy had severe back pain throughout his life.

August 12, 1944 Joseph P. Kennedy, Jr., a naval pilot in World War II, was killed when his plane exploded over the English Channel during a volunteer mission.

May 13, 1948 Kathleen (Kick) Kennedy was killed in an airplane crash in France. Her British husband, the Marquess of Hartington, had been killed in action in Normandy in 1944, after four months of marriage.

December 19, 1961 Joseph P. Kennedy suffered a near-fatal stroke while playing golf at Palm Beach, Florida. It left him unable to speak and paralyzed on his right side.

August 9, 1963 Patrick Bouvier Kennedy, the third child of President and Mrs. John F. Kennedy, died in a Boston hospital two days after his premature birth. He had hyaline membrane disease.

November 22, 1963   President John F. Kennedy was assassinated by Lee Harvey Oswald as he and Jackie rode through the streets of Dallas, Texas in a motorcade.

June 19, 1964   Ted Kennedy narrowly escaped death when his small plane crashed en route to the Democratic convention in Springfield, Massachusetts, where he had just been nominated for his first full term. He suffered a broken back and spent six months in the hospital.

June 6, 1968   Robert F. Kennedy was shot by Sirhan Sirhan in the Los Angeles hotel where he addressed campaign workers after winning the Democratic primary in California.

July 18, 1969   Mary Jo Kopechne drowned when the car in which she and Senator Kennedy were driving plunged off a bridge at Chappaquiddick.

November 17, 1973   Ted Kennedy, Jr.'s leg was amputated after he developed bone cancer.

April 25, 1984   David Kennedy, age twenty-eight, son of Bobby and Ethel, died in a Palm Beach hotel after a drug overdose.

Notes

The assessment of Edward M. Kennedy is the author's own, based on close study and observation of the senator, his life and work, and numerous talks with family members and friends. The views offered are buttressed by facts, statements, and opinions of numerous other persons who have known Ted Kennedy.

Documentation of sources and statements which the author deemed necessary follows: (*Oral histories in the J.F.K. Library are abbreviated "O.H."*)

To Begin

CIA plot to assassinate Castro: Details are in the report of the *Senate Select Committee to Study Governmental Activities With Respect to Intelligence Activities*, chaired by Senator Frank Church, issued in 1975. Alleged Assassination Plots Involving Foreign Leaders, pp. 129–130.

Barry Goldwater statement: *Chicago Tribune*, June 27, 1975.

Giancana statement: Giancana, *Double Cross*, p. 293.

Jackie refurbishing White House: The most authoritative work on the subject is *Jacqueline Kennedy, The White House Years*, by Mary Van Rennselaer Thayer (Little, Brown, 1967).

Jack "can't fight old man": Collier, Horowitz, *The Kennedys*, p. 202.

Bobby and McCarthy: Krock, *Memoirs*, p. 342. Also see Cohn on McCarthy by Roy Cohn, (New American Library, 1968).

Jack on civil rights and liberalism: Reeves, *A Question of Character*, p. 239; Burner, West, *The Torch Is Passed*, pp. 151–92; Wofford, *Of Kennedys and Kings*, passim.

ONE: *The Annointed*

Seigenthaler and Burke accounts: author interviews.
"Large arrow": *New York Times*, June 17, 1979.
RFK assassination, rites and funeral train: Author interviews with columnist Pete Hamill, Dave Powers, Pierre Salinger, John Seigenthaler and Richard Drayne. Also Salinger, *With Kennedy*; Plimpton and Stein, *American Journey*, and files of *New York Times*, *Los Angeles Times* and *Boston Globe*. The Plimpton, Stein book, containing recollections of RFK from hundreds who had known him well during what Truman Capote called "the ride of the century," is especially revelatory of the man.
Ted in hospital washroom: *Boston Globe*, July 10, 1985.
Ted and sharpshooter: *New York Times*, op. cit.
Jackie and Air Force One: Kenneth O'Donnell, author interview.
Motorcycle salute: Ray O'Connell, author interview.
Ted's grief: Joan Kennedy, Richard Drayne, David Hackett, author interviews; Dallas, *Kennedy Case*, p. 312–22; *New York Times*, June 16, 1968; *New York Times Magazine*, June 17, 1974; *McCall's Magazine*, February, 1974; *Look*, March 4, 1969.
Ted "ghosts at his side": Wills, *Kennedy Imprisonment*, p. 8.
Closeness of RFK and Ted: Luella Hennessey, Kennedy nurse, author interviews.
Ted and Bobby in London: Hennessey, author interviews; files of Press Association, Fleet Street, London; JFK Library files; author's personal files.

TWO: *Two Teddys*

Bad Ted comments: Wooten, *Washington Post*, June 17, 1971; *Newsweek*, December 9, 1992; Kelly *GQ*, February 1990; *New York Times*, April 18, 1991; Reeves and Wills, author interviews; Carr, *Boston Herald*, August 14 and October 28, 1991.
Good Ted comments: Hatch, *Washington Post Magazine*, April 29, 1990; Warner, *Chicago Sun-Times*, July 8, 1971; *Boston Globe*, July 16, 1989; Tip O'Neill and Simpson, author interviews; Lichtman, *Time* magazine, April 29, 1991.
Ted in Senate: *Congressional Record*, Jan. 21, 1992, 553–54; Melody Miller, Ted's deputy press aide, author interview.

THREE: *The Baleful Influence*

"Scum of creation," Cameron, *Rose*, p. 25.
Took to money: Koskoff, *Joseph P. Kennedy*, p. 18. See Goodwin, *The Fitzgeralds and the Kennedys*, and Koskoff for best accounts of early Kennedys in the United States. Also see Whalen, *Founding Father: The Story of Joseph P. Kennedy*, Rose Kennedy, *Times to Remember*, and Cameron for early Rose and Joe.
Lyons interview with Joe, Sr., *Boston Globe*, November 10, 1940.
FDR and Jack: Collier, Horowitz, op. cit., p. 110.
Jack's letter, Choate archives.
Bobby and football: Lawford, *That Shining Hour*, Knowles, OH, JFK Library; Lamar, author interview.
Bobby baseball story: Author interview with former Senator Fred R. Harris of Oklahoma.
Ted thrown overboard: Ted's own account in *As We Remember Joe*, a collection of recollections assembled by JFK and privately printed in 1945.

Kennedy competitiveness: Burns, *Edward Kennedy and the Camelot Legacy*, p. 26.

Joe, Sr., disciplining Ted: Rose Kennedy, op. cit., p. 113, and passim.

Ted and parents' expectations: Clinch, *Kennedy Neurosis*. See Chapter 11, "The Making of Teddy," pap. 324–44; Rose Kennedy, op. cit., p. 133, 143.

Ted and relations with father: Dallas, op. cit., p. 284, 316; Milton Gwirtzman, OH, JFK Library; Rose Kennedy, op. cit., passim; *Time*, November 29, 1971; Reeves, author interview.

FOUR: *First Fumble*

Ted's scholastic record at Milton: Burns, op. cit., p. 42; Dean Hall, author interview; Hersh, *Education of Edward M. Kennedy*, p. 77; author interviews with classmates.

Jack at Choate: Horton, OH, JFK Library; St. John, Packard author interviews; Choate archives, which are a rich source of his scholastic record and pertinent documents, including letters to and from home.

Bobby at Portsmouth Priory: Priory archives; author interviews with Norris and classmates. Unlike Choate and Portsmouth Priory, Milton keeps Bobby's records in a cabinet behind the headmaster's desk, to which access is restricted.

Dr. Holcombe's assessment of the Kennedys" Author interviews.

Ted at Harvard: Author interviews with classmates noted in text, and with Lem Billings. Other sources: Collier, Horowitz, op. cit., quoting from Billings's private papers, p. 90; *National Enquirer*, October 19, 1976.

Ted and football at Harvard: Author interviews with Kenneth O'Donnell, classmates, and Ted; files of Harvard *Crimson* and *New York Times*.

Spanish test: Author interviews with Ted and classmates. See notes to chapter 7.

Ted in Army: Hersh, op. cit., p. 82; *New York Times Magazine*, July 26, 1960 and September 28, 1962.

Ted's rebellion: Burns, op. cit., p. 49; author interviews with Joan Kennedy and Ted.

Ted at Charlottesville: Collier, Horowitz, op. cit., p. 116; Burns, op. cit., p. 51; author interviews with residents.

Ted's study habits at Charlottesville: Frances Farmer, author interviews; Burns, op. cit., p. 5.

FIVE: *JOAN*

The story of the Bennet family's roots, Harry Bennett's background, Joan Kennedy's years as a schoolgirl, beauty contest winner and model, and her meeting and marriage to Ted came from author files and many author interviews over the years with: Andasia Bennett, widow of Harry, Sr., and Joan's step-grandmother; Joan, her sister Candace McMurrey, her father Harry Bennett, Harry's former employer, Bryan Houston, Nurse Hennessey, and Candy Jones. Many of the interviews with Joan and Candy were conducted between 1990 and 1992. Newspaper files, especially those of the *New York Daily News* and *Mount Vernon Daily Argus* were valuable sources for Joan's wedding, as were Lem Billings and officials of St. Joseph's Roman Catholic Church. The *News* published a picture of the newlyweds on its front page on November 30, 1958. See also, David, *Joan, the Reluctant Kennedy*, pp. 45–50.

Ted as Joan's only love: *Ladies' Home Journal*, October 1962.

Jack's authorship of *Profiles In Courage*: Reeves, op. cit., p. 127; Parmet, *Jack*, p. 80.

Joseph P. Kennedy planted spy: O'Neill, *Man of the House*, p. 82.
Bumper stickers: Lippman, *Senator Ted Kennedy*, p. 12.
Powers on Jack: Author interview.
Sell Jack like soap flakes: Reeves, op. cit., p. 14.
Account of Jack naming Bobby attorney general: Author interview with George
Smathers.

SIX: *Sexual Legacy*

Sex as part of Kennedy mystique: Wills, op. cit., p. 16.
Shelly Winters incident: Winters, *The Middle of My Century*, pp. 434–35.
Dick Tuck on Ted's philandering: *GQ*, October 1990.
Schowalter statement: Author interview.
"Piece of cake": *Boston Magazine*, July 1991.
Emptiness at core: *New Republic*, June 24, 1991.
Joe, Sr., no moral principles: Goodwin, op. cit., p. 351.
Father and sensual pleasure: Wills, op. cit., p. 19.
Never without a young woman: Koskoff, op. cit., p. 332.
Father's sensual pleasure: Wills, op. cit., p. 19.
Jack watching father: Collier, Horowitz, op. cit., p. 174.
Sons providing women: *People* magazine, May 27, 1991.
Joe, Sr., and women: Frank Saunders, *Torn Lace Curtain*, passim.
Toodles incident: Story recounted by Goodwin, Reeves, Whalen, op. cit.
Swanson and boat incident: Madsen, *Gloria and Joe*, pp. 239–40.
Swanson and Joe, Sr.: Madsen's book brings together all the tales about Joe and
Gloria circulating for years.
Swanson and Joe, Sr.: Swanson's book, *Swanson On Swanson*, finally disclosed the
truth about their relationship, rumored for years. Madsen's book has revealing new
material. Sex also *Rose*, op. cit., p. 117. The author had a fascinating talk with
Swanson in 1980 during which she deplored the Hollywood actresses who were
revealing intimate details of their sex lives. "Disgusting, horrible," she called the
tell-all books. Two years later, her own book was published.
    One of the most persistent stories about the Kennedys is that Joe fathered another
son who would have been positioned between Bobby and Teddy in the hierarchy. Joe
and Gloria reportedly had a boy, whom she named Joseph, and brought up with her
own two daughters, Gloria and Michelle, as her adopted child. Swanson denied the
story in 1971, two years after Joe's death. In the *New York Times*, October 10, 1971,
she was quoted as saying that rumors about the boy were spreading rapidly in
Hollywood. "They called him Kennedy's child," she said. "They called him Mr.
[Cecil B.] De Mille's child. Well, he was born in 1922, and I never laid eyes on
Joseph Kennedy until 1928."
    Bad case of satyriasis: Grobel, *Conversations With Capote*, pp. 180–81.
    Exner and Jack and Ted: Exner, *My Story*, pp. 88–89; Spada, *Peter Lawford*, p.
227. See also, *Vanity Fair* April, 1990. Exner denial that she slept with JFK and
Giancana at the same time: From Larry King Live, CNN, February, 1992.
    Ted and Patricia Seaton Lawford: Lawford, *The Peter Lawford Story*, pp. 154–56.
    Mary Daly statement: *Boston Magazine*, July, 1991.

SEVEN: *"Now It's Ted's Turn"*

Ted's rebellion: Interviews with Joan Kennedy; also *New Bedford Standard Times*,
May 26, 1962; *Time* January 2, 1961, and September 28, 1968; Lippman, op. cit., p.
13.

Jack and Ted on Senate and playboy remark: Martin, *A Hero for Our Time*, p. 439.
Ted's travels: Lippman, op. cit., p. 14.
Jack ribbing Ted: Martin, op. cit., p. 440.
Attempted deal with McCormack: O'Neill, op. cit., pp. 170–74.
Spanish test: Robert Healy, numerous interviews, latest in January, 1992. *Boston Globe*, March 30, 1962; *New York Times*, March 31, 1962.
Delegate's lament: *Newsweek*, June 18, 1962.
Ted on Jack's birthday: *Time*, June 15, 1962.
Ted campaigning and the debates: Gerald Doherty, Ted's campaign manager, Donald J. Dowd, overall Massachusetts coordinator, and Mrs. Dowd, author interviews; Levin, *Kennedy Campaigning*, pp. 19–20; Joe McCarthy, author interview; Milton Gwirtzman, OH; Saunders, op. cit., p. 140; Levin, *Edward Kennedy*, pp. 13–14, 223. The fullest accounts of the two debates are in the *Boston Globe*, August 28 and September 6, 1962.
Called father first: Gwirtzman, OH.
Stay out of pool: *Corpus Christi Caller-Times*, May 28, 1967.
Beaverbrook comment: Koskoff, op. cit., p. 71.
Eastland advice: Bobby Baker, *Wheeling and Dealing in the White House*, p. 101.
Jolly Roger statement: *Newsweek*, January 4, 1963.
Tunney on Ted in Senate: Lippman, op. cit., p. 272.
Irish pol statement: *Saturday Evening Post*, January 14, 1963.
Ted and Ed McCormack today: Author interview with McCormack, 1992.
Ted and Jack's assassination: Gwirtzman, OH; Manchester, *Death of a President*, pp. 197–99, 254–55, 549.

EIGHT: *A Grand Wake*

Ted and wake: L. J. Davis, *Onassis*, p. 114; John H. Davis, *The Kennedys*, p. 445; Burns, op. cit., p. 107.
Cushing comment: Manchester, op. cit., p. 590.
Rose and assassination of Jack: Saunders, op. cit., passim; Dallas, op. cit., p. 19.
Ted's reaction: Nurse Hennessey, author interview.

NINE: *Joan on the Rocks*

For fuller account of Joan's early years in Washington, see David, *Joan, The Reluctant Kennedy*. *New York Times*, May 10, 1970, has good description of McLean house.
Kennedy women ignoring Joan: Wills, op. cit., pp. 39–40.
Jackie on Joan: Goodwin, op. cit., pp. 171–72.
Ted's plane crash: Author interviews with Joan Kennedy, Birch and Marvella Bayh, Dave Powers, Jimmy Breslin, Don Dowd; Guthman, *We Band of Brothers*, p. 285. Also files of *Boston Globe, New York Times*.
Ted's painting: *Boston Sunday Herald*, July 6, 1965.
Joan campaigning: Doherty, Eddie Martin, Don and Phoebe Dowd, Tommy Joyce, author interviews.
Jack's philandering: Bryant, *Dog Days at the White House*, p. 33; Kelley, *Jackie Oh!*, p. 78.
Joan's concert: William Smith, assistant conductor, Philadelphia Orchestra, author interview.
Reporter's comment on Joan: Arthur Egan, *Manchester Union Leader*, author interview.
Ted drunk on Alaska flight: Hersh, op. cit., p. 380; John H. Davis, op. cit., p. 579; *Time*, June 17, 1979.

TEN: *More Wenching and Drinking*

EMK and heavy breathing: *New York Magazine*, June 3, 1991.
Elevator incident: *Conservative Digest*, February 1988.
Marina incident: Confidential source.
Blonde-of-the-Week: *Conservative Digest*, February, 1988.
Incident in newspaper office: Confidential source.
Rude behavior to African delegation: *GQ*, February 1990.
Ted abstaining: *Newsweek*, December 9, 1991.
Capote comment: Grobel, op. cit., p. 271.
Helga Wagner: John H. Davis, op. cit., p. 579.
Helga Wagner and Llana Campbell: John H. Davis, op. cit., p. 579.
Sailing incident: *New Hampshire Sunday News*, September 3, 1972; *Manchester Union Leader*, September 4, 1972.
Incident at debutante party: *Vanity Fair*, April 1990.
Chronicle of Ted's romances: *TV-Radio Mirror*, September, 1971; *London Mirror*, October 18, 1971; *Washington Post*, June 22, 1975; Liz Smith, December 20, 1974, December 20, 1978, June 13, 1983; *Boston Globe*, November 27, 1984; *New York Post*, February 16, June 17, and December 21, 1985; *Boston Herald*, January 20, 1989, and July 15, 1991; *GQ*, October 1990; *New York Daily News*, April 8, 1991; *Time*, April 29, 1991; *People* magazine, April 21, 1991; *Vanity Fair*, October 1991.
Congressmen's sexual exploits: Riegle, *O Congress*, p. 46; Miller, *Fishbait*, passim; confidential sources.

ELEVEN: *The Senators Kennedy*

Bobby greeted with skepticism: Schlesinger, *Robert Kennedy and His Times*, p. 733.
LBJ on Bobby: Johnson, *My Brother Lyndon*, pp. 159–81. See also Baker, op. cit., for LBJ's animosity to Bobby.
Washburn brothers: Schlesinger, op. cit., p. 729; Davis, op. cit., p. 528; author interviews with O'Neill; Lerner, *Ted and the Kennedy Legend*, p. 79.
Ted joking and Bobby getting first comment: *Wall Street Journal*, November 6, 1966.
"As any future President": Schlesinger, op. cit., p. 737.
Ted's maiden speech: The full text is in *Congressional Record*, April 9, 1964, p. 7375.
Ethel on violent films: Lem Billings, author interview.
Ted capable of staggering coup: English, *Divided They Stand*, p. 308.
Convention could be stampeded: English, op, cit., p. 308.
1968 Convention: files of *Washington Post*, *New York Times*, *Boston Globe*; Theodore H. White, *The Making of the President*, passim.
Ted on whip job: Lippman, op. cit. p. 144.
Edward M. Kennedy Foundation comment: Collier, Horowitz, op. cit., p. 326.
Bobby's bumbling at hearings: Burke, OH.
Bobby about to explode: Dun Gifford in Stein and Plimpton, *American Journey*, p. 182.
Ted enjoying Senate: Burke, OH.
Bobby as senator and presidential candidate: Stein, Plimpton, op. cit., pp. 192–94; author interviews with O'Neill; Lerner, *Ted and the Kennedy Legend*, p. 79; Davis, op. cit., p. 530.
Ted's program and speeches: From office of Senator Kennedy.

Ted and Ethel, re gunshots: Lem Billings, author interview.
Lowenstein certain Ted could win: English, *Divided They Stand* 308.
Democratic Convention: White, *Making of the President 1968*, passim; English, op. cit., passim; files of *New York Times* and *Chicago Tribune*.

TWELVE: *The Drowning of Mary Jo*

Consulted for this chapter were files of the *New York Times*, especially *New York Times Magazine*, July 14, 1974; *Time*, *Newsweek*, *Boston Globe*, *Ladies' Home Journal*, *McCall's*, *Washington Post*, and the following books: Leo Damore, *Senatorial Privilege: The Chappaquiddick Coverup* (Chicago: Regnery Gateway, 1988); Jack Olsen, *The Bridge at Chappaquiddick* (New York Ace Publishing Company, 1970); and the author's observations and interviews, as noted in the text. Ted's statements, Mary Jo's drinking, testimony of the Boiler Room girls, are in the official transcript of the inquest, published in 1970 in five volumes Docket Number 1522. Transcript is now in Boston Superior Court, transferred there from the Edgartown Superior Court.

THIRTEEN: *Teddy and Jackie and Ari*

Bobby's reaction: Fred Sparks, *The $20,000,000 Honeymoon* (New York, Bernard Geis Associates, 1970) p. 26.

Onassis's arrest: Willie Frischauer, *Onassis* (New York, Meredith Press), chapter 12.

Ted and Ari meeting: Willi Frischauer, *Onassis*, (London: Michael Joseph, 1976), pp. 208–209.

Jackie and prenuptial agreement: Nicholas Fraser, et al., *Aristotle Onassis* (Philadelphia: J. B. Lippincott, 1977, p. 252.)

Description of the *Christina*: Lester David and Jhan Robbins, *Jackie and Ari* (New York: Pocket Books), pp. 83–92.

Wedding: *Ibid.*, pp. 93–94; also Sparks, op. cit., passim; major newspapers, October 18, 1968.

The marriage: Confidential sources, plus Kelley, op. cit., pp. 283–96; Stephen Birmingham, *Jacqueline Bouvier Kennedy Onassis*, pp. 165–71; *Time* comment, October 25, 1968.

Ted's tastelessness at funeral: L. J. Davis, op. cit., pp. 4–5; Nigel Dempster, *Heiress: The Story of Christina Onassis* (New York: Grove Weidenfeld, 1989), p. 89.

See David and Robbins, op. cit., pp. 177–90 for full text of Onassis's will, to author's knowledge the only English translation to be published in the United States.

FOURTEEN: *The Best Chance*

Nomination a fait accompli: *Newsweek*, August 4, 1969.

Coming on like a tidal wave: Rather, *The Camera Never Blinks, The Palace Guard*, p. 116.

Memories fading fast: *New York Post*, May 28, 1971.

Nixon Dirty Tricks: Rather, op. cit., p. 167; Lasky comments, author interview; Rather, *The Camera Never Blinks*, p. 226; Anthony Lukas, *Nightmare*, pp. 16–17; Ehrlichman, *Witness to Power*, p. 292; Dean, *Blind Ambition* passim; Theodore H. White, *Breach of Faith: The Fall of Richard Nixon* (New York, Atheneum, Reader's Digest Press, p. 121). Testimony about the dirty tricks attempted against Ted was given at the Watergate hearings, chaired by Senator Sam J. Ervin, Jr. (D., N.C.). See

Watergate Hearings, Break-in and Cover-up, proceedings of the Senate Select Committee on Presidential campaign activities, as edited by staff of the *New York Times*, for good summary.

Historic opportunity lost: *New York Times*, July 13, 1988

FIFTEEN: *Joan's Agony*

Joan's phone call to the magazine editor: Confidential source. (Readers should note that the editor's wife also listened to the conversation.) The author has known and worked with the editor, who is highly respected in the publishing world, for forty years.

Ted, Jr.'s ordeal: Author interviews with Joan Kennedy, Dr. Covalt of Rusk Institute, officials at Georgetown University Hospital, Nurse Hennessey; *Daily Express* (London), December 1, 1973.

Joan's drinking: Author interviews with Joan, supplemented by newspaper and magazine files.

Joan in drunken stupor: Wills, op. cit., pp. 49–50.

Deterioration of marriage and denials: Author interviews with Joan, Harry Bennett, Candace McMurrey, Dick Drayne; *McCall's* magazine, August 1978; *Ladies Home Journal*, May 1979.

Joan in Boston and new independence: Author interviews with Joan, Joan Brandon, Mike Tunney, George Smathers, sources at Lesley College Graduate School of Education, Dr. Michael A. Greenwald, Candace McMurrey, Harry Bennett, supplemented by newspaper and magazine articles, especially: *New York Post*, January 23, 1981; *McCall's* magazine, August 1978; *Sunday Woman*, September 1978; *Star*, July 15, 1975; *Time* magazine, November 5, 1979. See also, Marcia Chellis, *Living With the Kennedys: The Joan Kennedy Story* (New York: Simon and Schuster, 1985).

A "new Ted Kennedy": Author interviews with aides and friends.

Betty Beale comments: Author interview.

Joan at Lesley College, her reasons for leaving Ted and efforts to control her drinking: Author interviews with Joan.

New independence and womens' movement: text of address from Ted's office.

Rose's and Harry Bennett's reaction at news of divorce: Author interviews.

Patrick's spinal tumor: Author interviews with Joan, Massachusetts General Hospital.

Evidence of Joan's recovery, men in her life: Author interview with Candace McMurrey.

Joan's book: In late 1922, Joan's book, *The Joys of Classical Music: A Guide for You and Your Family*, was published.

SIXTEEN: *The Reluctant Candidate*

Ted happiest in Senate: Lerner, op. cit., p. 161, 164, passim.

Ted doesn't foresee seeking presidency: *New York* magazine, March 24, 1975.

Smathers comment: Author interview.

Reeves and Parmet comments: Author interview.

Gwirtzman comment: *Esquire* magazine, February 1990.

Mudd comments: Author interview.

Teddy fall on ass: Wills, op. cit., p. 10.

Kandy Stroud comment: *New York Magazine*, March 24, 1975.

Rowan comment: *New York Post*, May 7, 1975.
Ted says no: *New York Times*, September 24, 1974; other major newspapers.
Tunney comment: *New York Daily News*, June 3, 1975.
Shriver comment: *New York Post*, May 28, 1975.
Ted says yes: All major newspapers, November 7, 1979.
O'Neill told Ted not to run: O'Neill, op. cit., p. 326–27, and author interviews.
Ted pressured by advisors: Lerner, op. cit., p. 183.
Trick Ted out like Don Quixote: *New Republic*, May 31, 1980.
Ellen Goodman on Ted: Cited in Collier, Horowitz, op. cit., p. 432.
Ted actually wanted to lose: *Newsweek*, February 18, 1980.
On Ted's teasing of press about presidency: Jack W. Germond and Jules Witcover of the *Baltimore Sun* and Jules Witcover of the *Washington Post* wrote in *Washingtonian* magazine (February, 1986) that Ted Kennedy was Lucy and the press corps was Charlie Brown. "Every four years," they said, "Lucy Kennedy would put the football down and urge all of us to kick it. Then, when we came running full-tilt to kick it... Lucy would yank it away, leaving us to go sprawling.";
Fairlie comment: *New Republic*, May 11, 1980.
Ted free to enjoy lifestyle: *U.S. News and World Report*, June 4, 1988.

SEVENTEEN: *Close Call*

Story of Hinckley waiting in Ted's reception room to assassinate Ted: Author interview with Gregory Craig, who was, as noted in text, an attorney for Hinckley.
Meeting in serving pantry: Howar, op. cit., p. 204.
Ted's children severely affected: *McCall's*, February 1974.
Ted's fatalism and reaction to loud noises: Author interview with Gerry Doherty.
Blow my head off: *New York Times Magazine*, June 24, 1979.
Rose asking Nixon to protect Ted: White, *Making of the President 1972*, p. 319.

EIGHTEEN: *Parenting*

Kennedys oriented toward kids more than to wives: Goodwin, op. cit., p. 786.
Kennedys as parents: Author's files.
Incident of boy with weight problem: Letter to *New York Post*, November 7, 1991.
Dispute with Teddy, Jr.: Ted pinned the note to the wall of his office.
Ted, Jr., and alcohol dependency: Young Ted admitted he checked into a rehabilitation facility for treatment of alcohol abuse in the summer of 1991, *Ladies' Home Journal*, March 1992.
Patrick and drug habit: *New York Times* (and other newspapers), December 10, 1991.
Kara experimenting with substances: Collier, Horowitz, op. cit., p. 414.
Caucus of young Kennedys: *Washingtonian* November 1988.

NINETEEN: *Senator at Work*

Ted and rail strike: Author interviews with union officials and his staff aides; *Boston Globe*, April 28, 1991.
Ted responsible for keeping Bork off Court: Newfield *New York Post*, July 10, 1992; Hatch, *Washingtonian* February, 1990.
Jack's story to young Kennedys: Author interviews with Nurse Hennessey.
Jack on loving his father: Fuchs, OH.
Korologos comment: *Business Week*, June 24, 1991.

Ted discussing legislative technique: *Worcester Telegram and Gazette*, March 16, 1990.

Hofstra address: Text from Ted's office; address given March 28, 1985. Author was present when Ted delivered his speech. So were about a dozen of his children, nephews, and nieces, who drew considerable attention from the audience in the Hofstra field house. Ted, ever mindful of the magnetism of the family, introduced Caroline and John, Jr., who drew wild applause.

Comment of Ted moderating views: *Boston Globe Magazine*, November 24, 1985.

Ted's speeches stressing need for change, cost-effective programs and address before Psychiatric Association: texts from Ted's office.

Ted's staff; Author interviews with present and former staff aides, particularly Gregory Craig and Dun Gifford. Also, Tim Wineman of Senate Disbursing Office; *Boston Herald*, July 14, 1992; *New York Times*, June 24, 1979; *Washington Post Magazine*, April 29, 1990.

TWENTY: *Palm Beach: Chappaquiddick Redux*

Similarity between Palm Beach and Chappaquiddick: *Time*, May 27, 1991, headlined its story of the case as follows: "When in doubt, obfuscate. Ted Kennedy's handling of the Palm Beach case echoes an old pattern of recklessness, evasion and irresonsibility."

Arena comments: *New York Times*, April 8, 1991.

Accounts of Ted, Willie, Patrick, and Bowman: Transcripts of the trial.

Mercer comments: *Esquire*, August, 1991.

Bowman's background: *New York Times*, April 17, 1991.

Ted in T-shirt: *New York Post*, April 5, 1991.

Statements made by principals in case: From Palm Beach police investigation file, which contained 1,500 pages of documents, interviews and depositions.

Critical comments on Ted's behavior: Author interviews with confidential sources, also major newspapers.

J.F.K., Jr., comments: Letter, *New York Times*, January 20, 1992.

Bowman at American Press Institute Forum: *Editor and Publisher*, September 26, 1992.

Turning point for Ted: *Esquire*, August, 1991; *Time*, May 27, 1991; *New York Post*, August 2, 1991.

TWENTY-ONE: *Crossroads*

Gifford, Smathers, Mudd comments: Author interviews.

Delaware voter's comment: *New York*, March 10, 1980.

Sex and political leaders: Many books and articles have told tales of senators and representatives having sexual adventures. "Fishbait" Miller, op. cit., tells some wonderful stories. Among them: A representative once stroked the bald pate of Speaker Nicholas Longworth and said with a smirk, "It feels just like my wife's behind." Longworth looked up from his newspaper, rubbed his head, and nodded. "I'll be damned if it doesn't," he said. See also Warren Weaver, Jr., *Both Your Houses: The Truth About Congress* (New York, Praeger, 1972). *Time*, August 22, 1961, has a good summary of the sex lives of past political leaders. See also Bruce Felknor, *Dirty Politics* (New York: Norton, 1966), for accounts of charges of sexual misconduct and campaign innuendo against presidential and congressional candidates.

Carroll comment on Ted's program: *New Republic*, June 24, 1991.

Curbstone comment: November, 1991.

Kempton comment: *New York Newsday*, November 1, 1991.
Material on Richard E. Burke: *Washington Post*, September 24, 1992; *New York Daily News*, September 27, 28, 29, 1992; *New York Times*, August 12, 1992; *New York Post*, September 25, 1992; *USA Today*, September 29, 1992; Maury Povich on *A Current Affair* (TV show); Melody Miller; Richard E. Burke, *The Senator: My Ten Years With Ted Kennedy* (New York, St. Martin's Press, 1992).
Hersh and Seigenthaler comments: Author interviews.

TWENTY-TWO: Cleaning Up His Act?

Culver incident: *Newsweek*, December 9, 1992.
Friends deeply concerned: Hersh, author interview.
Hatch comment: *U.S. News and World Report*, May 27, 1991; *Boston Herald*, May 23, 1991.
Ted meeting with freinds on drinking: Confidential sources; also Evans and Novak, *New York Post*, November 2, 1991.
Ted and Vicki: Details of wedding ceremony and Ted proposing from Doris Reggie, author interview. Their meeting and relationship: Personal friends; *Boston Globe*, April 2, 1992; *Boston Herald*, July 12, 1992; *Newsday*, March 24, 1992.
Interviews with Ted and Vicki: *Cape Cod Times*, *Boston Globe*, Boston Herald, September 8, 1992; *New York Times*, October 1, 1992.
Ted and Vickie's daughter: Photographers at pier.
Kennedy wealth: *Forbes* magazine, October 21, 1992; Collier, Horowitz, op. cit., p. 151.
O'Neill and Smathers comments: author interviews.
Ted focused: *Boston Globe*, July 5, 1992.

Select Bibliography

ABRAMS, HERBERT L. *The President Has Been Shot*. New York, London: Norton, 1992.

ALLEN, GARY. *Ted Kennedy: In Over His Head*. Atlanta, Los Angeles: '76 Press, 1980.

BACON, MARGARET, AND MARY BRUSH JONES. *Teen-Age Drinking*. New York: T. Y. Crowell, 1968

BAKER, BOBBY. *Wheeling and Dealing in the White House: Confessions of a Capitol Hill Operator*. New York: Norton, 1978.

BIRMINGHAM, STEPHEN. *Jacqueline Bouvier Kennedy Onassis*. New York: Grosset & Dunlap, 1970.

BLAIR, CLAY, JR., AND JOAN BLAIR. *The Search for JFK*. New York: Berkley, 1976.

BRYANT, TRAPHES, WITH FRANCES SPATZ LEIGHTON. *Dog Days at the White House: The Outrageous Memoirs of the Presidential Kennel Keeper*. New York: Pocket Books, 1978.

BURNER, DAVID. *John F. Kennedy and a New Generation*. Boston: Little, Brown, 1988.

———— AND THOMAS R. WESTON. *The Torch Is Passed: The Kennedy Brothers and American Liberalism*. New York: Atheneum, 1984.

BURNS, JAMES MACGREGOR. *Edward Kennedy and the Camelot Legacy*. New York: Norton, 1976.

CALIFANO, JOSEPH A. *The Triumphs and Tragedies—Lyndon Johnson—The White House Years*. New York: Simon and Schuster, 1982.

CAMERON, GAIL. *Rose*. New York: Putnam's, 1971.

CLARKE, GERALD. *Capote: A Biography*. New York: Simon and Schuster, 1988.

COLLIER, PETER, AND DAVID HOROWITZ. *The Kennedys: An American Drama*. New York: Summit Books, 1984.

DALLAS, RITA, WITH JEANNE RATCLIFFE. *The Kennedy Case*. New York: Putnam's, 1973.

DAVID, LESTER. *Joan, the Reluctant Kennedy*. New York: Funk & Wagnalls, 1974.

———— AND IRENE DAVID. *Bobby Kennedy: The Making of a Folk Hero*. New York: Dodd, Mead, 1986.

————. *Ike and Mamie: The Story of the General and His Lady*. New York: Putnam's, 1981.

DAVIS, JOHN H. *The Kennedys: Dynasty and Disaster*. New York: McGraw Hill Book Company, 1984.

DAVIS, L. J. *Onassis: Aristotle and Christina*. New York: St. Martin's, 1986.

DEAN, JOHN W. *Blind Ambition: The White House Years*. New York: Simon and Schuster, 1976.

DEMPSTER, NIGEL. *Heiress: The Story of Christina Onassis*. New York: Grove, Weidenfeld, 1989.

DINEEN, JOSEPH F. *The Kennedy Family*. Boston and Toronto: Little, Brown, 1959.

EHRLICHMAN, JOHN. *Witness to Power: The Nixon Years*. New York: Simon and Schuster, 1982.

EVANS, ROWLAND, AND ROBERT NOVAK. *Lyndon B. Johnson: The Exercise of Power*. New York: New American Library, 1966.

EXNER, JUDITH. *My Story*, as told to Ovid Demaris. New York: Grove Press, 1977.

ENGLISH, DAVID, AND THE STAFF OF THE *LONDON DAILY EXPRESS*. *Divided They Stand*. Englewood Cliffs, N.J.: Prentice-Hall, 1969.

GIANCANA, SAM, AND CHUCK GIANCANA. *Double Cross: The Explosive Inside Story of the Mobster Who Controlled America*. New York: Warner Books, 1992.

GOODWIN, DORIS KEARNS. *The Fitzgeralds and the Kennedys: An American Saga*. New York: Simon and Schuster, 1987.

GROBEL, LAWRENCE. *Conversations With Capote*. New York and Scarborough, Ont.: New American Library, 1985.

GUTHMAN, EDWIN. *We Band of Brothers*. New York: Harper & Row, 1971.

HERSH, BURTON. *The Education of Edward M. Kennedy: A Family Biography*. New York: William Morrow, 1972.

HEYMANN, C. DAVID. *A Woman Named Jackie: An Intimate Biography of Jacqueline Bouvier Kennedy Onassis*. New York: Lyle Stuart, 1989.

HONAN, WILLIAM H. *Ted Kennedy: Portrait of a Survivor*. New York: Quadrangle Books, 1972.

HOWAR, BARBARA. *Laughing All the Way*. New York: Stein and Day, 1973.

JOHNSON, SAM HOUSTON. *My Brother Lyndon*. New York: Cowles Book Company, 1969.

KENNEDY, ROSE FITZGERALD. *Times to Remember*. Garden City, N.Y.: Doubleday, 1974.

KENNEDY, JOHN F. *As We Remember Joe*. Privately printed, 1945.

KELLEY, KITTY. *Jackie Oh!* Secaucus, N.J.: Lyle Stuart, 1978.

KOSKOFF, DAVID E. *Joseph P. Kennedy: A Life and Times*. Englewood Cliffs, N.J.: Prentice-Hall, 1974.

KROCK, ARTHUR. *Memoirs: Sixty Years on the Firing Line*. New York: Funk & Wagnalls, 1968.

LAWFORD, PATRICIA KENNEDY, ED. *That Shining Hour*. Privately published.

LAWFORD, PATRICIA SEATON, WITH TED SCHWARTZ. *The Peter Lawford Story—Life With the Kennedys and the Rat Pack*. New York: Carroll and Graf, 1988.

LERNER, MAX. *Ted and the Kennedy Legend*. New York: St. Martin's, 1980.

LEVIN, MURRAY B. *Kennedy Campaigning*. Boston: Beacon Press, 1966.
_____ AND T. A. REPAK. *Edward Kennedy: The Myth of Leadership*. Boston: Houghton Mifflin, 1980.
LIPPMAN, THEO, JR. *Senator Ted Kennedy: The Career Behind the Image*. New York: Norton, 1976.
LUCAS, J. ANTHONY. *Nightmare: The Underside of the Nixon Years*. New York: Viking, 1973–76.
MADSEN, ALEX. *Gloria and Joe*. New York: Arbor House, 1988.
MANCHESTER, WILLIAM. *Death of a President*. New York: Harper & Row, 1967.
MARTIN, RALPH. *A Hero for Our Time*. New York: Macmillan, 1981.
MILLER, WILLIAM. *Fishbait: The Memoirs of the Congressional Doorkeeper*. Englewood Cliffs, N.J.: Prentice-Hall, 1977.
OATES, JOYCE CAROL. *Black Water*. New York: Dutton, 1992.
PARMET, HERBERT S. *Jack: The Struggles of John F. Kennedy*. New York: Dial, 1980.
PETRILLO, DANIEL J. *Robert F. Kennedy*. New York and Philadelphia: Chelsea House, 1989.
RATHER, DAN, AND GARY PAUL GATES. *The Palace Guard*. New York: Harper & Row, 1974.
_____ WITH MICKEY HERSHKOWITZ. *The Camera Never Blinks*. New York: William Morrow, 1977.
REEVES, THOMAS C. *A Question of Character: The Life of John F. Kennedy*. New York: Free Press, 1991.
RIEGLE, DONALD W., JR. *O Congress*. Garden City, N.Y.: Doubleday, 1972.
SALINGER, PIERRE. *With Kennedy*. Garden City, N.Y.: Doubleday, 1966.
SAUNDERS, FRANK, WITH JAMES SOUTHWOOD. *Torn Lace Curtain: Life With the Kennedys, Recalled by Their Personal Chauffeur*. New York: Holt, Rinehart, 1982.
SCHLESINGER, ARTHUR M., JR. *Robert Kennedy and His Times*. New York: Ballantine Books, 1979.
SHANNON, WILLIAM V. *The Kennedy Heritage*. New York: New York Times Books, 1968.
SORENSEN, THEODORE C. *The Kennedy Legacy*. New York: Macmillan, 1969.
SPADA, JAMES. *Peter Lawford: The Man Who Knew All the Secrets*. New York: Bantam Books, 1991.
STEIN, JEAN, AND GEORGE PLIMPTON. *American Journey: The Times of Robert Kennedy*. New York: Harcourt Brace, 1970.
SWANSON, GLORIA. *Swanson on Swanson*. New York: Random House, 1982.
WEISS, MURRAY, AND WILLIAM HOFFMAN. *Palm Beach Babylon: Sins, Scams and Scandals*. New York: Birch Lane Press, 1992.
WHALEN, RICHARD J. *The Founding Father: The Story of Joseph P. Kennedy*. New York: New American Library, 1964.
WHITE, THEODORE H. *The Making of the President 1968*. New York: Atheneum, 1969.
_____. *The Making of the President 1972*. New York: Atheneum, 1973.
WILLS, GARRY. *The Kennedy Imprisonment: A Meditation on Power*. Boston and Toronto: Little Brown, 1981.
WINTERS, SHELLEY. *The Middle of My Century*. New York: Atheneum, 1989.
WOFFORD, HARRIS. *Of Kennedys and Kings*. New York: Farrar, Straus, 1980.

INDEX